"This is a bank robbery in a rural area," (Northumberland Prosecutor) McKenney says. "It's a crime that concerned people. Chad is mentally ill, but he knows right from wrong. Even though he has medical problems, he has to be punished. I'm sorry his parents didn't identify his problem before that and take steps to address it. But I can't be held responsible for that."

Washington Post – January 26, 2003

"Eight hours later, Sheriff Wayne Middleton and his deputies completed their search of the house. They had strip-searched Chad, his sister, and the Wegkamps. When they left, they took Chad with them."

Richmond Times-Dispatch – February 24, 2003

"Chad Wegkamp was chained hand and foot when he was arraigned on robbery and other charges in Heathsville, August 15. Wegkamp could be sentenced to life in prison if convicted of robbery."

Northumberland Echo – August 22, 2001

"When police arrived at the Wegkamp home and identified themselves and their purpose they were told that the family would not cooperate without a warrant, according to Sheriff Middleton. At that point, Middleton ordered his deputies to surround the property while a warrant was obtained."... "During their search of the Wegkamp home, officers observed evidence of an alleged counterfeiting operation and immediately sought a new search warrant, according to McKenney."

Northern Neck News – August 22, 2001

THE NORTHUMBERLAND NIGHTMARE

WHEN JUSTICE IGNORES MENTAL ILLNESS

By

Paul L. Wegkamp, Jr., CPA

ISBN 0-7414-1847-9

Cover graphic by Jon Krause

Published by:

PUBLISHING.COM

1094 New Dehaven Street
Suite 100
West Conshohocken, PA 19428-2713
Info@buybooksontheweb.com
www.buybooksontheweb.com
Toll-free (877) BUY BOOK
Local Phone (610) 941-9999
Fax (610) 941-9959

Printed in the United States of America

Printed on Recycled Paper

Published May 2004

For Chad

CONTENTS

Preface

The following account of our experiences with our son's mental illness and the criminal justice system is, unfortunately, entirely true. I started keeping a detailed diary the day after my son's arrest for bank robbery and counterfeiting. It had been easy to reconstruct the events of the previous six months because my son's early struggles with schizophrenia were etched deeply in my mind. I had kept emails, court records, and medical records that provided an accurate chronology of events.

I normally would work on the diary every night, recording the day's events and how I felt about them. As a result, you will be reading my gut reactions and exactly how I felt as each day unfolded. For the most part, I resisted the urge to go back and "soften" the language or to expound on entries as time passed. It is important to me that the reader experiences the same raw emotions and roller coaster ride that my family was experiencing.

The dilemma I faced when I decided to publish my diary is that I had a mountain of material, and it was difficult to decide what should be included. As a result, I have omitted the significant events that transpired after my son's trial for bank robbery. This includes the unbelievable decision of the U.S. Attorneys' Office for the Eastern District of Virginia and the U.S Secret Service to prosecute my son on counterfeiting charges. It also does not include the subsequent coverage of our son's case by both the *Washington Post* and the *Richmond-Times Dispatch*, and it also omits the events that transpired when we filed a formal complaint against the Northumberland County Sheriff's Department. Perhaps all of this will be covered at another time.

However, the material I have included is more than enough to enable readers to form their own conclusions about the lessons behind our family's experience. I dare say, your perceptions of this country's criminal justice system will be altered, and for good reason.

FOREWORD

Both visitors and residents alike have referred to where we live as God's country. Not only is this area one of the best-kept secrets in the country, even many Virginians don't know it exists. Its geographical makeup is the reason behind the secret and it's great beauty. It is a long, hundred-mile stretch of land that is bordered by the historic Potomac River on the North, the Rappahannock River on the south, and the Chesapeake Bay to the East. It is referred to as the Northern Neck and its natural boundaries have provided the isolation that has led to the secret and the uniqueness of those who live here.

It is the birthplace of George Washington, James Madison, James Monroe, and Robert E. Lee and yet, there is not a single town within its boundaries that has a population of more than a few hundred people.

The area has an abundant array of wildlife. It is not uncommon to see a bald eagle soaring overhead in the morning and to find a raccoon in your garage at night. One morning I looked out our window and saw a school of dolphins playing in the river not more than a hundred feet from where I was standing. It's a boater's and fisherman's paradise.

The sunrises and sunsets are breathtaking. God spared no color or effort when he put his hand to this part of the earth's canvas.

The people who are born and raised here are the strong and sturdy type, church going, honest, very self-reliant and very conservative, and they appreciate what they have. If they have a fault, it would be a streak of stubbornness and a lack of tolerance for those who are different.

The locals refer to people who retire here, and those few that are not of retirement age that move in, as "come-heres." The reference is often made in a derogatory way, as there is a natural tendency by the locals (born-here's) not to share what they have with outsiders. There is also a little jealousy in that the come-heres generally are wealthier and a certain resentment because they don't like the come-here's telling them how to run things - which they often do. It is not unusual to hear stories of a born-here charging a come-here more for services rendered than they would one of their own.

Despite some of these quirks, this is a great place to live. We have the privilege of living on a small hill close to a river and an oyster house where both "crabbers" and "oystermen" ply their trade. The work ethic of these men is unbelievable and they take great pride in what they do, and deservedly so. In an industry that is enduring hard times, these men work day and night to make a living. Many of them will arrive between 4:00 AM and 5:00 AM to prepare their boats for the day's catch. I've seen some of them come back to the oyster house after spending ten hours on the water, go home for a few hours, come back and go out again. They work in all types of weather. One night during a violent rain, I went down to the shoreline to secure our canoe. The breakers on just the river itself were three feet high, which usually indicates that the breakers on the Chesapeake Bay are at least twice that. Looking out at this turbulent water, I saw the spot light on one of the crab boats searching for the oyster house as it was coming in to seek refuge from the storm!

When they are not out on the water they are using their time to keep their boats in good repair and all of them seem to be able to fix just about anything that either goes wrong with the boat itself or the engine that drives it. I have nothing but respect for these guys and I'm glad I know some of them.

The Northern Neck is divided into four large counties; we live in Northumberland County, which borders the Potomac River and the Chesapeake Bay. It has an area of approximately 220 square miles and a population of about 12,000 people. We arrived here about seven years ago, after having discovered the place quite by accident. I had responded to an ad in the *Washington Post* advertising a marina/restaurant for lease in Westmoreland County, which is north of Northumberland County.

Most men buy a sports car when they are having a mid-life crisis; I decided to buy this marina! After signing on the dotted line, we were hit with a major setback by the local health department. Because I had no prior restaurant experience and was new to the area they ruled that the marina was not "grandfathered" and would be subject to a much stricter health code that had just been passed. After spending thousands of dollars in restaurant and marina improvements and having to put up with the additional requirements of the local health inspectors, I wasn't able to get the marina open until after the critical Memorial Day weekend and things went downhill from there. It was my first introduction to local county bureaucracies and I'll never understand why they made it so difficult. In a county that was suffering over 10% unemployment, I had no choice but to shut down operations after only six months. At one time, I had 22 people on the payroll.

Then, we got lucky. After being resigned to the fact that I was probably going to have to return to Northern Virginia to find work, I found out that a local bank was looking for a Controller, which is my line of work. The pay was not what I was used to, but it afforded us an opportunity to stay in this beautiful area and I jumped at it.

We leased several homes our first couple of years before finding waterfront property we could afford. It was two-and-half acres on a hill overlooking a large expanse of the Great Wicomico River, with a two hundred-foot shoreline of white sandy beach. It was deep water, so we could build a dock and keep a sailboat. The river is a tributary for the Chesapeake Bay, which was just a mile away. There was an overgrowth of brush everywhere, but an attractive large Oak and evergreen trees framed the old house and water. There were bay windows in the kitchen and the upstairs study that allowed for a beautiful panoramic view of the river and the extended shoreline on the other side of the river over a half-mile away. Down the hill just seventy-five yards away was a working oyster house, which added to the overall ambiance of the place.

Debra absolutely loved it. Case closed, we bought the home and knew the joy someone feels when he or she knows they have secured the place where they want to live the rest of their lives.

Debra and I have had two children together, Chad who was born in 1982, and Ali who was born in 1985. I also have a daughter, Deana whom I had from an earlier marriage. Debra and Deana have had a close relationship. Deana has lived with us on occasion, having finished her high school years while she was living in our home in Northern Virginia.

Deana kind of spoiled us. Eager to please her Dad, she was never any trouble and just a sweet person. She has striking good looks and was Homecoming Princess both her freshman and sophomore years while attending a "Triple A" high school in

McLean, Virginia. She played varsity basketball and was an honor student. She always seemed to be just a little more mature than her peers. She attended Virginia Tech and graduated with a bachelor's degree in fashion merchandising. She is now living in Salt Lake City, Utah and works has a floor manager and buyer for a Nordstrom's department store. I have always been very proud of her and I love her dearly.

Chad has always been quiet and studious and very goal oriented. Extremely bright, he has won many academic awards and is one of the computer geniuses that you often find in his age category. When he was in sixth grade he won "student-of-the-year" in his middle school in Northern Virginia and we were approached by the school recommending that we put him in a school for the gifted. Like his older sister, he had a sweet disposition, was very responsible and did what he was asked to do. He liked a set routine. When he would get home from school he would go straight to his room and study, after finishing his studies he would take care of any personal needs such as making sure he had something nice to wear for the following day. He would wash and iron his own clothes and was very meticulous about his grooming habits. Only, after he would finish these tasks would he allow himself to relax and do something fun. He hated to be a bother to us. He would wear his shoes until the holes in the bottom of the soles were so big that he had to tell us he needed new shoes. He would rarely ever ask for anything. Through his computer skills he would "wheel-and-deal" by selling used computers that he had bought over the Internet and fixed up. He always had spending money and would often buy his own clothes. I'll never forget the day I got home and he had bought a used sports car with money he had saved up from his summer job and computer dealings.

Chad is the central figure in the story that follows. This book is my diary of the events from the onset of his mental illness to his trial for bank robbery. It is a story that few of us would ever imagined and one that parents around the country, and perhaps the world, should know about. From it, we learned a great deal, but, unfortunately, we learned too late. I hope what I have written will help others with similar problems cope more effectively with the obstacles and handicaps that confront the mentally ill and their families.

Ali travels to the beat of a different drummer. She is fearless, smart, opinionated, and has little respect for authority. You have to earn her respect. But she has a heart of gold and is extremely loyal to those who she sees as being loyal to her. She also is not afraid to fight someone else's battle if she thinks they have been wronged -- too much so. She is also one hell of an athlete.

As a young girl the whole family was involved in the very well organized Prince William County sports league and the Boy's and Girls Club leagues. I coached basketball for a number of years and Ali was one of my youngest and best players. We won league championships several years and finished second another year. During tryouts, Ali would out-run the boys. She was so competitive it was frightening; she refused to lose. Her basketball skills and softball skills as an eleven-year-old took a back seat to none of her peers.

These skills were evident when we first moved to Northumberland County. She was the starting basketball guard for the middle school as a sixth grader, and even though she was the youngest player on the 12 to 14 year-old Lancaster County girl's all-star softball team, she was one of the stars as they went far into the county playoffs. But Ali burned out. She had been playing organized sports since she was seven years old and overnight she refused to play any more. Then one day out of the blue she announced that she was going out for high school basketball, even though it had been three years since her last school game.

Ali gets some of her traits from Debra. Debra is also opinionated and can be very stubborn. But Debra is down to earth and genuine, there is nothing phony about her and she makes friends easily and I have always found that women really like Debra. Wherever we go it isn't long before she has made some close friends. She dislikes people who are haughty or may think they are better than someone else. She seems much more comfortable with the "blue collar" folk, but she also has made some very good friends with professional women. She does come from a blue-collar background where both her father and mother had to work very hard to make ends meet. There were five sisters in the family, with Debra being the second oldest. Debra often had to baby sit for her younger sisters while her parents were working.

Her older sister was five years older, and married when she was very young.

Debra did a four-year stint in the Navy where she received her initial training as a nurse. She would later follow that up with a degree in nursing and become a registered nurse.

Debra is also very good at what she does. She is a terrific nurse; her grasp of the medical field and its jargon is impressive, though she would never admit it. We constantly have people calling the house who need medical advice. She is also a great mother, who would do anything for her kids.

Debra and I were married in the Mormon temple in Salt Lake City. Through the years Debra has become inactive in the church, attending only on a rare occasion. I have been much more active and have tried to get the kids involved, but as they grew older it became harder to do. Chad was the exception; he would usually attend with me until he left to attend college at James Madison University (JMU), a prestigious college located in Harrisonburg, Virginia.

Welcome to my world and my family. I'm afraid that the ride ahead in these pages will not be a pleasant one. But it is one that is worth taking and should "open-a-few-eyes."

CHAPTER 1

SOMETHING IS WRONG WITH CHAD!

CHRISTMAS BREAK, DECEMBER 2000

I remember being so proud of Chad as I picked him up in Richmond upon his arrival on the shuttle bus from JMU. He looked every bit the college student. He got off the bus with one of his friends and they were both laughing and joking as they said good-bye to each other for the holidays. His first semester at JMU had been a resounding success. He had finished the semester with four B's and two D's. The D's were troublesome but I know many a parent who would have loved for their child to do as well for their first semester at a prestigious institution.

We had concerns when we had dropped Chad off four months earlier for his first experience away from home. He was still only seventeen and quite shy in social situations. We had come up to see him for parent's day, but other than that it was the only time we had seen or visited with him.

It was good to have him home for the holidays. We rented movies and played a lot of games against each other on the Playstation - I could never beat him! He surprised us one day by stripping the bathroom door and painting it before Debra and I got home from work. It was in bad shape and needed fixing and Chad decided it would be a nice thing to do for us.

The day we drove Chad back to JMU for the start of the semester, we took him out to lunch and then said good-bye. Little did we know, it would be the last time we would have a normal conversation with our son.

FEBRUARY, 2001

A bill we get in the mail surprises us. It is from the hospital in Harrisonburg. Apparently Chad was admitted to the emergency room for the treatment of a bloody and broken nose several weeks earlier! When we call to ask Chad about it, he says that he had gotten into a fight with someone at a fraternity party. Chad said he

1

had been spouting off about something and someone had hit him with a sucker punch. I try to get more details but Chad is not very forth coming and doesn't act like it is a big deal.

I am angry that someone has hit my son and wished I could have been there. But at least we know Chad isn't being a recluse and maybe he has learned a lesson. The fact that we would have never found out about it, if it weren't for the bill, bothers me.

SPRING BREAK, 2001

I drive up to Harrisonburg to get Chad and bring him home. He seems distant and doesn't really want to talk. I ask Chad how things are going, but he his mumbling so much and I can't hear him. Finally I give up and he sleeps for most of the trip back home.

This pattern continues for most of the week. Chad seems content to stay in his bedroom to play his video and computer games. He stays up until 2:00 AM or 3:00 AM each morning and is asleep when Debra and I go to work. He does have a friend over one day and goes out with some friends one night. Ali and Chad get into it a few times over what to watch on TV.

Chad needs the car one morning so he takes Debra to work and goes and gets her after work. Apparently, as Debra opens the door to get in, a container falls out that looks like it is some sort of self-made device for sniffing drugs. Debra is furious and demands an explanation from Chad, who says the device must belong to some of his friends that he had in the car the other night. Debra wants to believe him but is pretty sure Chad is not telling the truth. She can't believe that Chad could be so stupid - it could be grounds for her dismissal, since she works for a correctional facility, if someone had found that in her car. She lashes out at him and is further infuriated when Chad acts like it is no big deal. Unfortunately, Debra does not tell me about this incident until months later. She was afraid of how I would have reacted.

I do notice there seems to be tension in the house and that Chad seems to be the cause of it. I just assume that he is getting on everyone's nerves and don't think much about it. Deana's wedding is in a few weeks and it is Deana that is foremost on my mind right now, not Chad.

Debra takes Chad back to JMU, and I think everyone is a little relieved that he is gone.

DEANA'S WEDDING, MARCH 2001

Deana's wedding is on the 24th in Salt Lake City and we leave a week early to allow for some vacation time in Las Vegas and then some time with family in Utah, culminating in Deana's wedding. Chad has decided not to come; his professors will not allow him to make-up any assignments or tests he will miss. Debra will tell me later that she was relieved by his decision, she was afraid that Chad's behavior would not have changed from that of spring break and had the potential to ruin our vacation.

We are all excited to see everyone and Ali is especially excited about her visit to Vegas. She will also be a bridesmaid at Deana's wedding. I was actually raised in Las Vegas. We lived there when my father worked for an engineering firm that provided the Atomic Energy Commission with instrumentation and analysis of atomic and hydrogen weapons tests. As a young child I can still remember the ground shaking every time a bomb was set-off at the Nevada test-site.

We have a great time in Vegas! There is so much to see and do. We stay at the Mirage and enjoy the sights and sounds of the strip. The Venetian is incredible and the water show at the Bellagio is breath taking. We take in the Pirates of the Caribbean show and also see an incredible mime performance at the Excaliber.

We arrived on Friday, and on Sunday morning I leave Debra and Ali poolside and hustle up to St. George, Utah. My nephew is having a missionary farewell; he will be going to Geneva, Switzerland on his mission. They don't think I'm coming and I surprise everyone at the Church. Dad and Linda are there and it is good to see everyone.

On Monday we head up to St. George; but before we go I take Debra and Ali to see the neighborhood I grew up in.

We spend a day in St. George visiting with my brother, Karl and his wife Karen and their great kids. The next day Lisa, my sister-in-law who is also visiting family and will be at Deana's Wedding, hitches a ride with us and we head-up to Salt Lake City. We stop at Nordstrom's to visit Deana at work and then take her out to dinner that night at Trolley Square. It is good to see her, though kind of sad for me because I know we can never be as close as we used to be. This is going to be an extremely hectic week for her, as family and friends are literally coming in from all over the world. We won't see her again until the wedding.

The next day we head up to Logan, Utah to spend a couple of great days with Linda and Dad. Dad is looking well - Linda is taking good care of him. Dad has rented rooms for all of our side of the family at the Hilton Hotel where Deana is getting married. It is the same hotel where I used to work a graveyard shift as I was putting myself through school at the University of Utah.

On Saturday, we all head to the hotel to get checked in and then go up near the State Capital Building to the small, quaint Chapel where Deana is getting married. The Chapel is on a hill that gives a panoramic view of downtown Salt Lake and the expanding valley. We reunite with Karl, Karen and family and also Lisa. It is a nice wedding and I do fight back the tears as I give Deana away.

After the ceremony, we head back to the hotel for the wedding reception. It is such a large reception that the entire banquet room of the hotel has been rented. The reception is conducted in Polynesian style and it is beautifully done. We all have a great time.

That morning we awake and say our good-byes and head back to Vegas where we will catch a flight back to Virginia. We have no idea about the storm that is brewing for us there.

TUESDAY, APRIL 17TH

We get the phone call from hell tonight! Chad calls and tells us that he and some of his dorm buddies were arrested over the weekend and they spent the night in jail. As minors, they were arrested for being drunk and disorderly in public and for the unlawful possession of liquor. I'm in total shock, and it takes a minute for it to sink in. I think he's kidding and I ask him if he is just putting me on. He assures me that he is not. He says his court date has been set for May 31st! Ali is in the room and I tell her to go upstairs, we need to talk to Chad in private.

I tell Debra the news and hand the phone to her. She talks to Chad for a few minutes and then hands the phone back to me. She is trembling, and I'm still not thinking straight. I ask him exactly what happened. He says that he doesn't remember much except someone in the dorm called the cops on them and reported that they were being drunk and disorderly to the point that security couldn't handle them. I get the impression that Chad is talking about someone like a hall monitor or the dorm parents, or whatever.

I ask him if he is okay now and fight the urge to let him have it. I ask whether we need to get a lawyer for him and he says that he has already been assigned a court appointed attorney. Apparently, he has been arraigned before a judge. I ask him how's his schoolwork is going and he says not so good. I am getting the feeling that what Chad is telling us is just the "tip-of-the-iceberg." Debra gets back on the phone again and reminds him that on her side of the family there have been a number of alcoholics and that he is playing with fire. We talk to him for a few minutes more and then tell him we will call him tomorrow or the next day after we have had some time to digest what has happened.

Debra and I just look at each other after we hang up the phone; both of us are shaking our heads in disbelief. How can this happen. Debra and I have set a good example for Chad his whole life. Neither Debra nor I have ever smoked or drank. We have tried to teach our kids good principals to live by and now it seems like Chad could be self-destructing. You add this incident to the fight episode (I still don't know about the spring break drug episode at this point) and it certainly looks like Chad is headed in the wrong direction. I tell Debra that I'm fearful of Chad's status academically. I hope he hasn't ruined his whole semester.

I would like to think this is a temporary glitch and that Chad will learn from this and salvage the situation. We are certainly not the first parents who have had a child arrested for being intoxicated, but we never saw this coming, and Chad has never been this irresponsible. *What the hell is going on up there at JMU? How can a student be arrested and no one tells his parents?*

Needless to say, we don't get much sleep.

WEDNESDAY, APRIL 18TH

It is hard to concentrate at work, and I know I won't get anything done until I communicate to Chad what is on my mind today. At lunchtime I send him an email. I tell Chad that his actions of late have gone beyond the state of being a stupid college stunt and he has got a serious problem. I mention that I suspect I only know a portion of what he has been up to. I let him know that his actions are very immature and that whoever he is trying to impress, that they are not worth impressing. I close the email with the following message:

"Just about every religion and philosophy in this world teaches that happiness in this life can be traced to three things; your physical health, your mental health, and your spiritual health. Needless to say drinking negatively impacts all three areas quickly and then eventually, totally."

"The most mature thing you can do these next three weeks is to stay away from the booze, and do nothing but study, to try to get the best grades you possibly can. Your buddies will get along just fine without you."

"I love you and want the best for you. Dad"

THURSDAY, APRIL 19TH

At two o'clock in the afternoon I get a reply from Chad. I am pleased with his response, though saddened by another revelation. He says that he agrees with everything I've said and that he has been acting very immature. He then reveals that he was also arrested for the possession of marijuana! He said that most of the kids in his suite at the dorm are pot smokers and he had been foolish enough to get caught up in it. He says that his arrest has been a real wake-up call for him and he hasn't drank or smoked since the arrest. He then says that JMU has been in contact with him and, that for him to stay in school, he has to perform ten hours of community service and take a rehab class next semester.

Chad closes his email by saying: "My motivation has been lacking over the last two semesters and my grades will probably reflect this. I know that I am a very capable human being and there is no doubt that in my mind that next semester when I come back I will rock all of my classes. My GPA will be fine I'm sure, by the time I graduate. I have messed up time and time before, but I take solace in the fact that I know my heart will be and has always been in the right place and in the end, I will meet all of my obligations."

Despite the marijuana revelation I am feeling much better about things and I'm thinking maybe this really will only be a glitch in the road for Chad. I send Chad a short reply laying out some ground rules of what Debra and I expect from him when he gets home this summer. I ask him to check with his lawyer to

6

make sure that there is no chance that this incident will end up on his permanent record as long as he does everything the court tells him to do. I also warn him that raising his GPA is not as easy as he thinks and that even if he were to get straight A's the rest of his college career his GPA would end up around 3.5, assuming he finishes this year with a 2.0 average. I admonish him once again to hit the books hard these last three weeks.

A mere two-and-a-half hours latter, as I am getting ready to go home, I get a bizarre reply from Chad! Even though my return message is attached to the email he doesn't acknowledge it. Instead, he wants me to relay a message to Debra. He says he has really been feeling weird lately. He says his back feels locked like there is something wrong with his spinal cord, and he says his neck shoots off in weird directions at times and he is having trouble keeping his head still! He goes on to say that sometimes his eyes roll to the top of his head and his legs have been buckling under him. He also says that his heart is beating fast all the time and that some of his blood vessels expand for no reason. He then says, "I have no idea what is going on with me, but I don't feel normal. I don't feel like my normal self at all. I'm also stressing out all the time now because of this, and I'm getting paranoid. I always think everybody's talking about me and my eyes are always glassy white and I can see all sorts of blood vessels in my eyes." He closes his email by saying, "Maybe I have some whack condition or something, I'm sure it will pass, but maybe Mom can tell me exactly what is going on."

I stare at the monitor screen thinking what in the world! I have to read it again to make sure I got it right. I sit there for a minute a little dumbfounded and a little scared. I print the email and head for home, hoping that Debra will be there. She is. I explain briefly what is going on and I hand her the email so she can read for herself. She immediately puts in a call to Chad and he answers. Chad starts to tell her the same thing on the phone and Debra stops him from time to time to ask him a few questions about each symptom. Just then, Debra can hear Chad's roommate come into the room as Chad says hi to him. Chad tells Debra not to worry about it, whatever it was, it was only temporary, he is now feeling fine. Debra tells Chad that he needs to go to the school nurse to get checked out, and if he can't get in to see her, to go to the hospital. Chad promises her he will and then hangs up.

I look at Debra and ask her what in the world is going on! Debra thinks that he has been having anxiety attacks. We both discuss the fact that he is under a lot of stress right now with the arrest and the fact that he is not doing well in school and finals are coming up. I feel a little guilty wondering if my last email was the reason Chad had stressed out.

FRIDAY, APRIL 20TH

Debra calls Chad to see if he has gone to the school nurse or the hospital. Chad says that he has visited the school nurse and they told him there is nothing wrong with him. Debra tries calling our family doctor to see if she can prescribe something for Chad that will help alleviate the stress. The doctor is not in and her backup refuses.

WEDNESDAY, APRIL 26TH

I receive a letter today from James Madison University. The letter informs us that the University has found Chad "responsible for a Substance Abuse - Alcohol violation and a Substance Abuse - Drugs violation." The letter is from the Office of Judicial Affairs. It is brief and contains no details. There is also no mention of the fact that Chad had been arrested. As a parent: "Too Little Too Late" guys!

I am also struck by the surrealness of the letter. This is not part of the "American Dream" that every parent envisions for their child's future.

CHAPTER 2

THIS CAN'T BE HAPPENING!

WEDNESDAY, MAY 2ND

I call JMU today to find out more about their substance abuse policy and to verify what Chad has told us about what he is required to do. I have been thinking about Chad a lot lately. I have concerns whether Chad has been in contact with his court appointed attorney, and I am hoping that he is doing well on his finals this week.

Debra and I are going to pick him up on Friday.

FRIDAY, MAY 4TH

Harrisonburg is almost a four-hour drive for us. We leave the house at 7:30 AM and arrive at about 11:15 AM. On the way up Debra and I discuss various concerns that we both share for our kids.

I managed to weave our pickup through the parked cars of the other parents and find a space pretty close to Chad's dorm. The door to the dormitory is kept locked, and we use the outside phone to dial Chad's room. There is no answer. One of the other students lets us in, as they are passing through the doorway. We make our way up to Chad's room and run into him in the hallway. He looks haggard, and he is wearing a cap with the visor pulled low over his forehead, where you can barely see his eyes. He mumbles a hello and we ask how he is doing. He apparently just got up and he is not quite ready for us. We start taking down to the truck the things he has packed.

I notice that Chad doesn't look up as we pass other people in the hallways and out on the lawn. One or two students say hi to Chad as they pass and Chad barely acknowledges them. I just figure that Chad must be exhausted from his finals and is really tired and also a little reserved, since this is the first time we have seen him since his arrest.

Debra and I have already agreed that we are not going to keep Chad on a "guilt trip," and we try on the way home to keep the conversation light. When I ask Chad on how he did on his finals, he is noncommittal and mumbles his reply.

SUNDAY, MAY 6TH

Chad's first weekend home has been a strange one. He has barely come out of his room since we've arrived and seems to be sleeping days and on his computer all night. It is also very unusual that since we got home Chad hasn't bothered to unpack. His bags and various boxes have been left exactly where we put them. Chad is normally a bit of a clean freak and likes to have his room and his things well organized. I tell Debra not to worry about it. I think he is still unwinding from what he has been through for the past couple of months.

THURSDAY, MAY 10TH

The past few days have been hectic. I had a Red Cross finance committee meeting yesterday and a Virginia Quality Life board meeting early this morning. I spend most of the day interviewing applicants that have applied for a position in our department. I am losing my most valuable employee in a few weeks and she is going to be very tough to replace. In addition, the CFA exam is only a few weeks away and I've been trying to find the time to study for that.

Debra interrupts my studying tonight to let me know that she really has concerns about Chad. Not only has his strange behavior continued, but she has noticed a couple of other things. She doesn't think Chad has taken a bath since he's been home, and he seems to be mumbling to himself a lot. His bags are also still unpacked. Chad has always kept himself well manicured and he normally takes a shower every day. Debra mentions the weird email we got from Chad last month and she tells me that she thinks something is wrong. She has made an appointment to take Chad to see Dr. Duer next week. I have been so busy that I've had hardly interacted with Chad at all since he has been home. I nod my head in agreement and suggest that the fact that he knows he has to appear in court in a few weeks might have something to do with it.

At about 7:30 PM, we get the other phone call every parent dreads. Chad, Ali and her boy friend have gone to the movies. We have let Chad take our family car, which is a Toyota Camry. It is by far the best car I have ever owned, and I had just finished paying it off about six months earlier. Apparently, Chad is driving too fast as he comes over a hill just as he is entering Gloucester and doesn't have time to break properly before hitting a long line of cars that are backed up the hill from a stop light. He hits the car in front of him, which starts a chain reaction. Five different cars have been damaged, counting our own. Luckily no one is seriously injured.

It is Ali who is on the phone, and she reassures us that everyone is okay but they need a ride - the car wasn't so lucky. She said the police had it towed away somewhere. We ask Ali for her friend's phone number so we can call his folks, and then we tell Ali we are on our way and to meet us at the bowling alley, which is close by.

Well, at least no one is seriously injured, but I can only cringe knowing that I need to call my insurance company to let them know my teen-age son was responsible for a five-car accident.

When we get there, it takes us a while to find the kids, because for some reason they think it has taken us too long to get there. They have gone to other side of the highway, thinking maybe we are there. Chad has a cut lip and light burns on his arms where the airbag had exploded. There is no sign of the wreckage when we get there. Ali says that most of the cars were only slightly damaged, with the exception of the one immediately in front of us and our own. Chad still seems to be in a state of shock, and he claims that he wasn't going too fast and that the brakes didn't work right. Ali said she didn't think he was going that fast, either.

When we get home, I look at the citation Chad has been given. He has been cited for reckless driving, and his court date is set for June 13th. This is starting to turn into a nightmare.

MONDAY, MAY 14TH

I call our car insurance agent and they tell me to go ahead and get a rental car, it will be covered under our policy. They will try to get a claims adjuster out in a few days to assess the amount of damage. I still have not seen our car, and I don't even know where it has been taken. The kids are no help because they don't remember who towed it. After making a number of phone calls I finally locate it at a garage in Gloucester, forty-five miles away.

I put in a call to Jim Breeden, who is a prominent attorney in our area and has a great reputation for handling traffic related offenses. My boss knows him personally and has alerted him that I will be calling him to ask him to handle Chad's case. I don't want to take any chances on this, with so many people involved; there is no telling what they will do. I also need to get Chad's charges reduced. We are already paying $2,400 a year in car insurance premiums.

TUESDAY, MAY 15TH

Since Debra and I have spoken, I have been more observant when around Chad. He has been coming out of his bedroom more often to either watch a movie video or to take in a NBA playoff game. He does mumble a lot, but, still, I have had several normal conversations with him and I don't think Chad is as bad off as Debra seems to think he is. But what she tells me tonight, floors me!

She said she had made Chad go with her when she went to do some shopping in Tappahannock. One of her purposes was to see if she could get Chad to open up and tell her what's wrong. Chad told her that he was still having the same physical ailments that he had mentioned in his email, that he was hearing voices and he knew that everyone was talking about him. When Debra asked him what he thought was causing all this, he told her that something was wrong with his scrotum! When she asked him what he meant, he said, "When I lift my scrotum up, the voices talk to me!" Debra said she tried to remain calm, and then asked him what are the voices telling him. "They are calling me a faggot!" he said.

I don't know what to think now. I do wonder if Chad could possibly be putting Debra on. The appointment with Dr. Duer can come none too soon.

THURSDAY, MAY 17TH

Debra takes Chad to his doctor's appointment with Dr. Duer. She is seeing him under the pretense that she is going to check his scrotum. Debra waits in the waiting room while Dr. Duer examines Chad. After about fifteen minutes, she escorts Chad to the waiting room and asks Debra if she can see her alone. She tells her that, as far as she can see, there is absolutely nothing wrong with Chad's scrotum and that she told Chad that, but she agrees that Chad needs to see a psychiatrist.

For the next half-hour Dr. Duer tries to find a psychiatrist that will see Chad right away, to no avail. The best she can do is make an appointment for about a month away. Debra tells the doctor to wait, and she will see if she can find someone sooner through her contacts at work. Debra asks the doctor if she can prescribe something that will help Chad. Dr. Duer says it is best to wait until the psychiatrist can see Chad.

FRIDAY, MAY 18TH

Debra is able to find a psychiatrist who is willing to see Chad Friday, next week. His name is Mario Gomez and he practices out of Richmond. I am pleased for both Chad and Debra's sakes.

I try to call Chad's attorney in Harrisonburg to see what is going on about his defense. Chad apparently has made no effort to contact her, and doesn't have a clue on what he is supposed to do. She is not there and I leave a message for her to call me.

I get a call from the claims adjuster. They are going to total the car! I will be sent a check for the low blue-book value of the car, based on the fact that we had a lot of miles on it. This is not good news. The car had been a gem, and I think it easily had another 75,000 miles in it. I think to myself it looks like another four years of monthly car payments. The agent mentions that one of the reasons they are totaling it is that the air bag had been triggered and, apparently, it is very costly to replace the air bag. The thought crosses my mind that the air bag probably saved Chad from more serious injury. What a good car it had been. 185,000 miles of carefree driving and its last act was to protect Chad. It's funny how you can get a sentimental attachment to a car.

MONDAY, MAY 21ST

I go into Chad's room to get a computer manual, and I notice a letter on his desk from JMU. It's his grades for the semester. I am stunned! He has flunked one of his courses and has gotten three D's and a C in the others. He has been put on academic probation, so much for salvaging his grades. I quietly go back to my study. I decide not to say anything to Chad, at least not right now. What in the world is going on! I don't understand it. How does your kid go from being a star student, who is extremely goal oriented, to this? And it all happens it a matter of months. I am anxious now to see what the psychiatrist has to say. It has finally become obvious to me that we need professional help - something Debra knew the day we picked him up from school.

THURSDAY, MAY 24TH

Chad's strange behavior has continued this week, though I never seem to see the things that Debra keeps telling me about. I have been busy at nights studying for the exam, but every time I see Chad, he seems okay and we have normal conversations. I do notice though he is keeping strange hours; he is keeping to himself; and he never has cleaned up his room. Debra tells me that he told her he is still hearing voices and that his scrotum is really bothering him. He wants her to buy the best jock strap she can find to help support his scrotum. I still don't know what to think and I can't wait to hear what the psychiatrist has to say. Debra will be taking him to his appointment tomorrow.

I finally get a hold of Chad's attorney. She puts my mind at ease. She tells me that she handles a lot of these types of cases and because this is Chad's first drug offense he'll end up paying a hefty fine and will have to do some community work and attend some support classes. If he completes his community work and attends all of his classes, the violation will be taken off his record. She explains how to get to the courthouse and tells us to show up about fifteen minutes early, and she will brief us at that time. I ask her if I should bring Chad's high school transcript that shows he was an honor student? She says that's a good idea. She seems really nice and knowledgeable. I also get the impression that she works long hard hours, as she offered to meet with us anytime, whether it is the weekend or at night.

FRIDAY, MAY 25TH

I get a call at work from Debra in the late afternoon. The visit to the psychiatrist turned out to be a disaster. Upon arriving at the psychiatrist's office, Chad absolutely refused to stay for his visit! Debra had taken him there, again under the pretense that this doctor was a specialist and he was going to check Chad's scrotum. When they were filling out forms in the receptionist area, Chad realized where he was and got up and left. Debra followed him out into the hallway and pleaded with him for fifteen minutes to please go in. He absolutely refused. She even threatened that she would call the police to make him go in. Chad told her that there is nothing wrong with his head; it's his scrotum.

The trip to Richmond had taken over two hours. Debra has no choice but to return to the car and to go home. Chad doesn't say a word to her all the way home.

I am now mad at Chad. Debra had taken the day off work to do this. It wouldn't have killed him to go in and to see the doctor, and it certainly would have helped his mother's state of mind, and mine as well.

MONDAY, MAY 28TH

Debra calls Dr. Gomez's office and explains what happened. She asks them to please reschedule and she will make sure to get me involved in getting Chad there. The appointment is set for Thursday, June 8th. Debra calls me after making the appointment and I agree to take Chad this time.

I ask Ali to pick up Chad's transcript, while she is at school today. I have called ahead and they tell me they will have it ready.

Debra gets the most ridiculous traffic ticket today. A Virginia State Police officer stopped her and gave her a ticket for an expired inspection sticker. The only thing is, it's the rental car! We had no idea it was expired and certainly didn't think to look. You would think the officer would cut her a break, but he didn't.

We call the rental car company and they apologize profusely and tell us to bring the car back and they'll exchange it and reimburse us for the ticket. They also can't believe the officer actually went ahead and cited Debra.

THURSDAY, MAY 31ST

We leave early for Harrisonburg. Chad's court appearance isn't until 1:00 PM but we want to get there with plenty of time to spare. Ali stays home and I ask her to please not to get up to any mischief while we are gone. We have our hands full with Chad right now. We will be spending the night in Harrisonburg.

We ask Chad whether he has written the letter to JMU that they required for his reinstatement. He says no but he'll do it when we get to the hotel. The letter is due June 1st and we thought we would drop it off while we are there. The letter is part of the requirement that JMU has for their students who have been put on academic probation. In order to register for classes the following semester, the students have to explain in a letter what they have learned and what steps they are taking to insure it doesn't happen again. We have been after Chad all week to get it done, but he keeps procrastinating. We certainly don't want to do it for him, and we would like to think that he is still responsible enough to make sure it gets done.

Upon arriving, we have no trouble in finding the courthouse and have enough time to get a bite to eat. Other than a traffic ticket, this is the first time Debra and I have ever had to make an appearance of any kind in court. We are a little nervous, and Chad is being pretty quiet.

As instructed, we arrive at the courthouse fifteen minutes early, but Chad's attorney doesn't appear to be there! There are several courts in session, and we are not even sure which one we are supposed to be in. I had explained to the attorney that I was six feet tall and had a reddish beard with some gray, but she had not given me any of her identifiable features. There are many people passing by who could be attorneys, but no one stops and acknowledges us.

We are getting a little frantic, as it is just a few minutes before starting. We ask several people if they are Chad's attorney and no one is. We ask a guard if he knows which court session we are suppose to be in, and he indicates that it is the farthest one down the hall, but he is not sure. We wait until five minutes after 1:00 PM and then decide to go into the court session indicated by the guard.

We are now really nervous. The court is full of people and I have no idea if Chad's attorney is going to show up or even if we are in the right courtroom. The cases seem to drag on slowly. I tell Debra to wait here and I go back outside to see if it looks like anyone is looking for us - no luck. When I return to court, the case being heard concerns a young coed who has also been charged with a marijuana charge. This relieves my mind somewhat, and I decide that when Chad's name is called, all we can do is tell the Judge that we are here but Chad's court appointed attorney isn't.

When Chad's name is called I nudge him to stand up and start to get up myself to give my little speech when I see out of the corner of my eye someone approach us. It is Chad's attorney. She asks the Judge for a few minutes to meet with her client and explains she just got out of another court case, which ran overtime. She does look very professional, and I breathe a sigh of relief.

After hearing another case, Chad's name is called out again and both Chad and his attorney come forward. The discussion goes exactly as the attorney told me it would go, and the Judge levels a $500 fine and assigns Chad to the Alcohol Safety Action Program (ASAP) that will oversee Chad's community work and the classes he will be required to attend. If Chad successfully completes the program the charges against him will be dropped at his next court hearing in December.

We are then led to the clerk's office by the attorney, where we pay the fine. Then she takes us to a room where we pay another fee and sign Chad up for the ASAP program. They indicate that there is a separate ASAP program for our county and they will be getting in contact with Chad soon. They have taken his driver's license and he now has a restricted license. He is now only allowed to drive to and from his ASAP appointments and his place of employment.

We thank Chad's attorney for her time, and she tells us to feel free to call her if we have any questions or need assistance going forward.

We are all greatly relieved now that this is over, and we actually enjoy the rest of the day. We eat out at a nice restaurant and spend the night at the Marriott.

FRIDAY, JUNE 1ST

We take our time getting up and checking out of the hotel. We are going to drop Chad's letter off before we leave and are incredulous when we find Chad hasn't written it! We thought he was working on it last night. Chad said he did work on it but he didn't know what to say. I ask Chad, "Do you want to go back to school next year or what!?" We have already checked out of the hotel so we end up dictating to Chad in the car what to write. Chad needs to get his act together soon, or I don't know what we are going to do!

CHAPTER 3

DELUSIONS & HALLUCINATION

TUESDAY, JUNE 5TH

Ali and Debra have gone to Kilmarnock to get something for dinner. I am up in my study on my computer and Chad is in his room and I'm assuming that he is playing a computer game. I think I hear Chad talking to someone. I'm wondering who is there, and then I hear Chad raise his voice. I go downstairs to check it out. Chad is standing alone in the kitchen. I ask him who was he talking to. He says no one, and then he quickly goes to his room.

FRIDAY, JUNE 8TH

Chad knows he has no choice but to go with me today to see the psychiatrist. I will drag him there if I have to. But I don't want to use the "strong-arm" approach. I tell Chad that by going today; it will accomplish a number of things. One, it will make his mother happy and will get her off his back; and two, he will talk to someone who just might be able to help him with his scrotum problem. This is the first time I have spoken to Chad about his scrotum. He has never mentioned it to me, nor has he ever told me any of the things he has been telling Debra. It is as if it is important to him that his Dad thinks well of him, but he lets his guard down around Debra. I also promise him that if he goes today, his mother and I will pay for a specialist to examine his scrotum. All Chad says in reply is, "Okay."

Debra is really excited that Chad has agreed to go and tells me to make sure I tell Dr. Gomez everything that Chad has told her.

It is a strange feeling being in a psychiatrist's office. I know it is silly, but I have never been in one before and you can't help but be more alert than normal. I have never had a very high opinion of the work they do. My mother had gone to several, and she seemed to come out in worse shape then when she went in. I also once lived next to a prominent psychiatrist who had an affair, and his wife ended up committing suicide.

Dr. Gomez introduces himself and is very soft-spoken. So much so, that I can barely hear him. I am disappointed when he asks me to explain what problem Chad has been having while Chad is still in the room. This is very embarrassing for both Chad and me, and I know how uncomfortable Chad is around strangers to begin with. I explain how Debra and I both noticed that Chad had been acting strangely since he has been home from school, and he apparently has been hearing voices. I mentioned that we had taken him to see our family doctor and she agreed that he needed to see a psychiatrist. I do mention that Debra is afraid that Chad has schizophrenia. I also explain that Debra is a registered nurse, who works at a prison where a number of inmates have schizophrenia, so Debra is aware of the symptoms. However, I don't work up the nerve to tell the doctor about Chad's obsession with his scrotum. I am just afraid it will be too embarrassing for Chad.

Dr. Gomez then takes Chad to another room where he can talk to Chad alone. I am hoping that I did a reasonable job of explaining what has been happening. I am wishing that Debra was here, but she felt like Chad was still mad at her for tricking him into the last visit and things would go better if she wasn't there. I am also hoping that Chad tells Dr. Gomez about his scrotum.

They visit for about fifteen to twenty minutes before they return. The doctor says they had a nice visit and then starts to tell me a few things. He is speaking so softly and he has a bit of an accent. I can't hear half of the stuff he is telling me! I ask him to repeat himself several times, and then I just give up. The doctor does tell me that while it is too early to properly diagnose Chad, his first impression is that Chad is suffering from severe depression. He does not have schizophrenia. If he had schizophrenia, there would be no doubt about it; the symptoms would be so obvious. *That's a relief!*

Dr. Gomez then says that Chad has been under a lot of stress and that we shouldn't try to pressure him right now to do anything. He will be prescribing a light dosage of Prozac that Chad should take every day and that we should bring Chad back in about three weeks to monitor his progress.

I can't wait to get back home and to call Debra with the news. It is a load off my mind that whatever Chad is going through is not as serious as Debra thinks. This news, along with the fact that Chad has finally received some medication, should make Debra feel a lot better.

On the way home, I ask Chad what he and the doctor talked about. Chad doesn't say much in reply, except that he had mentioned how things had been going at JMU.

When I call Debra, I don't get the response I was hoping for. She is skeptical and asks me did I tell the doctor everything. I explain to her that Chad was with me when I was explaining things, so I never did mention Chad's obsession with his scrotum. I also don't know if Chad said anything about it when he was talking to Dr. Gomez alone. I get a little impatient with Debra and tell her, look, the doctor was very adamant that Chad did not have schizophrenia. After I said this and mention again that Chad would now be getting some medication, Debra seems more at ease.

SATURDAY, JUNE 9TH

Debra goes to get Chad's Prozac prescription filled. The dosage is only 10 milligrams, which she says is about as low as can be prescribed. Chad will not take it at first, but when Debra starts to get angry, he takes it.

TUESDAY, JUNE 12TH

I am getting concerned. We have heard nothing from the ASAP program since Chad's court date. Chad has been assigned to the Tri-River ASAP program that covers the Northern Neck and Middle Peninsula regions. I want Chad to take responsibility for this, and I've told him to be proactive in pursuing it. He claims he has made several phone calls and keeps leaving a recorded message, but no one calls. I make several phone calls today and find out that they only accept phone calls from 3:00 PM to 4:00 PM during the day, except on Wednesday, when they don't accept any calls!

I pass this news on to Chad and tell him to make sure he calls them on Thursday to find out what is going on. I know this is hard for Chad. He is extremely self-conscious right now, and it is

21

very hard for him to talk to complete strangers, even on the phone. However, I also don't think that Debra and I should have to do everything for him - he needs to take some responsibility for this mess he has gotten himself into.

THURSDAY, JUNE 14TH

I remind Chad as I leave for work that he is to call the ASAP people between 3 PM and 4 PM. He says he will. I call the house after 4:00 PM to see how it went. Chad said the person hung up on him! I said what! He says that he was trying to explain that his case had been transferred from Rockingham County, when the girl blurted out, "You are on drugs!" and hung the phone up on him.

I feel bad now. Chad hasn't done any drugs since his arrest in Rockingham, but his present mental state has caused Chad to lose whatever confidence he had when trying to talk to strangers. When he is under stress he mumbles, and his speech is somewhat slurred. I could understand why the social worker might think Chad was high, but that is no excuse for her to treat him the way she did. He was only trying to comply with whatever he was supposed to do. I thought social workers are supposed to be trained in this area and to be sympathetic towards people. I hope we just got one bad apple. I feel its best not to pressure Chad any further on this and, after I tell Debra the story, she says she will call them tomorrow to find out what is going on.

FRIDAY, JUNE 15TH

Debra told me that she did speak with ASAP and Chad has an appointment with them on Friday June 22nd. Chad has been on the Prozac now for a week. We have been asking him each day if he has been taking his pill and he says he has. I tell Debra that I think Chad has shown some improvement. With the exception of the ASAP phone call, Chad seems to have relaxed a bit to me and seems happier. Debra agrees that he does seem to be a little more relaxed but that Chad told her the other day he is still hearing voices. He wants to know when he is going to see the specialist about his scrotum.

I just shake my head when I hear this. Why Chad will only speak to Debra about what is going on and no one else is beyond me. Debra is not happy about this. She wishes that Chad would talk about it to others and me because it's driving her nuts! We discuss how Ali has been reacting to all this. We have not been open in our discussions around her. She is certainly aware that something is up with Chad, but we haven't let on to her just how serious it may be.

MONDAY, JUNE 18TH

Debra has worked two twelve hour shifts over the weekend and is now going to take Chad up to Harrisonburg to attend some meetings that are required for someone who is on academic probation. The day will turn into a nightmare for her.

As they head to the car, Debra remembers that she forgot some papers and goes back into the house to get them. As she comes back out, Chad is screaming at the top of his lungs "Shut the fuck up!" "Shut the fuck up!" He seems to be looking down the hill towards the oyster house. Horrified, Debra asks Chad who is he yelling at! Chad points towards the oyster house and says those people are screaming at him. She looks down the hill and she sees no one, and she even tries to see if she can hear anyone, Chad is so convincing. He is so upset he is physically trembling, and seems to be on the verge of tears. Debra speaks softly to Chad and reassures him that there is no one there.

Spooked, Debra debates whether to go on the trip. The meetings are mandatory, so Debra decides to go ahead. It seems like Chad has calmed down. They get about thirty miles and Chad starts complaining that his shoulder is hurting. They go a few miles more and he starts yelling that his shoulder is killing him. He is holding on to his shoulder and starts to cry.

Debra stops in Tappahannock and gets a shoulder sling and some Motrin for Chad. After Chad takes the Motrin and Debra helps him put on the shoulder sling, she waits a few minutes and sees if Chad is starting to feel any better. He complains that his shoulder is still hurting, so Debra decides to turn around and heads back home. Once there, Debra gives Chad a double dose of the Prozac, and Chad sleeps for the rest of the day.

Debra tells me the news when I get home from work. Once again, I just don't know what to think. Why do these things only seem to happen to Debra? Is Chad playing some kind of sick game with her? Was this all a show, so Chad wouldn't have to face anybody at JMU? Dr. Gomez, who is the expert, didn't seem to think that Chad was that sick.

Unfortunately, I realize that there are good answers to these questions. These things are only happening with Debra because she is around him a lot more than I am. I think Chad let's his guard down around her but not me. I think the idea of going to JMU was very stressful for Chad which, given his mental condition, could possibly have caused the trauma that Debra witnessed. I am also pretty sure that Chad was not straight with Dr. Gomez.

We have a very serious problem here, and I need to start waking up and realizing that this thing is not going to just go away on its own.

WEDNESDAY, JUNE 20TH

Debra has taken Chad to see Dr. Duck, an urologist, in Tappahannock. Debra had let the receptionist know when she made the appointment that Chad was having mental problems and he seemed to be obsessed with his "scrotum problem." On the way there, Chad tells Debra that he will kill himself if the doctor says there is nothing wrong with his scrotum. Debra thinks he is using a manner of speech, but she tells him please don't talk like that.

Chad is with the doctor for only a few minutes. When he approaches Debra in the waiting room he tells her that the doctor said there was nothing wrong with his scrotum.

When they get home Debra calls me with the news. I was almost hoping that the doctor would say that Chad is right; there is something wrong with his scrotum. Better than acknowledging that your kid is going nuts!

FRIDAY, JUNE 22ND

Debra takes Chad to the Tri-River ASAP offices in Urbanna. Chad's appointment was supposed to be for nine o'clock but they find out that there are a number of people who are being signed up and they are being taken in alphabetical order. They do not get to Chad until after ten, and they don't leave until after 11:00 AM. Debra said she was not allowed to meet with them, they only saw Chad. Chad said he had to pay a $125.00 fee and that he is supposed to be there every Friday for meetings. He is to pay $50.00 at each meeting. Not only will he be required to attend these meetings; he is also to attend AA meetings twice a week. In addition, he has to go see their psychologist once a month, and he has to pay a fee each time he goes. This is discouraging news for Debra and me. We no longer trust Chad with our car; we are going to have to take turns giving Chad rides. With all these meetings, it is going to be a major burden.

I ask Chad and Debra when he is supposed to start his community service. They both have a blank look on their faces. "Remember the Judge assigned Chad to do fifty hours of community service," I remind them. They said the ASAP people never brought the subject up!

SATURDAY, JUNE 23RD

Debra and I have been invited to a wedding reception for the daughter of one of our friends at church. They have a nice home and the reception is held in their back yard. It is a beautiful reception that is extremely well done. Many of our friends are there, and we have a great time. As I admire the bride and groom, I can't help but wonder what are the chances that we may be doing this someday soon for Chad and his bride. Probably, slim to none.

TUESDAY, JUNE 25TH

We meet with Jim Breeden, Chad's new lawyer, tonight to go over Chad's case, on July 11th. Jim may call Debra to be a witness. She had noticed before the accident that the brakes were getting soft and that maybe that was a contributing factor. Jim walks us through what his arguments will be and tells us that we need to get the reckless driving charged reduced, or we will be open to any lawsuits that the other people who were involved in the accident might want to file.

Jim is a likable guy. He is older, on the short side and he has long, light grayish, curly hair that sits on top of his head in disarray. He is very affable, wears bow ties, and gives the impression of being the absent-minded professor. He does appear to be very bright and seems to know the law backwards and forwards. I also get the impression that he is a workaholic.

On the way home, Debra and I have a serious talk about Chad. I was hoping that between the Prozac that Chad was taking and the fact that an urologist had informed Chad that there was nothing wrong with his scrotum, it would convince him that he didn't have a physical problem. But Chad has seemed to be more in the dumps lately, and Debra told me that after the visit to the doctor Chad told her, "that no one understands my problem except me. I know now that I'm going to have to fix it myself."

Chad's next appointment with Dr. Gomez is this Friday. Debra tells me that she is going to make sure that the doctor knows every detail of what has been going on. She tells me that she has looked up schizophrenia in her old textbooks and Chad is exhibiting all of the symptoms. She reminds me that her family has had a history of mental illness. Two cousins have committed suicide, and she is afraid of Chad doing the same thing. She tells me I need to wake up and smell the thorns!

FRIDAY, JUNE 29TH

Debra doesn't have much trouble in getting Chad to go with her to see Dr. Gomez. I think that part of the reason is Chad does like him. I know how important this visit is, and I tell Debra to call me as soon as she gets home.

Debra is upset when she calls me. She said that Chad got very angry with her when she spoke so frankly to the doctor, and she also says she was not able to convince Dr. Gomez that what Chad has is schizophrenia. He admitted that Chad is more ill than he originally thought and that Chad had been exhibiting some schizophrenic tendencies, but he still needed to do more psychotherapy before he could form a complete diagnosis. To me this is good news. I tell Debra this and she becomes exasperated with me.

She explains that when they got there that the doctor insisted that Chad be present when Debra explained what had been happening. Debra felt it important not to hold back and told Dr. Gomez everything that had been going on. She could tell that Chad was getting upset, especially when she started talking about his obsession with his scrotum. When she finished the doctor and Chad went to another room. She said that maybe they were gone about fifteen minutes before they returned.

26

Dr. Gomez started to tell Debra a few things, and she was having trouble understanding everything he was saying. The gist of it though was it is too early to draw any conclusions and that he needed to meet with Chad in about a month. He does prescribe Zyprexa, which is a medicine that treats schizophrenic disorders and he increases the dosage of Prozac.

The bottom line is that we still don't have a diagnosis as to what is wrong with Chad nor have we received any guidance on what we are supposed to do next, other than make sure Chad takes his medicine.

Debra tells me she thinks that Chad told the doctor what she said wasn't true. She also tells me that Chad confronted her in the car on the way home. He tells her that he can't believe she would tell a total stranger something he told her in confidence. He also told her that, "At least Dad would wait until I was not there before he would tell someone!"

WEDNESDAY, JULY 4TH

Two of Debra's four sisters are here to celebrate the July 4th holiday. Cindy is from Ohio and Carrie is from the state of Washington. Carrie's daughter, along with her high school band, is in the July 4th parade in Washington, D.C. They are all there today. Chad and I have elected to stay home. I do some yard work and then Chad and I watch a movie on TV.

Debra has taken a few days off. It's a welcome and needed break for Debra.

SUNDAY, JULY 8TH

After I get home from church, Debra tells me she needs to talk to me about Chad. We can't force Chad to take his medicine, and he gets upset when we get after him. Debra tells me that she has been counting his pills each day and he is not always taking them. She also tells me that the Zyprexa dosage is so light she doubts it would make much difference, even if he were taking it every day. She also tells me that Chad keeps asking her for $4,000 to fix his scrotum. Apparently, he has been on the Internet and has found some doctor that has told him that the cost for corrective surgery on an enlarged scrotum is $4,000. This is just great! Debra starts to cry and says she just can't take much more of this. She is also sick and tired of Chad always coming to her to talk about his scrotum, and no one else.

I don't know what to say. It seems to me that Chad has his good days and his bad days. It is so frustrating, because, as much as we want to influence his behavior, we know that putting pressure on him causes too much stress. Basically, all that Chad has been doing is sleeping, watching TV and playing games either on his Playstation or his computer. He can't hold a job and he isn't helping around the house. He has not done what was required of him by JMU to be reinstated, and it's beginning to look like Chad will be in no shape to attend school late next month.

I tell Debra I will try to talk to him about his scrotum problem and see if I can get him to open up more to me. But I also tell her that I want to wait until after his court date on July 11th. I don't want to cause him any unnecessary stress before then and risk having some kind of episode while in court. I also make a point that we need to make sure that Chad takes his medicine tomorrow and on the eleventh.

WEDNESDAY, JULY 11TH

Jim meets us a few minutes before court and goes over what has been happening. He tells us that he met with the police officer that had written Chad up for the reckless driving. The officer said that Chad was so scared and polite that the officer had felt sorry for him. Jim said that he will stress that both Ali and Chad will testify that they were not traveling at an excessive speed and that Debra will verify that the brakes probably needed service. Jim does learn that the prosecution will produce a witness that will testify that Chad was going too fast.

The hearing goes quickly, and I don't remember much about it, except that the officer did testify that he had measured the skid marks that Chad left and they were sixty feet long. The officer does testify that Chad was very cooperative and that there were no drugs or alcohol involved. The Judge reduces the penalty from reckless driving to improper driving. Jim informs me that under this penalty no civil suit can be filed against us.

Debra and I are relieved when we leave the courthouse and head back home. The thought does cross my mind that we have had to bail Chad out of serious trouble twice now in just six weeks.

MONDAY, JULY 16TH

Chad has another ASAP meeting tonight. Our weeks are now filled with ASAP meetings. I took Chad to see the ASAP psychologist today at a counseling center in Gloucester. Chad had to pay some sort of administrative fee. He has now paid ASAP over $600.00. We are making him pay all of the ASAP fees out of his own savings. He doesn't have much left.

He hates going to the meetings and considers them a complete waste of time. So do we, and we are fearful that this whole ASAP thing is putting too much stress on Chad. He says the meetings are extremely boring and all everyone does is talk. He also says that he never says anything because he knows everyone is looking at him and talking about him behind his back. Oh, boy!!

Debra has been driving Chad to all his meetings and has to wait for them to end. One time she went to get some groceries, and when she got back Chad was beside himself. The meeting had gotten over early, and he freaked out when he came out and Debra wasn't there.

I'm wondering if today the psychologist might have picked up on any of Chad's problems. When I inquire of Chad on how it went, he says that the guy asked him some questions and that was it. Chad didn't volunteer any information and apparently the guy was just going through the motions. How could they call that a great counseling session? I am becoming less and less impressed with this ASAP program.

THURSDAY, JULY 19TH

Chad's behavior is changing for the worst. He is now muttering to himself all the time. More than once, he has asked me in a demanding tone what did I say to him when I wasn't even looking at him or talking to him. He is also now walking around the house with his left hand at the top of his pants pulling them up to give him more support. Debra was in his bedroom the other day and noticed that he had been cutting round holes in his briefs at various angles! What the hell is going on! Where is this going, and when will it ever end?

When we ask Chad if he is taking his medicine he says yes.

FRIDAY, JULY 20TH

I meet with my one of my Vice-Chairs of the Red Cross Chapter. It is our annual meeting next week where we select the officers for the upcoming year. I feel guilty, but now is a good time to step down. Normally, the chairperson serves a three-year stint; I have been the Chairman for two years and the Treasurer for three years before that. The chapter has tripled in size and our donations have doubled during my tenure, but there is still some things left undone. I'm afraid that our problems with Chad are going to demand more and more of my time, and I also need more time to study and to do more repair work around the house. The Vice-Chair is energetic and talented and I know she would make a great Chairperson. She graciously accepts the nomination, and it is a load off my mind.

SATURDAY, JULY 21ST

I'm in my study when Ali approaches me and asks, "Dad, what is wrong with Chad?" Ali certainly knows that Chad has been having problems, and she has had an experience with him yesterday that really spooked her.

They were outside just messing around and having some fun with our dog, Lacy. There were several of our neighbors down on their dock and it looked like they had some friends with them. As they are playing, Chad abruptly comes to a halt and starts staring at the people on the dock. "What did they say?" Chad asks Ali. Ali hasn't heard a thing, and she turns to look at the people on the dock. They are still at the end of their dock about a hundred yards away, and they are not even looking in Chad and Ali's direction. "Those people are talking about me!" Chad says raising his voice. Ali quickly tells Chad to "chill" and tells him they are not talking about him, and she can't even hear them. Ali says it looks like Chad is listening intently and is getting angry. He yells out, "They are calling me a faggot!" Ali quickly tells Chad to shut-up, they are not talking about him, and she ushers him into the house. Ali then says, "Chad was just shaking, he really believed that those people were calling him that!" Ali said she was scared and just spent the rest of the afternoon in her room.

I tell Ali that Chad is not right, he is mentally ill and that her mother and I are doing all we can to help him. I tell her that we are hoping his medication will make him better and that we are all just going to have to wait until the doctors tell us what to do next. We talk some more about Chad's symptoms, and then Ali leaves. I can only imagine how this is affecting Ali, she and Chad have grown up together. Not only has Chad been her big brother, he has been her best friend throughout the years.

CHAPTER 4

SELF-MUTILATION

SUNDAY, JULY 22ND

Today is the day I decide to have a serious talk with Chad about what is wrong with him. I know it is going to be hard to get him to open up. I think Chad is hoping that I just think this is just a rough spot he's going through and he's still the same ol' Chad. I have two goals: one, to try and at least get him to thinking that maybe his scrotum is okay and two, to find out for sure if he has been taking his medicine and to impress upon him the importance of the medicine. To a lesser extent, I am hoping that we can work out together some sort of attack on how we are going to lick this thing.

After lunch I grab Chad out of his room and tell him that I want to talk to him and to please come to my study. I can tell by the look on his face that he is surprised and that he really doesn't want to do it. Reluctantly, he follows me up the stairs. I start out by telling him that I know he is uncomfortable and he doesn't want to talk about what is going on. I ask him to please bear with me for a few minutes, answer a few questions, and let me know what he is thinking. I can tell he is itching to leave, and we haven't even started. He is standing and staring at the floor with his arms folded.

I let him know that I understand he is going through a tough time and I want to help him. I start asking him some open-ended questions hoping to get him to start talking. It doesn't work at first, but he does say that he just wishes everyone would leave him alone. He knows that everybody is talking about him. I ask him if he still is hearing voices. He doesn't say anything. I ask him if his scrotum is still bothering him. He says yes. He says he needs $4,000 to get it fixed. I tell Chad, even if we had the $4,000, I wouldn't let him get the surgery because all the experts say that there is nothing wrong with his scrotum. "I know what they said and they're wrong!" Chad replies. "But don't worry about it Dad, I got it under control. I'm the only one who understands what is

32

wrong with me and I'm going to take care of it," I ask him what does he mean by that. He just shrugs his shoulders.

The conversation is not going the way I hoped it would. I feel bad about telling him that he is not going to get the money from us. Chad has never asked us for money, until now. I wonder what he is thinking about our refusal to give him any. Here he is, not knowing what is happening to him - probably scared to death; and he is asking us for help; and we are telling him no.

I try to change the direction of the conversation by asking what are his future plans. He says that he wants to get the ASAP stuff behind him and get his scrotum fixed and then return to JMU in January. I latch on to his desire to return to JMU. I have also been wondering if it is a possibility to get him straightened out enough that he could return to school by then. I point out that in order for that to happen he needs to take his medication as prescribed, and he needs to start taking more responsibility for doing those things that are necessary to get him there. I point out that we still have not gotten any guidance from ASAP about how Chad is supposed to fill the community service requirement of his probation.

I ask him has he been taking his medicine and he replies, "Sometimes." I ask him why he doesn't take it all the time. He tells me that he hates the way it knocks him out. He says it makes him feel so tired that he can't even think, and he wants to be alert. I tell him that I think he would find, if he took his medicine all of the time, the voices and the scrotum problem would go away. He doesn't say anything and I can tell he doesn't believe me.

I try to end the conversation on a positive note. I tell him that his mother and I are going to be there for him, and we are going to keep taking him to the experts until we can get this thing worked out. In return I ask him to meet us halfway by taking his medicine and being proactive in getting the community hours done as required. He agrees and we shake hands and I give him a hug and pat him on the back. I tell him to hang in there.

I have not gotten Chad to open up as much as I would have liked, but I'm hoping that it has given Chad some encouragement. It has also made me realize all the more just how obsessed Chad is with his perceived scrotum problem.

TUESDAY, JULY 24TH

I get a call from Chad and I can tell he is almost in tears. He tells me that he had tried for almost an hour to get through to ASAP during the one hour designated calling time. He said he finally got through and the girl hung up on him again. He was trying to tell her that he didn't know what he was supposed to be doing about his community service requirement when she blurted out that he was high on drugs. She also said, who did he think he was kidding and he better not call here again until he got his life straightened out and she hung up. I don't know what to say to Chad. I know it has not been easy for him to stick with it and to make that phone call, only to be put down like that. Does this girl have any idea what kind of damage she has just done! How can she be so rude and incompetent at the same time? There is nothing I can do. They hold all the cards. Even if I decide to call and try to explain the situation to her, I will have to wait until tomorrow during the designated calling time and hope that I get through.

THURSDAY, JULY 26TH

Debra comes up to my study after work, and she is crying. Debra is not a crier. In twenty years of marriage, before all of this started happening with Chad, I could have counted on one hand the number of times I've seen her cry. She tells me that she found Lidocaine and steri-strip bandages in Chad's room. She said Chad had been asking her for several weeks for Lidocaine, and Debra had refused to get it for him. I have a quizzical look on my face. I have no idea what she is talking about. She says, "Paul, Chad tried to perform surgery on himself!"

I am stunned! Debra says that she confronted Chad, and he admitted that one day about week ago, when we were gone, he had boiled some surgical scissors and proceeded to try and to cut off one of his testicles. He stopped because he said it hurt so badly! He apparently, had found something on the Internet that had procedures on how this type of surgery is performed. I sit there like an idiot. I asked Debra, "Do you really think Chad was telling you the truth or is this a way to get the $4,000 from us?" "Paul, he is crazy, can't you get that through your head!"

For the first time, we talk about having Chad committed to a mental hospital. It is obvious that the treatment that Chad is getting from Dr. Gomez is not working. Debra also informs me that you can't just drive up to mental hospital and say, here take my kid, he's crazy. Chad is an adult with rights. Debra, through her tears, also says that, "Paul, I'm afraid if we have Chad committed, he will never forgive me."

We decide before we take that drastic step, that we will take him to another specialist to see if we have better luck with his treatment. In the mean time we need to stay after him about his medicine.

After Debra leaves, I find myself staring out the bay window into the blackness of the night. This is all just so surreal, it can't be happening. My son was supposed to be somebody - he was so gifted and had so much potential. A schizophrenic was not what I had envisioned! There is just got to be a way to fix this.

I think back to the day Chad was born. There were complications. They couldn't get him out. They had to use forceps, and then it took a team of doctors to get him to breathe properly; he had such a high heart rate. Once everything had settled down, they wrapped Chad up in a small blanket and gave him to me to hold. He was beautiful! As the little guy was looking up at me with large brown eyes, I made a silent promise to him that I would always be there for him, and no one would ever hurt him.

But how do you fight this! How do you protect him from this!

MONDAY, JULY 30TH

Debra has found a psychologist that has a great reputation. We are told that he spends a lot of time with his patients, and they all like him. His name is Douglas Bloomfield and he also works out of Richmond. The earliest appointment she could get was for August 14th. We are hoping and praying that this guy will be able to do something for Chad.

FRIDAY, AUGUST 3RD

At around 9:30 AM, we get a call that our bank branch in Irvington has been robbed! Our internal auditor and myself hustle down to Irvington, which is only about five miles from our offices. Upon arriving, we find our Senior Vice President assisting the police in surrounding the scene with crime tape. The branch is very small, and there are only two employees. The branch manager is standing outside, visibly shaken. The other employee is inside giving to the police a description of what happened. Luckily, no one is injured. But this guy had pointed a gun at them. The branch manager was very complimentary of her fellow employee who had taken the brunt of the robbery. Apparently, the guy had been waving the gun at her only a few feet away from her face.

There is not much we can do but to console our fellow employee. Once the police leave, the internal auditor along with our security compliance officer will count the money and try to determine how much was taken. The police are currently searching for the culprit, but it is beginning to look like he got away.

WEDNESDAY, AUGUST 8TH

Our teller and bank branch manager are now receiving counseling. One of them has returned to work but the other one is still very emotionally upset, and it might be several weeks before she can return. Meanwhile, the local papers have all come out and, of course, the robbery is big news.

THURSDAY, AUGUST 9TH

We can't believe it! We receive another call today telling us that the same branch in Irvington has been robbed again. But this time the police nabbed the thief, and they were able to determine it was the same guy that robbed us last week. Our poor bank employees! It is the same branch manager that was robbed last week. She had to deal with the gun again and is so upset that she faints before the day is through.

SUNDAY, AUGUST 12TH

I decide not to go to church. I feel guilty that I have not really spent any quality time with Chad since we picked him up from JMU. We get up late and eat brunch together while watching the sports news. We then go outside and play catch with the softball. It has been a long time since we played catch. We go out to the large field in front our house. Lacy chases the ball as we throw it to each other. It's a hot, muggy day. We take our shirts off to catch some rays. We spend more than an hour chasing flies and fielding grounders. We have worked up a sweat, so we go back inside to cool off. We watch a ball game for about hour and then decide to go to my office to get on the Internet, the power supply on my computer at home having failed. Chad is always teasing me about what a dinosaur my computer is compared to the one he has built for himself. I always tease him back saying that at least I have the Internet and until, he is willing to pay for the hookup and the phone service, he better shut-up! We are thinking that maybe we can find a cheap nonbrand state-of-the-art computer on EBAY. I have never used EBAY, but Chad has.

We spend some time getting me registered on EBAY and then we start looking for computers. EBAY is very user friendly, and we quickly find the type of computers we are looking for. I am surprised by the size of the selection and, with Chad's help, I'm able to find several computers that meet our specifications. The computer I want will still be on auction for another hour, so we do some surfing on the net. We will wait until the last minute before I submit my bid, as there are two other people who have already placed bids. When it becomes time to bid, I misspell my new password and we miss out! Chad has a good laugh, and I feel stupid. I go to my second choice, and it will be another hour before bidding stops. It's a "Dutch Auction" so I have no problem getting the computer. All in all, we spend about four hours on the Internet before we return home. Chad has been very patient with me, and we have had a lot of fun. We watch a rental movie that night. It has been a good day.

CHAPTER 5

THE BANK ROBBERY

We have learned by sad experience that it is the nature and disposition of almost all men, as soon as they get a little authority, as they suppose, they will immediately begin to exercise unrighteous dominion.

Joseph Smith

MONDAY AUGUST 13TH

Today, Chad will make the biggest mistake of his life. It is a day that I would do anything to get back.

As best as I have been able to put the pieces of information together, the following occurred: Debra had worked a twelve-hour shift on Sunday and was sleeping in. I left for work early that morning arriving around 7:30 AM. After I left, Chad had gotten up and changed the tags on Debra's car to the old tags that had been on the Camry. He then found Debra's keys and drove to Heathsville, which is about 23 miles from our house. At around 9:00 AM, he walked into a bank and robbed it! The bank was 100 yards from the Sheriff's office and the County Court House. Court was in session, and it was estimated that there were more than a dozen police vehicles parked nearby. After robbing the bank, I was told he walked calmly to the car and waited for traffic to clear before pulling out onto the road, heading east.

Unbelievably, he drove all the way home without being stopped. There are only two roads that head east out of Heathsville. He then hid the money and replaced the original tags leaving the old tags where he found them. A short time later, Debra got up and drove to Kilmarnock to take care of some errands. Chad was in his bedroom when she left.

At around 10:00 AM I heard from a coworker that the bank had been robbed in Heathsville. I don't give it much thought, other than I know it isn't going to help our own bank employees

38

stay calm. I'm just glad it wasn't our bank, and frankly, I had gotten my fill of bank robberies last week. A few hours later a coworker heard on the radio that no one was physically hurt and that they had gotten a partial ID on the tags. I remember thinking; "Good - it shouldn't take long to get the guy."

I get a call from Debra around 1:30 PM asking me if I had heard about the robbery. She said she had been pulled over by some detectives stating that her vehicle matched the description of the one seen "fleeing the bank." She assured them that she hadn't robbed the bank, and they asked a few questions before letting her go. I tell my coworkers that my wife has been stopped, and everyone starts referring to her as the bandit!

The rest of the day is routine. Debra has the day off, and when I get home that night all of us watch some TV and do a few chores. No matter how hard we try, neither one of us can remember Chad doing anything that day that would tip us off that something was wrong. He was still exhibiting some schizophrenia traits, but no more so than what we were getting accustomed to.

TUESDAY AUGUST 14TH

Today will be the worst day of our lives and the ultimate day in this nightmare that has no end. We are going to take Chad to see the psychologist in the afternoon. I go to work early again and Debra picks me up from work around 12:00 PM. Chad sits up front as we drive to Richmond. Chad really doesn't want to go, and we try to placate him by reminding him that we have chosen this doctor because he has the reputation of taking the time needed to really talk to his patients. We ask him has he taken his medicine. He says, yes. We want Chad to be as lucent as possible for his first session with the new doctor.

Dr. Bloomfield seems friendly and easy to communicate with. We are disappointed though when he indicates that it is best to review Chad's problems with Chad being present. I've got to tell you, whoever the experts are that decided this is the best way to approach a new patient - they're wrong! Remembering how Chad reacted to Debra when she was frank with Dr. Gomez, we temper our comments. We do point out that Chad has been diagnosed as severely depressed and we don't think he is making progress. We also mention that Chad has been hearing voices and we still fear his diagnosis might be more serious. We don't mention his obsession with his scrotum. We are hoping that Chad will bring that up when he meets with Dr. Bloomfield privately. We have tried to stress to Chad that these doctors will be in a much better position to help him if he is honest with them.

Dr. Bloomfield spends about 40 minutes with Chad. He tells us there are some administrative matters that need to be taken care of, and he has us sign some paperwork. He has Chad sign a disclaimer, saying something to the effect that it relieves Dr. Bloomfield of any responsibility if Chad should do something irrational. I am surprised when Chad seems to perk up and in a demanding tone, asks the doctor what does this mean. He explains that it means that if Chad should go out and shoot somebody, the doctor won't be held responsible. The doctor then tells us that it still too early for him to form a diagnosis, but he feels that Chad is not as bad off as we seem to think he is. The doctor says he seems to be of "medium depression" brought on by his poor showing at JMU after having been an honor student in high school. It is obvious that Chad has not told the doctor the whole story. We set up his next appointment and then leave. Our questions concerning when will Chad reach the stage that he can return to school can wait until next time.

We haven't had lunch, so we stop at the diner in Ukrops in Mechanicsville on the way home. I load up at the salad bar and then after the cashier rings it up, I realize I don't have any money. I have to go find Debra to bail me out. The three of us sit down and have a pleasant late afternoon lunch. We get back to Kilmarnock shortly after 5:00 PM. Debra and Chad return home in her car while I stop at work to check for messages. I don't have any messages, so I head home about ten minutes after Debra. When I arrive, I see Debra talking to two detectives and I see her opening all the doors to the car. I think its funny that she has been stopped again for questioning, and I would find out later that they had followed her in to our driveway.

As I get out of the car and approach them, I hear them apologizing for having to bother her again, and I hear Debra tell them to please go ahead and search the car. They have not asked to search it, Debra has volunteered the action thinking that maybe, after they have had a chance to look through it, they will leave her alone. They shake their heads no and reiterate that the car does fit the description of what they are looking for but the tags don't match the partial description they were given. They are pleasant enough and they do ask didn't we just get rid of a car a few months ago. We confirm that we did, but Debra says she has no idea what happened to the old tags. Debra didn't know that I had gone to Gloucester to remove the tags and get our personal belongings the day the insurance company told me they were going to "total" the car. Without thinking, I tell the detectives that I can clear this up in a minute, because I know where the old tags are. I hurry into the house, grab the tags and then let the detectives take the tags from me. There is a pause as they study the license plates. I can tell by the expression on their faces and the way they glance at each other that something is seriously wrong. They looked surprised and then I can see them get excited when they looked at each other.

I don't remember exactly what happened next. I just remember being in some kind of daze for the next few hours. They said something like, "Sir, we have to keep these plates as evidence." I demand that they give the plates back - they refuse. I tell both Chad and Debra to get into the house. I tell Chad to get upstairs to my office and I follow him there. I shut the door and say to Chad, "What the hell have you done?" He starts crying and says that he needed the money for his scrotum. I'm crushed, and I can't believe it! But his answer leaves me little doubt that we are in serious trouble. So much for the experts! I can't believe that I relied on them and not on Debra.

I grab the phone and call my boss at home. He is well connected, and he will know whom I should call, but he is not home yet. I leave a message for him to call me; it's an emergency. I go back outside to see what is happening, the Sheriff and his deputies are arriving in bunches! The Sheriff approaches me and says we should let him in to search the house. He explains that it will go much better for us if we let him in now. Meanwhile I'm looking at about a dozen deputies, all carrying guns, and they have the appearance of a bunch of rednecks. I tell the Sheriff to wait and I'll do whatever my attorney advises me to do. He doesn't like that answer and tells me that Chad will get many more years in the penitentiary if we don't cooperate. I ask him to just hold on until I get in touch with my lawyer.

I have no idea what to do. I have never done this before! I try frantically to reach somebody by phone with no luck. The

Sheriff says something like, "As far we know, your family could be in there destroying evidence." I go inside and have the whole family come out and sit on the porch, so the deputies can see us.

My boss returns my message. I then have the unpleasant, surreal task of having to tell him that my son is being accused of robbing a bank, and I ask him whom I should call. He tells me to hold on and he'll call me back. I also call Dad in Utah and then have to tell him the awful news. I ask if he has got Dale's number in Budapest and would he please try to reach him and have him call me. Certainly, my brother, a Director in the FBI, should be able to give me some good advice.

I sit outside with my family, waiting for the phone to ring. It's not much fun sitting there with all the deputies staring at us. The Sheriff is now telling Debra that I'm making a mistake and we should let them in now. I'm beginning to dislike this guy. My boss calls me back and says that the law firm we often use has a criminal practice and they will be calling me back. Unfortunately, they are tied up in preparing for a murder trial on Thursday, so he is not sure that one of the criminal lawyers will be able to call me right away. But he says that one of the lawyers I know will be calling me in a few minutes. He leaves me with several phone numbers, in case they have trouble getting through. Dad then calls and says he is having trouble getting in touch with Dale. He has his work number, but it is 2:30 in the morning there. There was a guard on duty, and he is trying to get in touch with Dale now.

I notice that even more people have arrived. I take heart in that most of them look a little more professional. A female deputy and an African American deputy are a welcome contrast to the majority of the deputies. The phone rings and it's the lawyer. He tells me that he has been in contact with the criminal lawyers and that one of them will probably be calling me within the hour. I walk away from everyone, and I do tell him that I think Chad did it. He tells me not to let the Sheriff in under any circumstances and to make them get a search warrant. I tell the Sheriff he needs to get a search warrant and hand the phone to him so my lawyer can also tell him. The lawyer also advises me to get everyone into the house.

The Sheriff warns me that if we flush a toilet or do anything that lead them to believe we are destroying evidence, they will storm the house. I tell my family to sit in the living room on the first floor and not to close any curtains. We have large windows so they can easily see what we are doing. It is around 6:45 PM. It has taken a little over an hour since the detectives seized the tags and I'd gotten in touch with a lawyer - it seemed like an eternity. Debra makes sure that Chad takes his medicine. We all sit on the couch. The Sheriff has had his men surround the house. We've got a bunch of rednecks staring through our windows.

I feel a little relieved, now that we are inside and they are outside. The feeling I have is horrible! I am dumbfounded and my thoughts are racing. I know they will probably get the search warrant, and it's only a matter of minutes before they do storm into the house. I can only hope that my first impression of that we are dealing with a bunch of rednecks is wrong.

I feel awful for Chad. I don't have a good grasp of what all the ramifications are, but I'm pretty sure he has ruined his life and possibly ours. My heart also goes out to Debra. I wish that I could protect her from this. We have had to struggle our whole marriage, and every time we seemed to have turned the corner we get hit with another setback. How could this have happened? I also wonder what impact this will have on Ali. The way she keeps her innermost feelings to herself, there is a good chance I'll never know. But strangely, I think her lack of respect for authority figures and her ability to act cool when put in a no-win situation will serve her well tonight. I also feel for Dad. I know he, too, must be going through hell right now! In some ways, it must even be harder for him, as he can only guess at what is currently happening.

My lawyer calls to make sure that we are okay and asks what the police are doing now. He says that we should hear from one of the criminal lawyers within the hour. Dale calls a few minutes later. Dad has filled him in on what is happening, and he asks what is the current situation. When I tell him that we are making the Sheriff get a warrant, I can tell from Dale's reply that he would have advised me differently. He says that, since you have chosen that route, that is fine and that my attorneys would have a better feel for how the law works in that part of Virginia. I ask Dale what he thinks will happen to Chad. He indicates that the best thing going for Chad is the fact that he is only eighteen years old and that this is his first offense. We talk briefly, and I tell Dale I will give him a call when everything settles down.

Lost in our own thoughts, we say little to each other. Chad has slouched down on the couch and pulled his cap over his eyes. Lacy knows something is wrong. She keeps moving back and forth between us, whimpering and wanted to be petted. We all need to use the bathroom but we are too scared to. I remember that my briefcase is out in the truck, and I fear that somehow the deputies will be able to seize it. I mention this to Debra, and then she remembers that she left her purse in the car. We debate on whether we should go out there and get the stuff and decide not to.

The minutes keep ticking away, and we have now been in the house sitting on the couch for about an hour. The sun is going down, I turn the lights on, so they can still see us. I look out the windows and there are cops and police cars everywhere. I swear, they think they have caught Al Capone. There are a number of deputies walking down by the river and out in the trees. It looks to me like they are already searching. I don't look long; the deputy at the window is staring at me. About twenty minutes later a curious thing happens. We hear a lot of noise outside and discover that the police are surrounding our house with their cars pulling right onto our lawn and pointing their headlights towards our windows. They all turn on their high beams. Our house is lit up like a Christmas tree. Talk about overkill - I wonder what our neighbors and the people out in their boats returning home from the bay are thinking. The cops must be having the time of their lives. The stupor I was in is giving way to a mixture of anger and frustration.

Bill Kopchak, the criminal lawyer, calls. He tells me that he is really busy right now but wants to know how we are making out. After I give him a quick rundown on what has happened he tells me its is likely that they will get the search warrant and to be prepared. I tell him that the Sheriff said he would storm the house if he had any suspicion we were destroying evidence. Bill says, just go about your business. He warns me to tell Chad that if he is arrested not to speak to them under any circumstances. He said that they would tell him that they are really his friends and they don't want to see him go to prison for ten to twenty years. They will say that if he will tell them everything he knows, they will put in a good word for him and everything will go much better. He also says they will flat out lie to him, if they think it will help their case. No matter what, he is not speak to them and must tell them that he has been advised by his lawyer not to say anything. He says to have Chad write that down on a piece of paper to give to them if he is arrested and to keep a copy for himself. He warns us not to discuss the matter over the phone because they also might get a phone tap. He says to call him tomorrow to tell him what the status is. He also tells me that because of the murder trial he is not going to have any time the next two days to devote to our case. In the meantime, he reiterates once again, that Chad is not to speak to anyone but the lawyers.

I take Chad into the kitchen and repeat what Bill has told me. He listens intently and says okay. I emphasize to him that they will probably keep him in the dark as to what is going on, but he is still to only speak to his attorneys even if it takes a week for them to get there. I have Chad write down his response as instructed by Bill and have him sign it. I tell him to give it to them as soon as they try to interrogate him. I don't know what more I can do to help him. I find that, even with all the emotions I am presently experiencing, including the still unbelievable fact that he has robbed a bank; my strongest emotion is to protect him. I'm afraid with all the pressure that the Sheriff deputies are going to put on him, it will bring on another psychotic episode and we will have lost him for good. Thank God that the first thing Debra thought of was to make sure he had taken his medicine!

The first lawyer calls me back again and wants to know if Bill has called and how things are going. Its around 9:00 PM and I'm thinking I better get my briefcase now or never. I tell the lawyer what I want to do and he says that's fine. I ask him to stay on the phone as I go out to the truck. I cause quite a stir as I step out of the house and start walking towards the truck with the cordless phone to my ear. The Sheriff asks me who is on the phone and what am I doing. I tell him that I'm going to get the briefcase out of the truck and I've got my lawyer on the phone. The deputies don't seem to know quite what to do. Several of them turn their flashlights on me and, as I take the briefcase out and start walking back to the house, I am surrounded by deputies who tell me that they want to search the briefcase. I have been giving the lawyer a play-by-play description that the deputies close by can hear. He says its okay to let them search it. I let them and get back into the house with briefcase in hand. I'm not sure what would have happened if I hadn't had my lawyer on the phone.

Its now around 9:30 PM, and the high beams from the cop cars are still aimed through our windows. We are wondering why is it taking so long to get the warrant; and if they don't get it soon, can we ask them to leave. They have now been on our property for four hours. About fifteen minutes later, we hear a loud commotion outside and then banging on our door. I answer the door, and the Sheriff shows me the search warrant and gives me a copy. The list of things that they are authorized to seize is surprisingly short. A backpack, the money, stocking cap, and a few articles of clothing are all that is listed. What is obviously missing is a weapon of some kind.

We are ordered to sit on the couch and not move. They post two deputies to keep an eye on us, the female deputy, and one of the deputies that looks like a redneck. It seems like every cop and detective in the county is in our house, which is probably the case. We are told that each one of us will be strip-searched. I am led to another room by one of the deputies and told to remove my shirt, shoes and socks. I am then patted down. First Debra and then Ali are led to another room where the female officer searches them. They are told to strip down to their underwear. We are returned to the couch with the same instructions not to move. I'm thinking, now its time to wake up.

In just a few minutes, my perception that many of the cops are rednecks is verified. They are hooping and hollering and having the times of their lives. We hear noises coming from all parts of the house, at first it's the sounds of drawers and cupboards being opened, then pounding and scraping. It is hard to describe what I am feeling. It seems so surreal and at the same time, disturbingly violent. The cops are definitely not the good guys to us. As the minutes drag on, the whooping and hollering increases. I can only surmise that they are finding pieces of evidence. From time to time I look at the faces of my family. Debra is white as a ghost, sitting bolt upright and staring straight ahead with her hands folded on her lap. It looks to me like she might faint at any second. Chad is still slumped on the couch with his cap pulled down over his eyes. He seems out of it, as if the medicine has taken effect. Ali looks determined; she refuses to let the deputies know for one second that they are getting to her. She is also struggling to keep Lacy under control. We have her on a short leash, but she is beside herself with all the commotion in the house. Meanwhile the two deputies that are guarding us are still staring at us. The female officer does seem to have a little bit of compassion in her eyes and she tries to pet Lacy to help settle her down.

After about an hour, we are ordered to stand in the kitchen while they search the living room. The search doesn't take long, but we are still required to stand there. The minutes continue to drag on, and I'm surprised that the deputies are still yelling and having such a good time. Surely, there can't be that must evidence. My study and our bedroom are located above the kitchen. While standing there we can hear the deputies stomping around. I can only shake my head, as I think of them going through my personal belongings in the study. Then we hear the sound of something being broken. We have worked so long and so hard to refurbish this house, and all we can do is stand there and watch these people trash it!

Another hour has passed, and Debra surprises me by asking the deputies can we return to the couch. The Sheriff himself gives the okay for us to return to our own couch in our own house.

A few minutes later I find out what the prolonged celebrations are all about. The Sheriff presents me with another search warrant. Apparently, Chad has scanned some money with his scanner, and now the police are also going to try to nail him for counterfeiting! Give me a break! This time the warrant is long and detailed. They have had the advantage of being in our house and going through our things, so they list anything and everything that could possibly tie any of us to the counterfeiting. Not only are they going to take Chad's computer, printer, and peripherals, they are going to take mine, as well. I can't believe they are also taking the monitors and speakers! Tell me, how do you make money with a monitor and stereo speakers. Just when you think things couldn't get any worse, they do.

A short while later, we hear the loudest celebration of the night. It is coming from the direction of the laundry room. Officers are hollering at the top of their lungs and exchanging high five's right in front of us. Officer Chuck (Chuckie) Wilkins approaches us with a smirk on his face as we sit on the couch and wishes us a *Merry Christmas*! I'm speechless. I can't believe that this man has just done this. I fight to control my anger. Ali shoots back with a "and a happy New Year!" Leave it to Ali to score the only points for our family on this horrible night.

And then the unthinkable happens. About a half-hour later, Officer Chuck Wilkins returns and approaches us again and flippantly says to us, "Now you're all going to jail!" Here is this officer in full uniform, badge on his chest, and a gun on his hip verbally threatening us in our own home. I'm pretty sure that what we are dealing with here is a redneck that just can't seem to control his testosterone levels. However, he has now given us all something else to think about. I look over at Debra and she is still as pale as a ghost. All I can do is sit there and let him do this to my family. How can anybody be this cruel? I look at the two deputies that are guarding us to see if there is any reaction from them - I don't see any. I wonder if they would have the courage to testify against their own captain!

It is now around 10:30 to 11:00 PM. I notice that Chad has fallen asleep. I can't believe he can sleep at a time like this. It just goes to show how far out of it he is, testifying to the strength of his medicine. We watch as the deputies continue to remove our personal belongings out of the house. It seems to me that they are taking more than what was on the search warrant, and as I try to examine the warrants again, I realize I don't have them with me. I'm pretty sure I have left the first one where I was stripped search. I ask the guard if I can go get it. He says, no. I start to ask him if he could get it for me. He yells at me to shut-up!

The next few hours drag on. I can't imagine what is taking so long. A tow truck has pulled up and taken our car away - they do allow Debra to keep her purse.

WEDNESDAY AUGUST 15TH

It is now around 12:30 AM and Debra has gotten her color back. I can tell she is now angry. We have not been allowed to go to the bathroom or eat for seven hours now. Some of the deputies have been standing around within earshot talking about their exciting day as if we aren't even there. Debra looks over at me and says loudly, "When are these people going to leave my house?" I am caught by surprise but relieved to see that Debra no longer looks like she is at death's door. I motion for Debra to stay calm and shrug my shoulders, indicating that I don't have any idea. Luckily the guards pretend they hadn't heard her.

Chad is still asleep, and my thoughts are now focused on what is going to happen to him. I haven't said anything to Debra, but I notice from my vantage point, though it is difficult to see outside, what looks like a paddy wagon. They pull it right on our front lawn, which has been soaked by rainfall for the past week. A paddy wagon has arrived for my son. No words can describe the feeling. I'm not even sure if it is meant for all us - thanks to Chuck Wilkins.

For some reason, the minutes seemed to drag even slower as all of us are thinking surely they are going to leave any minute now. Around 12:30 AM, the Sheriff, surrounded by a few deputies and detectives, marches into our living room to arrest our son. He proclaims loudly that "Chad you are under arrest for...." He realizes that Chad is asleep and stops. It kind of ruined the moment for him. We wake Chad up and the Sheriff again announces the arrest. They handcuff him and start to take him away. Debra gets up, asking can she hug him before they take him away. They tell her no, and she repeats what we told them earlier that he is not right and he is mentally ill. They don't seem to be paying any attention, but they do take his medicine when she hands it to them. I don't remember much of the next half-hour, except Debra and me hugging and sharing a short cry.

At around 1:00 AM, for some reason, these assholes are still in my home. I kind of come back to reality, as both Debra and Ali are asking me why are they still here. I motion to them to stay quiet. It is amazing how helpless I am to do anything. We just have to sit there and take it. My best guess is they are tying up loose ends, and they are taking their time about it. An acquaintance of ours that is a state trooper and lives just down the road shows up. She comes in to apparently console us and tell us how sorry she is for us. But right now, we no longer trust anybody wearing a uniform. We still have the two guards watching, and we are still not allowed to move from the couch.

It is about 1:30 AM now, and at least the rednecks have quieted down. I do see a little backslapping, as the Sheriff, calls the bank President to report that they have caught the bank robber. Finally, at around 1:45 AM the last officer leaves.

Our house is in shambles, not to mention our lives.

49

CHAPTER 6

THE COMMUNITY REACTS

We numbly use the bathroom and Ali who has not eaten for fourteen hours grabs a bite to eat. I don't know what to say and I can't remember any of us saying much of anything as we go to bed and try to get some sleep.

I can't sleep. My thoughts are with Chad. I'm wondering if those rednecks are going to cause Chad to have another psychotic episode. My thoughts are racing all over the place. I'm trying to think back to the day of the bank robbery and trying to recall anything unusual that might have tipped us off. I can't even remember what day it was. I'm very concerned for my job and Debra's job. This has got to be embarrassing for the bank, at the very least. I'm wondering how both of us are even going to get to work with just one car. I'm thinking of the amount of damage this going to do to our reputations and thinking that we might have to move. What impact is this going to have on Ali; her high school is only a few blocks from the bank that was robbed. I'm wondering what weapon Chad must have used. I can at least recall that no one was hurt. Thank God.

I continue to lie there as the minutes tick by with my thoughts still racing. What is going to happen to Chad? Is he in a safe place? What kind of time is he going to have to serve? What is the best thing we can do for him now? What are we going to do about money? I glance over at the bedside clock and notice that it is about 4:30 AM.

I must have dozed off, because the next time I look at the clock it is about 6:00 AM. I'm surprised because I really don't feel tired. If anything, I feel like I've had a shot of adrenaline, and I am up and out of bed. I don't know what to do next. It's too early to call anyone. I figure I might as well get ready and go to work. There is not much I can do. The attorneys will be tied up today with preparing for their murder trial. I think we are somewhat lucky with the timing. The Northumberland local papers go to press Monday nights and the Lancaster County paper goes to press on Tuesday nights. If we are lucky the news might not even break until early next week. If I can go to work today it will allow me to break the news to my coworkers personally, and it will be one less day taken off when I get to that stage where I need to take days off.

I should have known better. I would find out later that the Sheriff's Department was eager to have the news out, so they contacted the local radio stations and newspapers early in the morning.

I kept a meeting I had scheduled with our branch manager first thing that morning in Gloucester. On the way back to the office, as I was crossing the Rappahannock River on the Norris bridge, the local radio station broadcasts that it has an important announcement. They announce "Chad Lawrence Wegkamp of 448 Wicomico View Lane has been arrested for the robbery of...," It hits me like a ton of bricks. I can't believe it. I just can't believe it. I have worked with people at the radio station in my role as Red Cross Chairman. I know several of them personally. The person who read the broadcast is Joanne Chewning, our neighbor. They not only mention our name perfectly (which is very unusual) they also give out our complete street address. Why? I understand the need to let the public know that the bank robber has been apprehended but why all the detail and why would people who know me do this? The person, who robbed our bank twice at gunpoint in the same week, just a week earlier, didn't get this kind of treatment.

I am only ten minutes away from the office but it is too late for me to break the news personally. They all listen to this radio station. It is the only station whose reception is strong enough to pick up clearly in our building. As I pull into the parking lot I have no idea what to say to people. As I walk into the building, everyone ignores me like nothing is happening. Apparently, they have known for a while. There is an email on my computer that has been sent out by my boss to all the bank employees announcing the news. The email is well written as it expresses concern for Debra and me and at the same time lets our bank employees know that the Sheriff's Department has arrested a suspect.

I ask the people who report to me and the other coworkers in our department to please come by my office. Several of them say, "Paul you don't have to say anything to us, our hearts and prayers are with you and your family." I tell them I'm sorry I didn't get a chance to tell them before they heard it on the radio. These are people who I have worked closely with for over the past five years. It is hard to keep my composure. Several of them who have met Chad can't believe that he would be capable of such a thing. I explain that he has schizophrenia but I keep the meeting short.

It is obvious that I need to get home. I'm fearful of what Debra is going through right now, as she is there alone. Ali did go to school. I'm sure the school corridors are buzzing right now. Before I go, I ask John what particulars he knows about the bank robbery. I ask him has he heard anything about a weapon, because none was listed on the search warrant. What he tells me is awful. They had gotten word that the robber was extremely frightening. He had a stocking mask pulled over his face that revealed very little of his skin color, and one witness had even thought he was black. Apparently, he was vulgar and aggressive and told them he would kill them all if they didn't do what he said. He revealed no weapon but did have a backpack and they had no idea what was in the backpack. They said he was dressed very well in kaki slacks and a polo shirt. They said that after he had them put money in the backpack, he walked calmly out to the car and looked both ways before pulling out into traffic.

I asked John if he knew how much money Chad had gotten and he didn't know. John then told me that several executives from Bank of Lancaster had called and expressed their concerns for us and left a message that they would not be aggressive in prosecuting Chad. This bit of news come as a surprise and was very comforting, even though I knew it was most likely out of their hands. The part that was comforting was the fact that they made the effort to let us know that they were sensitive to our feelings and what we must be going through. He also let's me know that the bank was supportive of me, and the last thing they wanted me to worry about was my job. What a relief, and how fortunate we are to be dealing with such good people.

I want to go directly home but there is no food in the house. I stop at the store to get some things to hold us over. It is a weird feeling going into the store. You certainly don't want to meet anyone you know, and there are definite feelings of paranoia. Debra seems to be doing okay. She is depressed but so far there has been no crank phone calls. Just the opposite has happened. A number of friends have called and said they are there for us and please let us know if there is anything they can do. She tells me that she has called the Sheriff's Department and they have not been helpful in telling us where they have taken Chad. One thing we will learn over the next several days is that no one in the legal system will make any effort to let us know anything about what is happening to Chad. He is eighteen, they consider him an adult and, as far as they are concerned, we might as well be Mr. and Mrs. Joe Blow. Debra has made an appointment to see our family doctor that afternoon. She wants to get some Prozac to calm her nerves. She is concerned that I might need the truck for something else that afternoon. We are already dealing with the fact that we just have the one vehicle.

We discuss for a few minutes the day of the bank robbery, trying to remember anything that would have tipped us off that Chad had done it. We also discuss whether we should use the lawyers we have contacted or maybe we should let Chad take his lumps with a court appointed attorney. Debra is for the latter and correctly points out that we have no money and now is maybe the time for tough love. I don't want to get into argument and I brush the subject off. But I am definitely worried about how we are going to pay for it. I'm under the impression that, because of the relationship the bank has with the law firm, they will allow me to make payments over a period of time, but I'm not sure. I put in a call to them, as they requested, to let them know the current situation and to ask them about the financing. The secretary tells me that they are tied up and she will give them the message.

I decide to have a look around the house to see how much damage was done from the night before. It is not a pleasant experience. Chad's room has been totally ransacked. They have taken everything that was of value to him. It looks like they used a crowbar to look behind the ceiling vent. It is bent up pretty bad. All they would have had to do was to go upstairs and pull the vent covering off and they would have had full access to it. Upstairs, they knocked a hole in the wall and tore up some floorboards in my study. It is comical in that they actually threw cloths and bags to cover up the holes. I wonder just what purpose they thought that was going to serve. Needless to say, the whole house is in disarray. It looks like whenever they came to a box or a drawer their approach was just to empty the contents onto the floor and then maybe shove everything back in when they were done. They had brought our ladder from outside to get up into the attic and then left the ladder. Outside, the damage to the front lawn is substantial. Wherever they had pulled their vehicles onto the lawn they had left tire damage. The tow truck dug into the lawn as much as two feet leaving trenches 40 feet long. They had also dug up the lawn over the septic tank. I took pictures of everything. I ask Debra whether she has seen all the damage upstairs. She shakes her head no and says she feels like she has been raped. She says that they have seen some personal stuff that even I haven't seen.

The attorneys call, they are both on a speakerphone. I fill them in on what is happening and then tell them that I am assuming that I will be able to pay their bill over a period of time. I am informed that I thought wrong and that they will require a $10,000 retainer fee up front. I choke on the news and tell them I don't think there is anyway I can do that. They stand firm and say that the bank certainly thinks a lot of me and why can't I just borrow the money from them? I ask their opinions of court appointed attorneys and they tell me; "not much...if it were my son I wouldn't take the chance." They tell me to think it over. They say that the work they have done so far was on a pro bono basis and to leave word with their secretaries tomorrow if I want them to take the case.

As I get off the phone, I don't know what to think. I had already made up my mind that this was the route I wanted to take. For the first time I realize this may not even be possible, we may have no choice but to go with the court appointed attorney. Between Deana's wedding and Chad's tuition and subsequent problems, we have already spent any savings that we had. I also realize that I need to find out more about the caliber of the court appointed attorneys as fast as possible.

I don't have any luck. The few people I can think of who might have some insights are either away or don't know anything. I call Dad and we talk about it. He tried to get of hold of his good friend who used to be a city attorney in Utah. However, he is also away from town. I would love to talk to him; we used to play on the same basketball team. He is very knowledgeable and a straight shooter. Dad thinks he'll be back this weekend, but I need to make my decision before then.

Debra has a good talk with the doctor. Between her visit with the doctor and the Prozac she calms down considerably. The phone is ringing constantly. The calls are split between people returning my calls, more friends wishing us well, and a lot of calls from high school kids trying to get the latest scoop from Ali. It appears that this thing has actually made Ali look very cool to a lot of the kids in school. In a way, it's a relief not to have to worry about how Ali basically is going to be treated. I know she will still run into some people with pretty nasty mouths, but at least it looks like they will be in the minority.

As we talk over the phone it is very hard not to be forthright in our conversations and to talk specifics. However, we do hear a slight clicking noise when we pick up and we have a friend arrive by car to tell us that the clicking on her end of the line was quite pronounced. I can't believe that they have gone through the trouble of wire-tapping our phones. Don't these guys have anything better to do - like go to class and learn how to treat people with civility?

Dale calls to see how everything is going. We talk about what is likely going to happen to Chad. Dale tells me there is even a chance that the FBI might get involved. A bank robbery is considered a federal crime. However, he says the chances are slim that they would pursue it given that it was a small bank in a rural area and the crime was committed by an eighteen year old without a weapon. Dale says again that the best thing Chad has going for him is the fact that he is only eighteen and a first-time offender.

Our friend, who lives down the street, brings us a full course dinner; it looked like she had cooked most of the day for us. We are very appreciative and I can tell the kind act lifts Debra's spirit, as well as my own. I talk on the phone until 11:00 PM and finally go to bed to try to get some sleep even though I don't feel tired at all - I'm so wired.

THURSDAY AUGUST 16TH

I am up early trying to think of what I can do at this time of the morning that will help. I fight the urge to start calling people until at least 7:30 AM. I decide that one thing I can do today that is at least somewhat constructive is to get caught up on the yard work in between phone calls. Debra is up early also and is trying to reach her boss, who for some reason has not returned Debra's calls from the day before. We are worried about her job. The correctional facility has no tolerance with any of its workers getting in trouble. They even have a policy that if one of the members of your immediate family has been convicted of drug use, it's grounds for dismissal. I am also uneasy about this because Debra is supposed to be at work today and she is not planning on going back anytime soon. If Debra loses her job, we will be in serious trouble.

Debra has no luck in contacting her boss but does find out from a friend that Chad has been admitted to the Northern Neck Regional Jail. He is being kept in medical for observation. I am amazed that neither the Sheriff's Department nor the jail has even bothered to try and contact us to tell us what they have done with our son.

Debra was also told that Chad's arraignment is for 9:00 AM tomorrow. I'm not sure what the purpose of the arraignment is, but I do know that it would be best that he had legal representation. I'm not sure where I'm going to get the $10,000, but two possibilities have come to mind. One is to go ahead and borrow from the bank. I'm not sure how that is going to go. We already have a 1st and a 2nd mortgage with them. The second possibility is to ask Dale if he would lend me the money. I know he has substantial savings, but I don't want to drag him into this. The thought has occurred to me that this has got to be uncomfortable for Dale, given his employment with the FBI.

I make several phone calls in pursuit of financing ideas and keep trying to get some solid feedback on the effectiveness of court appointed attorneys. I talk with my boss John, who encourages me to call the bank president and indicates that the president has expressed a willingness to help in anyway he can. John says he is surprised with the tack the law firm took with me. John also questions the advisability of going with a court appointed attorney. This is all encouraging news; and when I relay it to Debra, she is upset.

Debra can't believe that I'm pursuing the action of hiring the law firm. She reiterates that we have got to face the music and realize that our son is a "fuck-up." He will never amount to anything, and we have got to quit bailing him out of trouble. It is time for him to face the music, and it is time for us to get on with our lives. We are outside and she is shouting at me. Ali has left for school, but I know there are several watermen down at the oyster house. I don't want to include them in our discussion. I reply angrily to Debra that she better calm down or I'm not going to discuss this with her.

She glares at me, and then in a softer tone says what guarantees do we have that the result will be any different if we do go with the court appointed attorney. She also makes the point that we need to think about Ali and her college education and how we have not been able to do anything for her lately because of all the money and time we have already spent on Chad this year. She also reminds me that the $10,000 is only a retainer - the final bill could be much higher. She says she will be there personally for Chad every chance she gets, but we can't let this ruin us financially.

I can't deny that her argument is a good one, and if I had gotten any feedback stating that the court appointed attorneys do a good job, she would probably win me over. But my gut is telling me that the way to go is to get the best attorneys available. I also feel that in this rural area this is a big event, with the possibility that Chad could be used as an example of what can happen to any more bank robbers. The way the Sheriff's Department reacted, you would have thought it was the crime of the century. I also feel that if we don't do everything we can to help Chad, no one else will. His entire future is predicated on the actions we take right now. We are all he has got.

I express these feelings to Debra and she asks me why am I doing this. I thought I just explained it to her and I ask her what do you mean? "Why?" We are shouting at each other now and Debra says in a threatening tone that I better not do this. She turns and goes into the house. I don't know what to do, but given Chad's condition I don't think now is the time for tough love.

I realize that I might be putting our marriage on the line, but I call the attorney's office and leave a message that I do want them to represent Chad tomorrow at his arraignment in Circuit Court. I now wonder, if I'm going to have to travel this route without Debra's support.

I need some gas for the lawnmower, so I take a quick drive to the corner market. While there, I pick up the Rappahannock

Record and I'm surprised to see that the robbery has made the front page. The way the article is boxed is a pretty good indication that they stopped the presses to publish it. The article is not long but factual. Of course it spells out Chad's full name and gives the general location of where we live. It also reports that Chad wore a black ski mask. I had no idea where he had gotten that, which raised the question of when did he get it. The article mentions that neither the bank nor the Sheriff's Department would disclose information about whether a weapon had been used. I guess it's not the crime of the century if no weapon was used. The article also reports that no one was injured and that Chad would be arraigned on Friday, August 17th. All I had to do was to buy the paper to find out when Chad would be arraigned. Apparently it's okay to give the local newspaper the information but not the accused's parents!

I ask Debra if she wants to see the article and she says no. She tells me that she found out that we probably won't be able to see Chad until next Tuesday from 10:00 AM to 11:00 AM, which is the regular visiting hour for an inmate in medical. She did find that Chad could request a special visit. Apparently, these visits are granted if for some reason the person can't receive visitors during regular visiting hours or for other special circumstances. Debra's friend at the jail will give this information to Chad. I can't believe that the legal authorities are going to make us wait that long before we can see him.

Debra also informs me that her sister, Cindy, will be arriving tonight from Ohio to give us some moral support. At first, I don't think its such a great idea and then it occurs to me that Cindy will be a great help in keeping Debra's spirits up and will be another witness for us.

We get a call from some church members who are bringing over dinner for us tonight. We have received a number of phone calls again today from friends, church members, and coworkers wishing us the best. Debra comments on how this outpouring of love and concern is really helping her. I can second that. Just about every one of our black friends has called us or arrived at our home with baked goods. Several of them express no surprise when we tell them how the Sheriff's Department treated us. "Now you know how it feels,' is a remark that we will hear more than once.

One of Debra's friend, a sweet older black woman, gives us $50.00 to help us and will not allow us to return it.

A number of our friends from Church drop by, and we discuss with them what has happened to us, and the pitfalls we have all encountered in raising our kids. They are here until the sun goes down and are leaving just as Cindy pulls in.

That evening, I discuss with Dad what might happen at the arraignment tomorrow. I am concerned that I haven't received any verification from the attorneys that they have gotten my message and will be there for Chad. I had spoken to BJ from the firm earlier, and he told me not to worry - he had also left a message. He indicated that the murder trial was going on into the night. John also called and reiterated that the bank will support me, and I tell him that I will try to see the bank President tomorrow after the arraignment.

I receive a call from Jim at about midnight. Their murder trial has just ended and they had won the case. He told me that Bill Kopchak would be there tomorrow at 9:00 AM. I haven't met Bill and want to know how I can recognize him. Jim laughs and says, "Just look for the tall, dark and handsome guy with black hair."

FRIDAY, AUGUST 17TH

We get up early and, needless to say, we are all a little nervous. We are excited about the prospect of seeing Chad and hope we will be able to meet with him. We arrive early hoping to meet with the attorney before the court is in session. We are surprised to find several members of our Church there to lend their support. We introduce Cindy and talk while keeping an eye out for the attorney. A lot of people are coming, and a number of the deputies that were at our house are there; including our favorite, Captain Wilkins. We will find out later that there was no reason for all of them to be there. They basically came to participate in the circus and to show off.

It is almost 9:00 AM and there is no sign of Bill. Remembering our experience in Rockingham, I suggest to everyone we better go in. We have to file past Wilkins, and I give him a cold hard stare. He doesn't like it. What's he going to do? Wish us a merry Christmas! Not this time. We are surrounded by our friends instead of rednecks wearing guns. As we file in, there is very little space available, except up front, which suits us fine. I keep an eye out for Bill. They start on their docket. After a few minutes, a lawyer-looking type that fits the description Jim gave me, goes through the gate and takes a seat at the attorney's desk. We catch each other's eyes and he comes over and introduces himself quietly. He says that he will be meeting with us shortly. I can relax a little now, knowing that he is here.

It isn't long for they call out Chad's name. A number of the deputies scurry to the door located at a right angle behind the Judge's pulpit. A big production is about to begin as they bring in the notorious bank robber. Leading the way are two deputies with Chad behind them, and then there are two more guards behind Chad. What we see is awful. Chad is chained to the hilt. He is handcuffed to chains that surround his waist, which lead down to his feet, which are also chained. He is wearing the bar-stripped prison garb and hasn't shaved. He looks dirty and disheveled. They obviously haven't let him shower or even bothered to give him a comb. He looks every bit the part of a thief. We can tell that he is scared. He will not look up during the entire proceedings, except for one small glimpse at us and a bit of a wave hampered by the chains.

It is an indescribable feeling to watch your own son under these circumstances. It is definitely surreal and you want to be able to tell everyone that this is a good kid with a lot of talent who just had the ill fortune of being struck with schizophrenia in the prime of his life. But you can't. You just have to sit there and watch the Sheriff's Department, the jailhouse, the media and the courts all extract their pound of flesh. I have to keep reminding myself that Chad did terrorize some good, innocent people, because I was becoming convinced that we are not the bad guys in this story.

As the proceedings begin, the Judge seems to think that Chad will be receiving a court appointed attorney. The prosecutor informs the Judge that he doesn't think that is the case and then Bill speaks up, saying that the family has retained them. He further explains that he has not yet had an opportunity to meet with Chad or his family and he asks the Judge for a two-hour recess so he can do so. The prosecutor questions the need for two hours and the Judge allows the recess but shortens it to one hour.

Bill leads us to a conference room. We go through formal introductions, and I hand him a ten thousand-dollar check and ask him not to deposit it until Monday - he has no problem with that. He asks us for some background on Chad and on the events of the past few weeks. He also asks us what are the results we are hoping for. We tell him that our goal is not to get him off but to get him the help that he needs. Bill says good - he says that the prosecution obviously has a mountain of evidence and our approach should be to emphasize Chad's mental state at the time of the robbery. He says that this approach could eventually lead to Chad not being prosecuted for the crime and being committed to a state mental institution where he can get some help. Bill also reports that the prosecutor is a fair person and good to work with. He mentions that the prosecutor has already given him his complete file on Chad - something that he doesn't have to do. We cut our meeting short so Bill can spend the rest of the hour with Chad. We ask him to see if he can arrange for us to see Chad after the proceedings, because we haven't been allowed to talk to him since the arrest. He says he thinks he will be able to arrange that.

They bring Chad back in as the court reconvenes. Our attorney asks for more time to prepare his case and to have Chad adequately evaluated. The prosecution indicates that they don't have any objection, and the Judge sets the time for September 14th, to hold a preliminary court hearing. We don't know exactly what this means, but we hope that Bill can fill us in. As they are taking Chad through the back door, Debra thinks that the bailiff is waving for us to follow. I'm not paying attention until she grabs my arm and says they have indicated that we should follow them. I think it's a bit strange, but I'm guessing that the attorney was successful in arranging for us to meet with Chad. I hurry after her, and as soon as we passed through the door I can tell we screwed up. There is a surprised look on the bailiff's and deputies faces. Chad is standing right there and Debra does manage to hug him, as we hear someone exclaim, "What are they doing here?" Two deputies burst through the door right behind us and the officers are telling us in no uncertain terms that we have to leave. I give Chad a quick pat on the arm and tell him to hang in there. Debra tells him to make sure and ask for a special visit; Chad nods his head to indicate that he knows what she is talking about. We sheepishly return to the courtroom, and I'm thinking, *Nice going Debra!* But she doesn't care; she got a chance to give Chad a hug.

Bill motions for us to follow him to the clerk's office where we sign a paper and pay a court fee. He explains to us that he had a good talk with Chad and was impressed with his demeanor. He said Chad was very contrite and willing to go along with any suggestion we would all make. Bill also said that Chad admitted that he had been lying to us about taking his medicine. Bill also said that he would try to meet with Chad over the weekend to get a full statement from him and to further assess the situation. We remind Bill that Chad has been on his medicine for a few days now, so he will be talking to Chad in a more normal state.

As we drive home, we talk about the proceedings and what will happen next. We are all impressed with Bill and are hoping we have done the right thing. We want to take Cindy out to lunch but decide it's not a good idea. I'm anxious to get home and then get to the bank to talk to Jeff Szyperski, the bank President. I'm hoping that check doesn't bounce as high as a kite.

Jeff is available when I call Jeff's secretary and set up a time. I feel uncomfortable as I walk into Jeff's office. I feel awful about the predicament my son has put the bank in. Our bank and the bank he robbed have been friendly competitors for years. For the most part, our senior management and directors are either acquaintances or friends with the senior management and directors of the other bank. Over the years, our bank has developed a reputation has the "white collar" bank while their bank has the reputation as the "blue collar" bank.

I apologize to Jeff for what has happened, but he quickly brushes it aside, acknowledging that there is some embarrassment but there are bigger issues involved such as our welfare and that of our son. He wants to know how Debra and I are doing and how Chad is doing. I fill him in on what I know of the details and also make sure that he understands that the Sheriff's Department has also accused Chad with counterfeiting. We both discuss the fact that neither one us knew that it was against the law to scan money in the privacy of our homes. I assure Jeff that Chad never made any attempt to try and pass any of it. As a matter of fact, he had thrown most of it away. We talk about what is going to happen to Chad. We talk about the tough love approach versus trying to get him the best attorneys we can. Jeff indicates that from what he knows of the court systems, he would strongly encourage the latter approach. He also makes a good point that we don't want to be in a position several years from now where we will be second-guessing ourselves as Chad spends more time in jail.

Jeff has prepared some loan papers for me to sign. He mentions that under the hardship rules we could bust our 401K plan and get the funds from there to repay the loan. This is an approach I hadn't thought of. He says to let him know if there is anything else he can do. Jeff is ten years my junior, but as far as I'm concerned, he comes across as wise beyond his years.

Once home, I mention to Debra that we can repay the loan with my 401K savings, and that seems to take a load off her mind. We can settle down now that we have raised the $10,000, whereas just hours before, we didn't think it was going to be possible. Debra has been visiting with Cindy. I'm starting to realize how lucky we were that Cindy could make it down.

Later on that afternoon, a church member brings another home cooked meal to us. While visiting someone pounds on our door. Debra says now what and our visitor exclaim what in the world is that! Fearfully, I approach the door expecting another Sheriff's deputy. Instead, it's a neighbor down the street upset because apparently Lacy scratched their new truck. I'm not sure what she wants us to do about it, especially when I hear her son who is behind her say it wasn't Lacy - it was their dog. Debra, who is friends with the neighbor, apologizes and says that we will pay for any damage. I can't believe that they would bother us with something as trivial as this at a time like this.

I spend more time on the phone that night. I really miss not being able to research items over the Internet.

SATURDAY, AUGUST 18TH

Debra and Cindy relax this morning and don't do much of anything but watch TV and visit. No one is in the mood to go out anywhere. I keep myself busy by working on the yard.

At lunchtime, I'm looking out the kitchen bay windows towards the water and I realize that I can't see our canoe! We keep it down by the water and tie it to some large shrubbery limbs to secure it. I walk down towards the river and I don't see it anywhere! This is not a cheap canoe. It is twenty-two-footer made out of indestructible material that I paid over $800 for several years earlier. I also can't believe that the tide would have taken it out, because it was tied and pulled out of the water and it was full of rainwater that I hadn't dumped out from the previous week. I can't believe that someone would steal it! I then remember that I had seen the Sheriff's deputies poking down around the canoe when I had looked out the kitchen window before they got the search warrant. I'll bet they moved it around enough that it loosened the tie and left it close enough to the water that a high tide could have taken it out!

I spend an hour looking for it and then give it up and return to the house. What more can happen this week?

We are surprised, to say the least, when we get a collect call from Chad. We are so excited we almost manage to cut him off as we fumble with the phone. There is a message up front giving details on how to set up phone privileges with an inmate. We are given a number that we can call to make the necessary arrangements and to make a deposit. It is great to hear Chad's voice and he sounds fine. We ask him how he is doing and if he is getting his medicine. He says that he is getting the medicine and that he is no longer in Medical. They have moved him in with the general inmate population. We ask him if he has asked for a special visit. He said that he had made the request yesterday but hadn't heard anything back, and it was his understanding that the person who makes the decision doesn't work weekends. Why am I not surprised? We tell him to keep pushing for it, and we say at least we will finally get to see you on Tuesday. He then indicates that he thinks his visiting hours have changed now that he is no longer in Medical.

Debra and I keep passing the phone back and forth in our excitement and before we know it, a computerized voice comes across the line telling us that we only have two minutes left. We tell Chad we love him and to hang in there and that we will get the phone service set up. We had talked for fifteen minutes, and we are exhilarated by the fact that we have finally gotten to talk to Chad. We are also excited about the fact that it sounds like we will be able to talk to him daily once the phone service is set up. We do have concerns, however, about the fact that he has been moved into the general prison population. Since when is it a good idea to mix someone who is mentally ill with jail inmates? We will find in the weeks ahead just how naïve we are about the whole thing.

We also talk about the lack of response by the jailhouse officials to Chad's request for special visitation. It doesn't seem like it would take a long time to make that decision. Debra says she will call the jail on Monday to see if Chad's visiting hours has changed and also to see if she can find out anything about his request.

I get a call from Dad later on in the day saying that he has talked to Blaine and filled him in on what has happened. Blaine is back in town and Dad gives me his number and let's me know that Blaine is expecting my call. He says that Blaine was quite complimentary of Utah court appointed attorneys and that it is not a bad route to go. Blaine also expresses his concern for us and told Dad to tell us that, as bad as it seems right now, with the passage of time we will eventually be able to get on with our lives and get over what has happened. Blaine has had one of his relatives run afoul of the law. He knows what he is talking about.

I call Blaine later that night. It has been years since we have talked so we exchange pleasantries for a while. It is good to talk to him. As I get to the trouble we been having, Blaine quickly says: "You and Debra are not in any trouble - it's the other guy." I have to laugh; Blaine has always been able to look at things with an objective point of view. We talk at length about the pros and cons of going with a court appointed attorney. He basically says that there are many good ones in Utah and they often bring to the table an astute understanding of how the various local judges and courts look at different types of criminal activities, many of them are very knowledgeable and work hard. About the only negative thing he says is that sometimes they are overworked to the point that they don't always have the time needed to do the proper job.

We also talk at length about the fact that we are leaning towards the "insanity" approach in defending Chad. Blaine is skeptical and says that is a tough one to prove these days. He says that the laws were rewritten years ago making it much tougher to win with an insanity plea. He says the basic approach to that defense now, taken by the prosecution, is to say "Yes, we agree your son is mentally ill, as a matter of fact we think he's a "looney-tooney;" but guess what, he can still tell the difference between right and wrong." And apparently that is all the prosecution has to do, no matter how mentally ill the person is, to convince the judge or jury that he should be punished like anyone else.

I also talked with Blaine concerning the treatment we had received from the Sheriff's Department. He surprises me when I tell him how Captain Wilkins treated us. Blaine says I would march down there tomorrow and file a complaint. When I tell him that our attorney's have advised us not to do that and not to make any waves, I can hear the disgust in Blaine's voice. He points out that my attorneys should know what they are talking about and he would say follow their advice. He briefly discusses how his experience as a city prosecutor would sometimes put him at odds with the actions of the police department and how they wanted things resolved. An effort to be fair to all parties involved would often result in an outcome the police didn't like, and they would let him know it. Finally, Blaine just quit and opened his own law practice and got away from criminal law.

It was an interesting discussion and very insightful. After thanking Blaine for his time I reflected on what he had told me. His points about the court appointed attorneys and the type of defense we would be making were contrary to the decision I had made, and the course we were pursuing. I hope we have chosen the right course. I do have a suspicion that the court appointed attorneys in rural Virginia don't have the same caseloads, work ethics or talent as the Utah attorneys.

SUNDAY, AUGUST 19TH

Debra and Cindy take Ali school shopping in Northern Virginia. They make a stop in Fredericksburg before they go up to Woodbridge and The Potomac Mills Mall. Shopping has always been a stress reliever for Debra. Having lived in Woodbridge for ten years she is very comfortable in that part of the woods. Whenever Debra makes a trip like that, I know she won't be home until late. I'm the opposite of Debra; I like to stay at home to relieve stress.

After they leave, I go into Chad's room and just sit down to reflect on the past week. As I look at the shelves and desktops that contain mementos and trophies of his accomplishments, I'm struck by the awful turn of events. *What have you done Chad? What have you done to your life? It was this time last week when we were out on the lawn playing catch.* I know it can never be the same again. I can't help crying.

MONDAY, AUGUST 20TH

Going to work today is going to be awkward, not only for me but also for my coworkers. But I've got to get it over with sometime. It makes it easier knowing that I've done pretty much all I can for Chad, and it is now up to the attorneys. Debra made the comment last night that she is glad that we did go with the attorneys - she says she realizes she would be nervous as hell if we hadn't. Debra and Cindy will be at home. They end up going to Urbanna to do some sightseeing and to have some lunch.

Work is uneventful and helpful. I do get word, however, that one of the Northumberland newspaper editors had called an officer to confirm that I had worked for the bank. It helps to have my mind on something else. John does drop in to inquire about how everything is going. He says they were at a gathering of prominent community members over the weekend and the general consensus was nothing but heartfelt concern for Debra and me. Several people call and a number of coworkers drop by and ask me to please let them know if there is anything they can do. Every bit of news like this and kind word help tremendously.

As I drive home from work, the thought occurs to me that maybe somehow our canoe ended up in the cove on the other side of the oyster house. Sure enough, as I walk around the cove and ask permission from property owners if I can go down by their shoreline, one of them tells me they found a canoe half submerged the other day and they had pulled it out. He takes me down by the water and there it is. I can't thank him enough, and I also apologize for the commotion at our house the night Chad was arrested. He is a waterman and we have an interesting talk about how his business is doing as of late. After finishing our discussion, I paddle the canoe home; and I feel a lot better.

Chad calls that evening. It is good to know that we at least have a line of communication with him, even if someone is listening. He tells us that he met with Bill yesterday and pretty much told him everything. Being skeptical, we asked him if he told Bill about the voices he had been hearing and about his perceived problem with his scrotum. He says, yes. He also mentions that he has not heard anything about his request for a special visit, and he has also heard that regular visiting hours aren't until this Friday. I ask him what he thinks the delay is, and he says he has no idea. Again, we are only allotted fifteen minutes before the computerized operator cuts us off.

Debra calls her friend who works at the jail, and she confirms that Chad is right. Visiting hours for an inmate are on Friday's. She also tells us that Chad had only spent one night in Medical. The jail officials determined that he was okay to enter the general prison population, and it is very rare they ever decide otherwise. In other words, we had missed our opportunity to visit with Chad last week because he was in court during regular visiting hours, and it appears that the jail officials could care less about Chad's unique circumstances. We are at least hopeful that the fact that Chad was in court and the fact that we still have not been allowed to see our son will work in our favor and we will be granted a special visit.

Debra gets a piece of alarming news from her friend later on when she comes by the house. Apparently, after Chad had been arrested, a number of deputies had dropped by the next day to gloat over their great catch. During their bragging she heard one exclaim, "Not only is his Dad a Vice President of a bank but his mother made $50,000 last year and he still goes and robs a bank." She said she got so sick of their mouths, she told them that they don't know what they are talking about; she works with Debra and there is no way she makes that kind of money and her husband is not a Vice President of a bank.

After she leaves, Debra and I look at each other in disbelief. Not only am I at a Vice President level at the bank but also the deputy had nailed exactly what Debra had made last year after rounding it up, and allowing for overtime. Debra's salary is supposed to be a well-kept secret at the correctional facility she works at. It is amazing how we can't seem to free ourselves of these "keystone cops" and the amount of damage they are doing to us. I tell Debra I will speak with John tomorrow (he is in charge of the personnel policies at the bank) to see what course of action he recommends. We both go to bed wondering how a deputy at the low end of the totem pole found out what Debra was making.

We don't know it when we wake up, but today will be almost as bad as last Tuesday.

Debra calls me at the office and tells me she has worked up the nerve to go to the grocery store and asks me if there is anything I need. Shortly thereafter John walks into my office, with a concerned look on his face and he asks me what is Debra doing today. I tell him she is going to the store. He says you might want to call her and tell her to stay home. Some friends of the bank have called and said you will not believe the Northumberland County newspapers - they are just awful! John doesn't have any details other than Chad is front-page news and there is a picture of him as he is being escorted from jail. I quickly give Debra a call back and she is crying. She has already gotten the news from a friend. That same feeling of helplessness I had a week ago has just returned.

I wasn't expecting this. The bank robbery is a week old and no one was hurt, but obviously the editors have decided that they are going to sensationalize this thing to the hilt. They are going to make money off of our misfortune. The only thing I can think to do is to give the attorney's a call. Bill is out of town and Jim is tied up. I'm angry and have already made up my mind if there is any possible way, I will sue these newspapers.

We now have to prepare ourselves for another round of embarrassment and being the talk of the whole Northern Neck, and then some. The question of whether we are ever going to be able to lead normal lives again in this area have returned.

After debating whether I should contribute fifty cents to the wallet of the editor, I get the only one of the two newspapers that is carried here in Kilmarnock. I have decided that I'm going to need to see it so I know what I'm talking about later.

As far as I'm concerned, the statement that the newspaper was just awful is an understatement. In bold headlines the article proclaims, "Robbery suspect nabbed." In the middle of the article our last name "Wegkamp" appears in box format written in large, bold, red ink font followed by "could face life in prison if convicted" also written in large, bold, red ink font. The article is basically a propaganda piece for the Sheriff's Department. By distorting the facts, using elements of the truth, and omitting pertinent facts, they create a sensationalized story that not only paints the wrong picture of Chad but also totally damages the reputation of the entire family. We are the only Wegkamp's in the whole region - which makes us an easy mark for the editors. This point can't be emphasized enough. We are "come-heres" without any extended family in the area.

The picture of Chad is a parent's worst nightmare. It is a large photo, showing Chad in his prison garb, being escorted by two deputies. The quote under the photo, printed in a large black font, is "Chad Wegkamp was chained hand and foot when he was arraigned on robbery and other charges in Heathsville August 15."

The paper triumphs the "fast police work" and quotes Prosecutor McKenney praising the efforts of Sheriff Middleton and Captain Chuck Wilkens in their efforts to solve the case. There is no mention of the fact that we had voluntarily provided the tags to the detectives that had given them the evidence they needed to obtain a search warrant. Nor is there any mention of the fact that Chad is mentally ill and didn't have a weapon. In fact, the paper implies that he might have had a butterfly knife because the police seized one out of our home. The paper does make a point of giving my full name and making sure the reader understands that it was my home that had been searched.

Even though the counterfeiting charge is a misdemeanor, the article gives it as much ink as the bank robbery, going into great detail about what was seized and could be used as evidence. Of course, there is no mention of the fact that Chad had never tried to use any of it and had already discarded it.

Altogether, the article and photo cover almost half of the front page. I will never have the same opinion of the press ever again.

Chad calls tonight and tells us that the major of the jail has refused his request for a special visit. It has been a week since he has been arrested, and we still haven't been able to meet with him. That's great therapy for a teenager who is mentally ill - deny him visits from his family! The only explanation is that Chad had requested the visit be at night, to accommodate our schedule, and no visitation is allowed at nights. No attempt is made to try to work with Chad and suggest what might be convenient time for all.

It's been a lousy day.

I didn't get much sleep. Everyone is up early. Cindy will be returning to Ohio today. It's been great having her here. She has been a tremendous help to Debra.

Debra has still not returned to work and is taking Prozac daily. She plans on going to work on Monday. She definitely doesn't want anything to interfere with our visit to Chad during regular visiting hours on Friday.

Bill Kopchak is back and returns my phone call. I tell him I've got a laundry list of things that I want to talk to him about. We set up a time for Monday. He asks me to bring a copy of the newspaper articles.

At lunchtime I go to several places to find a copy of the Northern Neck News. It's the local paper out of Richmond County, which is located just to the northwest of us.

I can't believe this article is even worse than the other. The photo is the largest color photo I've ever seen on the front of a newspaper in this region. The caption underneath reads; "Police lead Chad Wegkamp from the Northumberland Courthouse to a squad car after his Aug. 17 arraignment. Wegkamp, 18, is charged with 3 felony counts, including grand larceny and counterfeiting." It looks like the picture was snapped just seconds before the other photo was taken. The coverage is unbelievable - it actually takes up more than a third of the front page and then spills over to take a chunk of the second page.

The article is vicious. It not only contains the half-truths of the previous paper, it adds a few more. It quotes Sheriff Middleton as saying that the family refused to cooperate, and not only is my name mentioned more than once but Debra's also. The article also states "during their search of the Wegkamp home, officers observed evidence of an alleged counterfeiting operation and immediately sought a new search warrant." It is obvious that a standard of ethics and fairness do not exist at either paper. It is also obvious that the Northumberland newspapers are bedfellows with the Northumberland Sheriff's Department.

I take some solace later in the afternoon when I get a few phone calls from friends saying how disgusting the newspaper articles were. I'm hoping that at least a few people called the newspapers to express the same sentiment.

CHAPTER 7

THE NORTHERN NECK REGIONAL JAIL

THURSDAY, AUGUST 23RD

We are excited about our visit with Chad tomorrow, and we're wondering if we can bring him anything. I call the jail and they tell me no. I try not to think of the reality of the situation. I still wonder, as if at any moment now, I'm going to wake up from the worst dream I've ever had.

I have weird experience standing in line at the local grocery store. An old lady in front of me has bought the paper, and is reading the story on Chad, with the photo of Chad in plain sight. The cashier comments on the story, but I can't quite make out what she said. This is so surreal! It just can't be happening!

John tells me that he went to a dinner party the night before and the topic of conversation was the newspaper articles. No one can believe the sensationalism, and no one can remember any story getting that kind of coverage. The general consensus is that this is just another example of why these papers are held in so little regard.

While I'm sitting on the couch and watching TV, Debra approaches me with a white piece of paper in her hands and a funny look on her face. "This is how they found out how much money I made last year!" she says as she hands me the slip of paper. It's her last pay stub for the year 2000. It was on the window seal in the laundry room where the deputies had found the money!

FRIDAY, AUGUST 24TH

I wake up at 4:30 in the morning because I am so excited to see Chad. As usual, even though I'm awake, I still feel like I'm in a dream-like state. I lie in bed for an hour reflecting on what to say to Chad. I'm even a little concerned that maybe we will run out of things to say. I'm also wondering whether security at the jail will be as Debra describes the security at her prison. I also can't help but think of the reality that today I will be visiting my son in jail. The excitement of seeing my son gives way to that dark shroud and the feeling of a heavy weight on my chest.

I get up and start getting ready. By 6:30 I'm ready to go - even though the regional jail is only about 45 miles away. Debra is up and also getting ready. The visiting hours start at 9:00 AM and we are both ready to leave by 7:30. Debra wants to stop at the garbage dump along the way. I'm amazed that she can even be thinking of a domestic chore at this point in time. I tell her that I will stop at the dump on my way to work.

We decide to leave early and arrive twenty minutes early. Along the way we share our excitement, and Debra describes once again on what it will be like, based on her experience at the correctional facility.

As we enter the facility, we realize quickly that our experience will not go as smoothly as hoped. There are no signs, receptionists, or guards. There is nothing or no one to assist us. Further inspection of the room reveals a booth-like structure at the far end of the reception area. It reminds me of the old type of booth where you would buy movie tickets. However, instead of windows, there appears to be ominous black windows where they can see you but you can't see them. You have no idea how many people are in the booth.

Not knowing what to do, we sit down on some chairs next to some people who also look like visitors. Then we notice a few more people come in and go up to the booth, and it looks like they are pressing a button and announcing whom they are. I soon realize they are visitors announcing what prisoner they have come to see. I quickly scramble up to the booth and notice there is a small sign pointing to a button indicating that if you need assistance press the button. I press the button and call out my son's name. A female voice replies, "Okay" and that's it. I have no idea what "okay" means. Does it mean that we will now finally get to meet with our son? Are we supposed to go somewhere else? Are we supposed to wait until someone comes and gets us? Frustrated, I sit down next to Debra and wait - noticing that it seems to be what everyone else is doing. I say to Debra, "I guess we are just going to have to follow the lead of the pack." I glance at my watch; its 9:00 AM.

We wait another five minutes and, all of a sudden, most of the visitors rush to get in line in front of the booth; we do the same. We are half way down the line. There are about twenty-five visitors, including some children; most of the visitors are minorities. I don't know what the signal was that alerted everybody, but I notice that the people at the front of the line are once again pushing the button and talking to someone they can't see. The voice is asking for a picture ID and slipping out a form through a sliding metal drawer for the visitor to sign.

The line is moving excruciatingly slow. Part of the hang-up is the unseen voice keeps sending out the sign-in form without a pen. The visitor then has to press the button again to ask for a pen. While standing there, my heart sinks when I notice the first visitors to sign in are going through a door up the hall to our right, and behind the door I catch a glimpse of booths like you see in the movies. The booths are small with thick glass extending from the desktops to the ceiling. Inside each booth is a telephone receiver. We are going to have to talk to Chad through a telephone. We will be unable to touch him or talk to him in a civilized manner.

One of the visitors, standing in line in front of us, is an attractive young mother who has her hands full with two shoeless, small children, a boy and a girl who are hyperactive. As she approaches the window and presses the button, the boy breaks free from her arms and immediately runs for a door to the left of us marked "no admittance." She frantically puts the girl down and races to grab the other. She stops the boy just as he is opening the door; meanwhile the girl is amusing herself by continuously pressing the button. I couldn't help but hope that there was a loud buzzer attached to that button!

It is 9:25 AM when we make it back to the window. We are grateful that the visitor in front of us has left the pen outside the drawer. I press the button and announce once again that we are here to see Chad. There is no answer. Not wanting to agitate the omnipresent God behind the window, we both stand there and wait. I can feel the person behind us getting restless and I don't blame him. After about a minute, I press the button once again. Finally, the drawer is rolled out to us but no instructions are given. We assume she wants our photo IDs so we put our driver licenses in the drawer and it is withdrawn. A minute later the sign-in sheet is rolled out to us and we fill it out and quickly place it back in the drawer. The form sits there and whoever is behind the window makes no effort to pull the drawer back in. I start to fiddle with it to no avail. Finally, the drawer is pulled back. I assume we are done and all we have to do now is wait for our driver's licenses to be returned to us. Of course, our licenses are not returned to us promptly and after waiting another minute, I finally push the button and ask are we going to get our licenses back. Another 15 seconds pass and with no verbal reply our licenses are rolled out to us.

I glance at my watch; it is now almost 9:35 AM. It has taken almost ten minutes to sign in. We still don't know for sure where to go but we head for the same room where the other visitors are going. Upon entering the room, there is a lot of commotion as the visitors are jockeying for a booth. To our dismay there are only ten booths in total. We grab the last one available, which is the one right by the door with the least bit of privacy. We are both frantically looking for Chad, thinking that he might be waiting at one of the other booths. We don't see him anywhere.

Other visitors are now entering the room and are upset that there are no booths available. I have Debra sit down on the stool at our booth to secure it. We can see through the glass windows at the doorway where the prisoners enter. We stare at the doorway hoping that Chad will come through it. I notice a middle-age heavyset woman sitting in the booth next to ours who is also waiting to see a prisoner. I ask her if the waiting is usually this long? She said, "No, this is unusual." There is a lot of noise as the visitors talk to the inmates. There is virtually no privacy. There are only small partitions between the booths, much like you would see at a line of telephones at an airport.

I glance at my watch - it is now 9:40 AM and still there is no sign of our son. The crowding in the room is getting worse as the last of the visitors are coming in. Each booth has one small footstool; most of the visitors are standing. The young children are running amok playing hide and seek between people's legs and under the booths. The room is getting hot and stuffy. I feel like we are cattle and that the Northern Neck Regional Jail has about as much respect for visitors as it has for its inmates.

It is now 9:45 AM and Debra and I are becoming more and more frantic. I'm beginning to wonder whether we do have the right room or if something has happened to Chad. I know if Chad doesn't get to see us, he'll be crushed; we'll be crushed! We are now the only booth that doesn't have an inmate present. I can see several visitors mumbling that we should move so they can visit their inmate who is present, one of whom is gesturing to us to move. I'm thinking that something has gone terribly wrong and we do need to move so those visitors can speak to their loved one. Just then, at 9:48 AM, Chad walks through the door. What a relief!

Chad sees us through the glass and begins to cry. They appear to be tears of remorse and of relief to finally be close to some people who love him. I know he doesn't want the other inmates to see him cry so I try to suppress my tears and immediately start asking him questions concerning the conditions at the jail. He composes himself and begins to answer my questions. Debra and I take turns talking to him. We are now oblivious to the conditions around us - concentrating on our conversation with Chad. Most of it is small talk knowing full well that "big brother" could be watching and listening. Chad has no stool to sit on, and he is hunched over in an awkward position, as the telephone line is not long enough to allow him to stand up straight.

Chad presses the possibility of his getting out on bond and has a lot of questions about what the lawyers are doing.

At about 10:40, a female guard comes into the room and starts telling inmates their time is up and they need to leave. It's not clear whether the message is for just some of the inmates in the room or all of them. We are thinking because Chad came out so late, the message doesn't apply to him. We continue to talk to Chad for about another minute, when she makes it clear that all inmates are to leave the room immediately. We barely have time to say goodbye. So much for our two-hour visit. No effort is made by the prison staff to explain to the visitors why the inmates were brought out so late and why they had to leave early.

As we leave the jailhouse, I am struck by how close we came to not being able to visit with Chad at all. If we had been back further in the line or if Chad had been brought out just a few minutes later, we may not have been able to visit with him. We would have had to wait another seven days.

I cannot believe how callous this system is. Here we have a seriously mentally ill eighteen-year-old boy who needs the support of his mother and father more than ever, and it took nine days since his arrest before we are even allowed to sit down with him under horrible conditions.

MONDAY, AUGUST 27TH

Debra returned to work today. We now have to deal with trying to get to two jobs with one car. It takes over an hour to take Debra to her job and then to turn in the opposite direction and head to my job, a distance of 65 miles. We will be putting 130 commuting miles a day on the truck.

We talk about my meeting today with the attorney. We are hoping that he can shed some light on what happens next and what we can do to defend ourselves against the vicious media attacks on the whole family and the abuse we endured when the house was searched.

I take a quick lunch and go the American Civil Liberties Union site on the Internet. I am surprised to find instructions on how to file a grievance against a police officer. I feel empowered by this information, and I can't wait to share it with the attorney to see if it's okay to pursue it.

When I bring up the subject, the attorney looks at me like I'm the one that is crazy. He explains that the success of their law firm is partly attributable to the good relationships they have established over the years with the law enforcement agencies, courts, and prosecutors. If I do anything that upsets this relationship, all bets are off for Chad. I also mention the subject of whether I can do anything about the media attacks and distortions. He explains that, "the media can say anything they want because they can always hide behind the First Amendment and anything I try to do is more fodder for them."

In other words, if I try to defend my family against the media onslaught and the verbal abuse we have endured, Chad will do more time. I know the attorney is right, but I can't help but wonder if he would have felt any differently if it were his family that was going through this instead of mine.

We focus on what we are going to do for Chad. Bill mentions that the two hours he had spent with Chad previously has left him no doubt that Chad is "completely loco" and is in

77

desperate need of help. We discuss his defense. He confirms to me that we are not looking to get him off but to get him the help that he needs. We discuss what legal motions are going to be made. One motion will be to petition the court to get a full expert diagnosis of Chad's condition. We spend some time discussing who the expert should be. Bill says that he is open to suggestions and asks me to get with Debra to see if she knows of anyone.

Bill also states that Chad is going to need to plead guilty to the crime in order to plead insanity. You can't have it both ways. You can't plead insanity and innocent of the crime at the same time. He also states that Chad needs to agree to do this before we move forward. He is going to try and set up a meeting between all of us at the jailhouse on Thursday.

When Chad calls that night, I inform him of my conversation with the attorney. I can tell he is very excited about the meeting. We have an agreement with Chad that he calls us every night at 6:15 PM. I look forward to his phone calls, not only for the opportunity to chat with him, but just to hear that he is all right. It occurs to me that if he misses a call I will worry about him.

I also talk with Dad that night about the latest developments. He makes a comment about how Chad's brain is still there with all of its potential but somehow a wire has gotten loose. If only we could get that wire reconnected!

TUESDAY, AUGUST 28TH

Debra finally gets hold of Dr. Gomez. Apparently, there has been a mix up and we have been leaving messages to the wrong Gomez brother, who is also a psychiatrist. Debra explains to Dr. Gomez that based on Chad's last few letters and phone calls it is apparent that the medicine is not working. Gomez ups Chad's dosage of both the Prozac and Zyprexa.

I get a phone call from the attorney in the late afternoon. There is some good news and a little bit of bad news. He has gotten hold of Dr. Peck, a noted psychiatrist who specializes in schizophrenia. Bill has worked with him before and Dr. Gomez also thinks highly of him. Dr. Peck has told Bill that he is very concerned that Chad is being kept with the general prison population. He tells the attorney that time is of the essence and that the sooner we can get him into treatment the better. From what Bill relates to me, Dr. Peck confirms just about everything I read on the National Institute of Mental Health's website about the harm a prison can inflict on schizophrenics.

Dr. Peck indicates that there is a mental facility in Richmond called Tuckers that has a separate wing for mentally ill patients involved in court cases. The goal will be to get Chad out on a special bond that will allow him to be treated while he is awaiting the outcome of court proceedings.

Bill also states that he has arranged a meeting for Thursday at 2:30 PM. The bad news is that the jailhouse officials have indicated that the parents will not be allowed to be at the meeting. Bill has protested and states that the meeting is for the planning and strategy of Chad's defense and will impact Chad and his parents for the rest of their lives. Bill is told that the matter will be referred to the major at the prison and that the major will call him tomorrow with his answer. Unbelievable! Absolutely unbelievable! Is there an admiral or a general we could appeal to? How about a Commander-in-Chief?

Debra has been off Prozac for a couple of days now. She takes Chad's phone call and gets upset when all he wants to talk about is his scrotum. She cuts him off sharply and hands the phone to me. Chad seems a little perplexed and confused. I change the subject to the New York Yankees and keep talking to him like nothing has happened. When I get off the phone, Debra is still steaming and complains bitterly about how Chad only wants to discuss his scrotum problem with her and no one else. I want to say to Debra, *remember he is one sick puppy right now and when he calls us he is looking for emotional support--not to be treated rudely.* But I think better of it!

Our night ends on a good note. Ali gets home from her basketball team's first game of the season with the news that they won big. She started and had a great game finishing with eleven points and a "bunch of rebounds." "You should have seen the three-pointer I made Dad; it was sweet!"

WEDNESDAY, AUGUST 29TH

We leave for work at 6:00 in the morning. Debra is still upset over last's night phone call. She mentions that maybe she ought to go back on Prozac. I don't say anything.

79

At 12:30 PM I get a phone call from Bill that confirms that the meeting is on for Thursday. He hesitates and then informs me that Major Ted Hull of the Northern Neck Regional Jail has refused to let us attend the meeting that will decide the future for our mentally ill son. What he will do is allow us to talk to Chad using the visitor's booth after the meeting. As a father, I feel helpless. It is impossible to put into words the feelings I am having.

Debra is running an errand when Chad's 6:15 phone call comes in. I can tell he has taken the higher dose of medicine. He is not alert. However, he perks up when I tell him that the meeting with the attorneys is tomorrow and that we will get to see him afterwards. He indicates that he is unsure on what to do. I tell him to agree to whatever the attorney tells him.

THURSDAY, AUGUST 30TH

Debra and I scramble early in the morning to put together some background information on Chad. Bill needs this information to prepare for their meeting with Chad. He will also be sending some of this information to the prosecutor. Upon arrival at work, I fax the information to the attorney's office. Debra will get a phone call a few hours later as Bill tries to decipher her handwriting.

I am nervous and by lunchtime I'm pretty much useless at work. Not only am I nervous about how the meeting will go with Chad, but I also know in my gut that things will not go smoothly at the jail. I leave work at 1:30 PM. It will take about thirty-five minutes to get to Debra's job and about twenty minutes from there to the jailhouse. The radio is playing "Tears in Heaven" by Eric Clapton." Even though my son has not met a tragic death, I can still relate.

It is, as I fear, they won't let us see Chad. The girl on the other side of the one-way window says she has received no notification of a special visit. We explain to her that our attorneys spoke with Major Hull yesterday and told us to be here at three o'clock. She asks us to sit down until she can check out our story. A few minutes later she tells us we have to leave because she can't find anyone to verify our story. Luckily for us, our attorneys come through the door and explain the situation to her. They motion to us to sit down and then confirm with us that we will be able to talk to Chad when they have finished.

The attorney's exit through a security door and are gone about twenty-five minutes. While we are waiting a prison official walks out into the foyer. I notice he is checking us out, and by the way he keeps passing in front of us, it is obvious that he wants us to check him out. The man is obviously preoccupied with his self-importance.

A security door opens to our left, we can see our attorneys standing behind a glass plate and there are booths just like the ones we encountered the previous Friday. It is about 3:25 PM and the voice calls from the booth for us to come forward and sign in. She informs us that she goes home at 4:15 and we only have until then. She also informs us that because we are being granted a special visit, we cannot come and visit our son tomorrow during regular visiting hours. Why am I not surprised!

When we pass through the security door on our left, I notice that there are eight booths with phone receivers. Why wasn't this room opened last week when there were more visitors and inmates than phones? Chad comes through the door. We are relieved to see that he looks okay. However, he does look pale and his hair has gotten darker from the lack of sun. He also looks like he has lost some weight and his beard is growing out.

I begin talking to him over the phone receiver. I ask him how he is doing and he says okay. It's an awkward situation because only one of us can speak to him at a time and the attorney's are standing right next to him. I don't feel comfortable asking him about what he has discussed with the attorneys. There is always that fear that someone is listening. Debra and I chat about fifteen minutes and then the attorney's motion that they are coming around to our side of the booth.

They tell us that the guard said that we only have until four o'clock. They don't seem concerned that anyone could be listening, as they begin to tell us what they have discussed with Chad and what he has agreed to do. At one point, Bill takes the phone and repeats to Chad what was agreed upon, so we can hear. As Bill speaks, Chad nods in agreement. Basically, nothing has changed from the strategy that was discussed previously. The good news is that we are lucky enough to be working with a prosecuting attorney who is capable of being able to show some compassion; though he is concerned about how the public will react if Chad is given bail. He has agreed to allow Chad to be transferred to Tucker's special wing for evaluation and treatment. Chad will plead guilty. The attorney's think that the transfer can be accomplished before the 10th of September. They also indicate that they are working hard to have our things returned to us as quickly as possible.

Chad asks what will happen later. Is there still a chance this could go to trial? All the attorneys say is that this will be determined at a later date, depending on the diagnosis and treatment that Chad gets at Tucker's.

There is only about five minutes left. The attorneys excuse themselves so we can spend that time talking with Chad. We ask him if he is pleased with how things are going. He says he is, and we encourage him to hang in there until the transfer.

As we leave the jail, we are pleased with the progress the attorneys have made and are hopeful that we will not have to deal with the jail ever again. But we have both noticed that Chad's medicine is still not having the desired effect. He was nervous and picking at his face and continuously pulling up his prison uniform as we were talking to him. He also told Debra that he was still hearing voices and that his scrotum was bothering him. His transfer can come none too soon.

We also discuss the fact that the attorneys have indicated that for procedural and insurance reasons we will have to continue using Dr. Gomez. We are not happy about this. We felt that if Dr. Gomez had been more competent in the beginning, none of this would have happened. However, we do feel that he certainly should be responsive now that we have his attention.

On the way home, we stop and get this week's edition of the Northern Neck News. There is not a word about Chad. You would think they would have followed up with their sensationalized story from the week before. You would think they might have disclosed that further investigation revealed that Chad was a former honor student at Northumberland High School and finished in the top ten percent of his class and was voted the best accounting and business student of the year. You would think they would have mentioned that Chad had just recently been struck with schizophrenia and that he actually robbed the bank without a weapon and it was unbelievable that he made it home without being caught. As one prominent member of the community commented, "These local newspaper editors don't have the talent or take the time needed to actually come up with good, substantive news reporting." May I make a suggestion, Mr. Editor? How about a good journalistic piece on the abuse of mentally ill inmates by the local jail or a piece on how mistrusted and disliked the Sheriff's Department is among a large percentage of the county's population.

Debra and I also discuss an interesting tidbit that was reaffirmed by some comments made by the attorney's today. We have learned from conversations with friends at work, and from what the attorneys have told us, that the local sheriff's departments from the neighboring counties are in constant competition with one another. It is apparently a big deal that the Sheriff's Department in Northumberland County caught their bank robber in less time then the Sheriff's Department in Lancaster County caught theirs. This even helped explain why the Northumberland papers gave it so much sensationalized coverage in comparison to the Lancaster paper. It's nice to know that these guys have got their priorities right!

Debra and I also discuss how we have to watch ourselves around our coworkers. We are under tremendous stress, and we have found that it helps to relieve stress when we can poke fun at the situation and at ourselves. I have cracked a few jokes at work, and have seen that look of how can you be joking at a time like this. For an example, one thing we have joked about is that if we'd known our son was going to be arrested that night, we would have asked him to connect the Playstation before he leaves. Our direct TV, VCR, stereo system, telephone lines, and computers were all hooked up on the same wires, cables, and remotes. Chad is the only one who knows exactly how to do it, and the cops took everything but the Playstation and TV! Debra said that when her coworkers asked her that morning where she got her new shoes, she joked that she got them with the money Chad gave her! Her coworkers told her, "not funny!"

FRIDAY, AUGUST 31ST

Work is going to be a hassle today. It is month end, which is a busy time for any accountant. John is gone, so I also fill in for him during the quarterly advisory committee meeting, which will be held in the late afternoon.

I get a big boost in the morning when the bank offers me the use of the company car until we get our car returned. I am also told that the refinancing on our home should be completed in a week or two.

The advisory committee meeting goes well. However, it is embarrassing when the discussion centers on our own recent robberies.

The phone call with Chad that night is disturbing. He tells us that the jailhouse officials destroyed the computer articles I sent him. One article was on the new monitors that are now available and the other was on the most cost-effective upgrades you can do for your computer. Hardly the kind of information that someone could use planning a jailbreak! The sad thing is that as much as Chad loves computers these articles would have helped him keep his mind off his troubles.

Chad tells me another story that makes me angry. One of the detectives, James Bruce, who was at the house the night Chad was arrested, took Chad's fingerprints. The guy seemed to take pleasure in causing Chad some pain as he did it. This guy, who was backed up by prison guards, told Chad to quit fighting him as he pulled, twisted and tugged at Chad's fingers so hard they cracked and Chad thought maybe they were broken. Chad asked the detective what his problem was, and the guy gave him a cold stare. It's nice to know we have such brave men in the Sheriff's Department. How much longer do I have to standby and do nothing.

CHAPTER 8

THREATS FROM THE SHERIFF'S DEPARTMENT

SATURDAY, SEPTEMBER 1ST

It is the start of the Labor Day weekend. I'm exhausted and, after I wake up later than usual, I found myself going back to sleep for another couple of hours. After I get up, Debra and I travel to Williamsburg, which is about eighty-five miles away, to pick up the company car. Upon arrival we notice that the inspection sticker has expired. We will not be able to use it until Tuesday after we can get it inspected.

That night we watch the movie "The Family Man" with Nicolas Cage. The movie is about a high-powered Wall Street bachelor who is given a glimpse of what life would have been like had he chosen to marry his college sweetheart. It would have been a good movie for Chad to watch. It is all about getting your priorities right.

SUNDAY, SEPTEMBER 2ND

I decide not to go to church today and go to work to get caught up. After working a few hours, I started thinking about the newspaper articles and start to do a "slow burn." I search the Internet to see if there is a practical way to sue the papers and their editors. It takes a few minutes, but I'm able to determine that the key search words are defamation, privacy, and libel. All three of these items are intertwined in a lawsuit filed by someone who is trying not to have their lives ruined by the "power of the press."

Defamation is a false statement that damages a person's reputation or exposes them to public hatred, contempt, or ridicule. The right of privacy includes the "right to be left alone." Libel is written or printed information that contains defamation.

From my review of the articles, it is obvious how an editor protects himself or his employer against a defamation lawsuit. They try to make sure there is at least an element of truth in what they are saying. From what I've researched, the key is whether or not a false statement had been made. It really doesn't matter how unfair or hurtful the article is, as long as there is some truth behind it. I do think, however, that these local papers did go too far in their distortion of the facts. I don't think our forefathers ever intended that the First Amendment was to be used to justify vicious attacks on a family's reputation.

In order to be successful in a libel lawsuit, the plaintiff has to prove that: (1) the statement was published to the general public, (2) the plaintiff was specifically identified, (3) defamatory statement was made, (4) the plaintiff was injured, and (5) the defendant was at fault. I know items one, two and five can easily be proven. Item three is the key and I think any reasonable person would find that the statements by the press that my wife and I refuse to cooperate with the police and that a counterfeiting operation was being run from our house were false. As far as item four is concerned, is there any question that the press has set up the whole family to be subjects of ridicule and contempt?

It is interesting to find in my reading that a lawyer advises his journalistic clients that the best protection against being sued for libel are the basic journalistic principles of truth, accuracy, and fairness.

I call Dad up later that day and tell him I'm still thinking of pursuing this. He advises me not to make waves at this point and wait and see how everything turns out. He also reminds me that Chad's lawyers have also advised against it. I don't want to be perceived as being obsessed with this, but I don't want the statute of limitations to run out before I decide to pursue it.

That afternoon I try to work myself into exhaustion. Before I go bed, I learn that Mike Mussina of the New York Yankees almost pitched a perfect game. The Yankees won, completing a three game sweep of the Boston Red Sox, which virtually assures the division title. If only life could be as predictable as the Yankees!

MONDAY, SEPTEMBER 3RD

Today is Labor Day. Even though I got the day off from work, I don't feel like enjoying it. I do some yard work and do a lot of writing in my diary. Ali and Debra are busy getting things ready for Ali's first day of school tomorrow.

I get a phone call from the attorneys advising me that things are not going as smoothly as planned. Apparently, Tucker's special wing for psychiatric patients is not as secure as originally believed and it was not meant to house prisoners. In other words, because we are using our house to secure a property bond, we could easily lose the house if Chad decides to walk away from Tuckers. Because he will be out of the prison system, there will be no law enforcement agencies checking on him.

It is imperative though that we have Chad examined by competent experts whose diagnosis can be used in his defense. The jail will not allow any doctors, other than their own, to enter the jail. The only other alternative we have is to allow state examiners to make the examination. The attorneys have been told that "unless they find Chad standing on a chair with a noose around his neck they will find him competent to stand trial." This is partly due to the fact that the state is in a budget crisis and there are no funds to support the already overcrowded state-mental-health-care facilities. Apparently the state gets no assistance from the federal government due to actions taken by the government during President Reagan's administration. These actions were directly related to the assassination attempt taken by the President's assailant who was mentally ill and ended up in a mental institution instead of receiving a prison sentence.

Debra and I have a decision to make, and we have to make it fast. The attorneys tell us that they need to know as soon as possible what route we want to take in order to be prepared for Monday's hearing. They suggest that maybe we should visit the facility before we make up our minds.

I give Debra a call. We discuss the fact that only three weeks ago we would have thought it was impossible for Chad to rob a bank. The way his mind is working now it is very conceivable that he could walk away. Basically, it comes down to what is more important, our home or our son. I call the attorneys back and tell them to proceed with the property bond.

Chad's phone call that night is disturbing. He sounds rough and gets upset when I explain to him that things are not going smoothly. I explain that it looks like there is a good chance that his stay at Tuckers will be brief and he'll probably be returned to the jail until his final hearing or trial. He starts mumbling something about "watch out for the police" and the movie "Clockwork Orange." I ask him what in the world is he talking about and remind him that he was the one that robbed the bank. He says never mind. I am more than happy when our phone time is up.

Our day ends on a high note, thanks to Ali. We attend her basketball game against the Middlesex County high school team. It is a physical, fast paced game and Ali shines. She has a great game, she garners a number of rebounds, assists, and finishes the game with twelve points. Her team wins easily and we are all elated.

THURSDAY, SEPTEMBER 6TH

The attorneys call and have indicated that they have been in touch with Dr. Gomez, and he is making arrangements for Chad. The hearing will be Monday at 9:00 AM and the attorneys have added a provision to the property bond allowing the Sheriff's deputies to escort Chad to Tuckers. This is apparently at the request of the prosecuting attorney. Another provision requires that Tuckers give our attorneys and the Sheriff Department twenty-four hours notice before they release Chad. We are also informed that Chad's court date for Rockingham County has been delayed to October 16th. We are also told that Dr. Gomez reports that Tuckers is secured and well staffed. We begin to feel a little better.

Chad's phone call is encouraging. He sounds much better than the night before, and I can tell that he is starting to get excited about the prospect of getting away from the jail. I let him know that we will not be visiting him on Friday. Debra and I both will be taking Monday off to attend his hearing.

I get a phone call from Dale. He has flown over from Budapest to attend some training meetings in Quantico. He indicates that he will drive down on Saturday to pay us a visit. I look forward to seeing him and getting his feedback on what he thinks about our situation.

SATURDAY, SEPTEMBER 8TH

I worked hard that morning out in the yard. We have over two and a half acres. Trees, shrubs, and the lawn grow like weeds during the summer months and Chad used to be here to help me. Debra is working twelve-hour shifts both today and tomorrow. Ali runs off to her boy friend's house.

Dale shows up earlier than expected, and we catch up on family news. I tell Dale in detail about the night of Chad's arrest. He just shakes his head from time to time in disbelief. We spend some time speculating on how Chad managed to rob a bank right next to the Sheriff's office and made it home twenty-three miles away, untouched.

We talk about the damage to the house, and he mentions that the FBI is required to reimburse a homeowner for any damages committed during a search. We also talk about the newspaper articles, and he encourages me to go after them.

I mention that, as badly as I want to go after all of these people who have made money or boosted their careers on the backs of my son and family, I can't! Family and friendships that have been forged since grade school control the whole infrastructure of the county. The prosecutor grew up with some of the Sheriff's deputies, they have relatives and friends on the bench, who in turn have relatives and friends working at the newspapers, jail, court houses, etc., etc. We are "come-heres." We are easy pickings for the county's legal system and all the entities that feed off of it. I have been advised by the lawyers not to make waves, because we could jeopardize the outcome for Chad. Again Dale just shakes his head.

We go out for an early dinner at the Northside Grille in Kilmarnock. It is one of the few restaurants in this area that manages to stay open year after year, year-round. The food is good, and we have a nice time. Unfortunately, when we reach home, there is a message on the answering machine from Chad, who was trying to call. I feel bad because I know how much the phone calls mean to all of us.

Dale decides to stay that night, and we plan on going on a canoe trip out the river to Chesapeake Bay and then cutting over near the menhaden fish factories in Reedville.

SUNDAY, SEPTEMBER 9TH

It is a beautiful day. We head out early and have a great time. I'm surprised by the lack of boats on the water. It is amazing how the boating dies down after Labor Day weekend. As we are heading back, a water safety patrol boat pulls up along side and orders us to stop. I can't believe it when he actually makes us try to keep the canoe still while we are out in the middle of the Great Wicomico River. He writes us a ticket for failure to wear a life jacket! I wonder if there is an air safety patrol! If there is, the way this summer is going, they'll get us next!

Dale heads back to Quantico after we get back, and I get back to the yard work. Chad calls late in the afternoon, and we spend most of the allotted time talking about what is supposed to happen tomorrow at his hearing. He sounds alert and excited.

MONDAY, SEPTEMBER 10TH

Debra and I arise early and we arrive at the courthouse early. A number of our friends from church are there to greet us. We are extremely grateful for their support, because we have no family within six hundred miles.

As we are passing through security, Debra nudges me and nods towards Chuck Wilkens standing nearby in full uniform.

While waiting for the Judge to come in, one of the detectives comes in and hands me another search warrant. This warrant gives specific permission to search the hard drives on the computer. Whatever! It's not like I have a choice.

The actual hearing only takes a few minutes. The attorneys and prosecutor met earlier in the morning to iron out the details. We are disappointed when they have Chad sit down on the left side of he courtroom. We are sitting in the first pew, but it is on the right side of the courtroom. Debra comments, "Is this some sort of psychological ploy by the court systems?" The prosecutor and Sheriff's deputies sit on the right side of the courtroom while the defendants and their lawyers are made to sit on the left.

After Chad is led out, Bill motions to us to follow him out to the clerk's office. We sign some papers, and Bill gives us a copy of the court order. Chad is being released on a twenty-five thousand-dollar property bond to Tuckers Pavilion at Chippenham Hospital. The Judge has ordered that both the Commonwealth's attorney and our attorneys be notified within twenty-four hours prior to Chad's discharge. Upon discharge, the bond is automatically revoked, and the Sheriff's Department will transport Chad to the jail.

I am surprised and delighted when Bill tells us to follow the Sheriff's deputies to Tuckers. We are to deliver Chad's clothing and condiments and to assist with the check-in; insurance arrangements will need to be made. Debra gives me a playful elbow to the ribs. We had argued that morning on whether we would be allowed to visit with Chad at Tuckers after his admission. I told her that I didn't think we would be allowed to see him until the next day.

We thank Bill for being able to arrange this; maybe now Chad will start getting the help that he needs. Bill tells us that the next step is to go see the magistrate in the Sheriff's office. He needs us to sign some papers to make the bond effective, because Chad will not be released until then.

We thank our friends for coming and hustle over to the Sheriff's office. We are told that he is tied up in meetings all morning. We are somewhat flabbergasted. We thought this would be a priority. We show the deputy on duty the court order, and he tells us to take a seat. There is a pay phone next to us, which starts ringing, and the deputy tells us to pick it up. It is the magistrate, who asks us what is going on and then tells us to come over to the old courthouse, where he is keeping appointments. His ten o'clock appointment hasn't arrived and he will try to squeeze us in.

The old courthouse is just a block away. On the way, Debra and I discuss whether this is going to go smoothly or not. The answer is "not." The magistrate, Bob Watkins, is a nice guy and is easy to talk to. The first thing he tells us is that he is going to have to have a copy of the deed and a copy of the last property tax assessment. Why didn't anyone tell us this earlier? We hustle back to the new courthouse to get a copy of the deed and then are instructed to go back to the old courthouse to get a copy of the latest property tax assessment.

When we get back, we feel lucky to find that the magistrate has taken care of his ten o'clock appointment and we have arrived before his eleven o'clock appointment. As he starts to fill out papers, he asks whether we have any liens on the house. The answer is yes; my bank has a lien. He then tells me that he will not be able to complete the bond without determining whether we have enough equity in the house to cover the bond. I quickly use the phone to call some of my coworkers who work in the loan department at the bank. I ask them to please drop what they are doing and to fax us the outstanding balance for our loan and a copy of the appraisal we had done on the house to secure the refinancing. About fifteen minutes later the faxes come. He is now able to finish the paper work and has determined that we have net equity of $73,000 in the house. We sign the papers - our house is now on the line.

We head back to the Sheriff's office to see what's next, by now its eleven o'clock. We tell the deputy that our attorneys indicated that we were supposed to follow the Sheriff's deputies to Tuckers and help check Chad in. He asks us to take a seat again while he goes and speaks to the Sheriff. He returns and tells us that we will not be allowed to follow the deputies and we are not to be in the vicinity of the hospital while they are checking him in. I guess they figure that it is during this time we will mastermind Chad's great escape! We will not let the Sheriff get us down. Chances are good we will get to see our son today! We hurry home to grab something to eat, make a few phone calls, and get my map of Richmond. We get a call from the magistrate; there is one more piece of paper we need to sign. We will have to hustle back to Heathsville, which changes the way we will go to Richmond.

After we sign the paper, we head straight for Richmond, which is about eighty-five miles to the west. We don't know Richmond well and we do get lost. We are in an area, south of Richmond that is not covered by the map. It seems like it takes forever, but we eventually find the hospital. It is now 2:30 PM as we go through the hospital doors. We notice that the Sheriff's car is parked at the entrance.

The admittance clerk tells us that the deputies had just arrived with Chad a few minutes before. We explain that we have Chad's clothes and the insurance information. She tells us to wait while she goes and checks with someone on what she is supposed to do. After about ten minutes, she returns and informs us that we will have to wait until the deputies leave, but it should only take a few minutes more.

We wait for over an hour. Finally, Debra inquires about whether they have forgotten about us. She is told that there doesn't seem to be a room available for Chad. We will find out later that it is not so much that there isn't a room - it just wasn't the right room. However, she does say that things are being worked out and that we should just wait a few minutes more. A few minutes more will turn into three-and-a-half hours. We notice that during this time the deputy's car is still parked by the entrance. I can't help but wonder if they have something to with the delay.

At 6:00 PM a nurse from Tuckers calls our name and tells us that Chad is now being processed and it should only be a few more minutes. She asks for the insurance information. We are now getting very excited and finally at 7:00 PM she comes and tells us we can now go see Chad!

As we arrive at Chad's floor there is a security door we have to pass through and we are required to sign in. The person who sits adjacent to the door unlocks it electronically and lets us in. We pass through one room full of patients and then see Chad in another room through a glass window. He sees us! He has a grin from ear to ear. I can't remember the last time I saw him smile like that. It is a good sign that the medicine is having an effect. People who are in the depths of schizophrenia are not capable of showing much emotion.

He meets us at the door. It is so good to be able to see him and hug him. We sit down at a nearby table and just talk. Debra had brought several magazines and candy for him. He is delighted. The atmosphere is relaxed and his surroundings seem nice. Chad was arrested August 14th. It has taken almost a month before we can actually sit down with him.

We talk at length about his time in the jail and how different it will be for him here. The nurse tells us his room is ready. It's a nice room, with a comfortable bed, plenty of drawers, and a private shower. He shares the room with one other patient.

It is 8:30 PM, visiting hours are over. We wish Chad good night and hug him once more as we are leaving. Debra tells him she will come again tomorrow. Of course, we get lost trying to find our way out of Richmond. We arrive home at 10:40 PM. It has been a long day.

TUESDAY, SEPTEMBER 11TH

Terrorists strike the World Trade Towers and the Pentagon. I can't believe it! How can people do this to other people? It just seems so unfathomable. Dad will tell me that when he turned his TV on at nine o'clock in Utah, the first image he saw was the

Towers burning. For the first few minutes, he thought he was watching the movie channel.

I have a friend who works for Phillip Morris in New York. I hope she is okay. The best I can remember, I don't recall her saying anything about her office or condominium being near the Towers. I think about Dale and what impact this will have on him.

Debra phones Chad and tells him she won't be able to make it. He sounds really disappointed. Given the chaotic conditions of the day - it doesn't sound like a good time to be driving into Richmond. We have heard that a number of roads have been closed by the Federal buildings.

WEDNESDAY, SEPTEMBER 12TH

I try to get a hold of a law firm that would be willing to prosecute the local newspapers. No local firm is willing to do it. I get a hold of a firm in Charlottesville, who will get back to me. They are supposed to have expertise in the area. I don't have much hope that they will take it as I wasn't able to get past the law clerk.

Everyone in the office is talking about the terrorist's attack. Everyone is surprised that we haven't done anything in retaliation. Who cares that we don't know with a hundred percent certainty that Bin Laden did it. Don't we need to get them all?

We drive to Richmond after work to see Chad. I get a little scared when I first see him. It looks like he doesn't recognize us, and he has that "absent stare" that is associated with someone who is mentally ill, but he quickly comes around.

He is still excited to be in his new surroundings. He tells us that Dr. Gomez came by earlier and that he was later given a CAT scan. We talk extensively about the terrorist attack and what steps President Bush will be pursuing. It reminds me of discussions we had when he was younger.

Debra asks him if the doctor made any changes to his medicine. Chad said that he had increased his psychotic medicine to fifteen milligrams. Then he says something that we have been longing to hear. He thinks that there is a possibility that his scrotum problem may be a mental problem rather than a physical problem. It's nice to hear. Hopefully, it will last. Chad also says that the day he returns home for good, "…will be the happiest day in my life."

We leave at 8:30 PM, and again we get lost. We don't get home until after 11:00 PM.

THURSDAY, SEPTEMBER 13TH

Jim Breeden calls and tells me that he is still working with the prosecuting attorney on getting our things back. Jim suggests that part of the problem is that the Sheriff's Department just hasn't gotten the message yet; that they are not dealing with a hardened criminal, but with a mentally ill teenager.

The continued lack of compassion demonstrated by the Sheriff's Department has got me thinking again whether I want to pursue the verbal abuse charge. I call the Sheriff's Department to inquire about what the procedures are for filing a complaint and what is the statute of limitations. I'm mostly interested to know how much time I have before it becomes too late to lodge a complaint. I'm hoping that it will only take a minute to get the information I need, and I certainly don't have any intention of telling them who I am.

Of course the Sheriff's Department will not let me make a phone call like this. Upon requesting the information I am asked my name. I am put on hold for a minute and then I'm told I will be put through to Captain Wilkins. I tell her, "No, he is not the one I want to talk to." She laughs and then says hold on. I am put through to James Bruce; the detective who my son claimed was very rough with him at the finger printing. He is cordial enough and says there is a form I can pick up. He suggests, however, that I come down and they can take the complaint verbally. Yea right-- like I can trust these guys! I tell him thanks, but I will take care of it at a later date. I realize after I hung up that I forgot to ask about the statute of limitations. I'm also thinking they probably are having a good laugh right now.

Debra calls - she has talked with the nurse she has made friends with at Tuckers. The CAT scan shows solid physical proof that Chad is indeed dealing with schizophrenia. The scan shows that Chad has neurological damage in the form of enlarged cerebral ventricles. These are cavities in the brain filled with fluid. The cavities become enlarged because of the loss of brain tissue, putting pressure on the brain. The experts don't know if this pressure or the loss of brain tissue is the cause of schizophrenia. They only know that all schizophrenics have enlarged ventricles.

95

After talking with Debra, I search the Internet for articles on enlarged ventricles. While searching, I find the following definition of schizophrenia at the National Institute of Mental Health website: "it is the most chronic and disabling mental illness. It typically begins as a psychotic episode in young adulthood, with devastating hallucinations, delusions, social withdrawal, and blunted emotionality." I quit searching as I find more depressing articles.

I'm getting numerous phone calls throughout the past few days from people who still think I'm the local Red Cross Chairman. Most of them are inquiring on where they can donate blood or make donations to help the victims and their families in New York and DC. There are a lot of good people in the world, and I think a lot of them do live right here.

I get word that our loan refinancing has gone through and will start with the October 1st payment. The monthly reduction in payment is not as much as I hoped for. Money is definitely going to be tight until we get all the legal fees and medical fees paid off. It is gratifying; however, to see how much the bank is doing to help. They have not charged us a refinancing fee of any kind. We are in their debt in more ways than one!

After work, Debra drives to Richmond to see Chad. Even though I'm a little worried about Debra getting home okay, I stay behind to get caught up on some chores. Surprisingly, I get a phone call from Dale, who wants to know how things are going. He informs me that he will be trying to catch a flight to Germany tomorrow. From there he will fly to Budapest.

Debra gets home at 11:30 PM after having gone to visit Chad. She has to get up at 4:00 AM to go to work. She has been doing this all week. I don't know how she manages, but certainly no one can question her loyalty to her son.

FRIDAY, SEPTEMBER 14TH

Jim Breeden calls and tells us that Dr. Gomez has finished his evaluation, and he will send us a copy. He also asks if I know anything about someone calling the Sheriff's Department looking to lodge a complaint. I told him, "Yes it was me, but I'm presently leaning towards not doing it." I'm a bit disturbed to think that my call to the Sheriff's Department to inquire how to lodge a

96

complaint may become a factor in how my son's case will be handled.

Dale gives me a call at work. All international flights have been canceled. He asks if he can come over on Saturday night. It works fine for me. I'm glad to have my brother for company, but I feel for his family in Budapest. I'm sure they are anxious to have him home.

I leave work early to meet Debra at her job. The plan was to pick Debra up and go visit Chad in Richmond, using the Oldsmobile. We had been putting way too much mileage on the truck. But the Olds conks out on me on the way. It restarts okay, but we decide to take the truck to Richmond.

Our visit with Chad goes well. Chad is delighted when Debra brings him some food from MacDonald's. We talk about what we think is going to happen next. We really know very little. Part of the reason is the fact that the attorney's are also navigating "new waters."

We actually make our way home without getting lost. On the way, I stop in Warsaw and buy this week's edition of the Northern Neck News. Chad has made the front page again. No picture this time, but in bold black headlines its reads "Wegkamp to undergo psych evaluation." It had become brutally clear that, once entered in the ranks of accused felons, even a mentally ill teenager loses all rights of privacy.

SATURDAY, SEPTEMBER 15TH

I woke up this morning and looked out the window towards the river. *I'll be damned - the canoe is missing again!* I can't believe it - how embarrassing. I could swear that I tied it up good. I then notice that the tide is very high and quite rough and the wind is blowing quite hard. Further inspection reveals that the branch I had tied the canoe to had been ripped right off the tree. I get our binoculars and look across the river expanse and out towards Chesapeake Bay. I can't see it anywhere.

I go over to the oyster house and sheepishly tell a waterman that my canoe is missing again and ask him if he has seen it. I'm wondering if it might be in the cove next to the oyster house where it was spotted by them before. The fisherman indicates that it wouldn't be there. Given the direction of the currents and the winds the past few days, he states that it has probably carried across the river out towards the bay. He tells me he will keep an eye out for it. I walk around the cove and I don't see it. It doesn't look hopeful, and it's a lousy start for the weekend; but it seems pretty trivial given our current situation.

That morning, Debra and I chat about the phone call we had with Dad the night before. We learned that a first cousin of mine had been hospitalized for six months for mental illness and was presently still on medication. It had been kept quiet by the family and we had no idea.

Debra and I talk for over an hour about all the factors that could have been contributing factors to Chad's illness. He had trauma at birth. It had taken him about five minutes to breathe properly after he had been delivered with use of forceps. When he was two years old, he became deathly ill with the flu and reached a body temperature of 106 degrees. He showed OCD (obsessive-compulsive disorder) symptoms after that. At five years old, he had been diagnosed with a brain lesion. Now we find out that there is a history of mental illness on both sides of the family. It is almost like Chad never had a chance.

That afternoon we receive a magazine entitled "Stuff" in the mail that apparently Chad had just recently subscribed to. It appears to be a magazine written for young male audiences. I thumb through it and I don't see any pornography, but there is a scantily dressed young woman on the cover in a sexy pose. Debra flips when she sees it. "That's just what we need! Trash like this coming to the house at a time like this!" She calls up the magazine and cancels the subscription. I'm surprised she can cancel another adult's subscription but I don't think they want to argue with her.

Later on, she drives to Richmond to see Chad. Ali goes to a party with her friends and I wait at home for Dale. After he arrives we talk about how much the world has changed since he was here last Saturday. We chow down on hot dogs and chips while watching TV. We half-jokingly comment on how we both hope the country bombs some terrorists tonight, because there are no ball games to watch.

SUNDAY, SEPTEMBER 16TH

Dale and I talk about his situation at the FBI and the police-training academy he is overseeing in Budapest. He has not yet been pulled off this assignment to work on the terrorist attack. He expresses concerns that they might have to close the academy down. He is not sure what will happen with the funding, and his biggest problem is that instructors are flown out constantly from the U.S. to teach the classes. Given the problems that the airlines are having and increased security, he may not even be able to get the instructors he needs. He is going out with a realtor this morning to see what is available in the housing market.

Debra and I travel to Richmond to see Chad. I am anxious to see him today. He has now been at Tuckers a week, and there is no telling when they will come and take him back to jail. They are supposed to give our attorney's twenty-four hours notice but I certainly don't trust the Sheriff's Department.

It is great to see Chad. He is doing much better and we have a nice long visit. We talk about what we think will happen in the near future. We are thinking that he will probably have to stay in a mental institution anywhere from six months to a year. We also talk about a new game system that will be released by Microsoft for the Christmas holidays. We lament the fact that no matter where he ends up he probably will not have access to a computer. We then hit on the idea that one game system he might be able to have is the new Advance Gameboy, which is hand-held. I tell him I will get him one for Christmas, if he doesn't rob any more banks by then. He laughs!

On the way home I stop and get the book *Chicken Soup for Fathers* as a birthday present for my Dad, who is turning seventy years old on the 20th. Dad has been my crutch my whole life and he is by far the person I love the most on this earth. I hope that one day Chad will feel the same about me.

That evening before dusk, I notice that the river has calmed down and that the tide is out. I wade in up to my knees and start walking towards the bay, hoping to spot the canoe. After proceeding about a half mile I am surprised to spot what I think is the canoe. It is across the river pulled up on an embankment. It is too late to try to retrieve it tonight; tomorrow I will cross the Great Wicomico Bridge by car and try to find the spot.

MONDAY, SEPTEMBER 17TH

As lunchtime approaches, I realize that I've left Dad's birthday present at home. I head home for lunch hoping to maybe catch one of the watermen down at the oyster house. Maybe I can ask one of them to drop me off by the canoe and I'll paddle it home. I don't see anyone down at the oyster house so I grab Dad's present and head to the post office.

When I get back to the office I have a message that Bill has called. When I return the call I get a shock. He says he has two points that he wants to cover with me. He immediately starts scolding me like I'm a two-year-old. He says he can't believe that I called the Sheriff's Department and threatened one of the police officers! I said, "What!" He said that the bailiff at the courthouse also said that I had thrown my keys at him when we were there for the last court hearing. The combination of the deputy's lies and the tone that my own attorney was using set me off. I twice yelled into the phone, "Bullshit." Unfortunately, I have been told in the past, that when I lose my temper it is like the walls of Jerico come tumbling down. It has been years since I have lost my temper like that.

I ask Bill how he can believe this shit and whose side is he on anyway? I can't believe this topic has come up again, and I ask him do I need to get new attorneys. Bill softens his tone a bit and says that Chad is his client and he is looking out for him. *Like I'm not!* I resist the urge to remind Bill who is paying the bill.

I can't believe that the Sheriff's Department can stoop so low. You obviously can't call them and inquire about how to file a complaint without being accused of assaulting a police officer. The accusation that I threw the keys at the bailiff is ridiculous. I do remember as I passed through security that I dropped my keys in the basket instead of placing them in. Both Debra and our friends were with me at the time. When I tell everyone later about the accusation they are all incredulous, and we all can't help but laugh. This episode speaks volumes about what we are dealing with. I remember it was James Bruce I had talked to during the phone conversation. *I know your true colors now!*

I'm beginning to have suspicions about my attorneys. I understand now that the Sheriff's Department is quite capable of threatening us, and using Chad's predicament to protect one of their own. What I don't understand is why my attorneys seem to be so willing to be the messenger. I certainly don't doubt that Jim and Bill are doing everything they can to help Chad; but their desire to maintain great working relationships has left the rest of the family defenseless. I also have got to believe that there is something pretty unethical going on here. As far as I'm concerned, the basic thing that is happening is we are being told to keep our mouths shut or things will go worse for our son.

Bill's second point should have been his first. Chad is being discharged today and the Sheriff's Department is on their way to escort him back to jail! I really don't know what to do, but I do know that I want to talk to Debra. Bill tells me the next step will be to set a bond hearing. I apologize for yelling at him and he tells me he'll call as soon as he gets an update.

I call Debra, and we both realize there is really nothing we can do. Chad was really starting to make progress - it's a shame. Debra and I both end up later calling Tuckers and asking for the nurse on duty. We learn that they were surprised that the deputies showed up. They thought that Gomez had more testing to do - we will find out later that was indeed the case. They also indicate that they had given the deputies all of Chad's belongings and a list of the medicine he was taking.

After I hang up from talking to Debra, I find that the wall of Jerico must have come down because, even though I had my office door closed before I exploded, I notice two male bank officers standing just outside my door when I opened it. Poor guys, they probably don't know whether they are protecting me from someone else or if they are protecting me from myself. I appreciate their concern. I now find myself just as upset that I lost my temper as I am of being accused of assaulting a police officer.

I feel a little better when I hear from my friend in New York, She is fine - a bit scared - but fine. Her apartment is on 62nd and Broad, which is apparently a long ways from where the Trade Towers stood.

That night I am able to recover the canoe. I even manage to paddle it home in my suit without getting a ticket.

CHAPTER 9

AN UNREASONABLE BAIL

TUESDAY, SEPTEMBER 18TH

Bill calls and tells me that the bond hearing has been set for Monday at 11:00 AM. It will be at the General District Court with Judge Hyde presiding. He has also received a rough written draft of Gomez's evaluation. He stresses again that one of the things that will greatly aid in Chad's case would be the prosecutor's acceptance of the evaluation as is, without getting one of his own.

He then tells me to try to think of ways we can "sweeten the pie" when it comes to the bond proposal. I mention that one thing Debra and I can do is to arrange our work schedules so that at least one of us will be home with Chad at all times. Bill says that is exactly that type of stuff he needs. He encourages us over the next few days to try and think of anything else that might help persuade the Judge.

Chad calls that night and tells us that he had received no warning the previous day that the deputies were coming. They actually woke him up from a nap and gave him just a few minutes to get ready.

WEDNESDAY, SEPTEMBER 19TH

I get a call from Debra while at work. She has just talked to Dr. Gomez and it is good news. Dr. Gomez is excited that Chad has shown as much progress as he has. He says that he can tell that Chad has stopped hearing voices, and he is optimistic that Chad might be able to make a full recovery. He says that Chad is still fixated on his scrotum problem but that will pass in about three weeks. Debra inquires as to some of the details and is surprised to learn that Chad has also been diagnosed with having an Obsessive Compulsive Disorder. This is the reason he has fixated on his scrotum.

The fifteen milligrams of Zyprexa that Chad has been taking are for the hallucinations associated with the schizophrenia.

The sixty milligrams of Prozac he is being given is to help him deal with the Obsessive Compulsive Disorder.

I'm pleased to hear the good news, but I'm a bit guarded, knowing that he has been returned to the jail. Debra points out that there is a big difference between taking Prozac under the relaxing conditions at Tuckers and taking the same dosage while you are part of the general inmate population at the regional jail. *I wish we could get off this roller coaster ride.*

That night I watch the news and I am concerned about the comments that are being made concerning the need to expand law enforcement powers in light of the recent terrorist attacks. Given the recent offenses against my family's civil liberties, it scares me.

I am touched by an interview that Rosie O'Donnell gives. She talks about standing in line to pay for gas and the attendant appears to be a young man of Arab descent. As he takes the money, he keeps his head bowed and will not look up. Several of the customers in front of her try without success to engage him in conversation. As she gets to the window, she doesn't let go of the money, as he takes it, until he looks up. She tells him that he has nothing to be ashamed of and to keep his head up. He starts to cry as he thanks her.

I can't help but feel empathy for him and how he must have felt. I can remember how ashamed we felt. I can remember how hard it was for us to even go to the grocery store for fear of how people would react. We still have those feelings and we can tell how uncomfortable people are when they see us. I wonder how much time will have to pass before we can put these feelings behind us.

THURSDAY, SEPTEMBER 20TH

I met with Glen Spaulding today. He dropped by at my request. Glen was a former branch president in our church, a retired engineer, and a Kentucky basketball fan. I've always enjoyed talking to him. He has a wealth of knowledge, and I've always gotten good advice from him.

I ask him what his feelings are about Chad and what he thinks should be our tack in dealing with his mental illness. He really emphasizes that all our efforts should be based around "salvaging Chad." He is still so young and such a bright kid, and it is still quite possible that he could make a meaningful contribution to society. I tell him that Debra and I are not quite sure about how to treat him when we have him home. We want to keep him busy, but at the same time not put too much pressure on him. I also ask him how does he think the other church members will react if he comes to church.

Glen assures me that the members will love to see him and will try to support him in any way. He stresses patience and restates something I mentioned to Debra several weeks ago. We are all he's got - if we don't do it, who will?

I ask Glen, if it's possible, could he please attend the hearing on Monday. I tell him that I will need someone to bear witness that I didn't assault any of the deputies or the bailiff. He laughs and says sure.

I attend Ali's basketball game that night. They are playing one of their archrivals, Lancaster County. As the game starts, both teams are tight. Ali breaks the ice by hitting two consecutive jumpers right inside the key in front of the foul line. Her team leads four to nothing and her coach immediately takes her out. She will not get back into the game until midway through the 2nd quarter. Please don't ask me what his reasoning was. Sometimes it's hard being a parent.

FRIDAY, SEPTEMBER 21ST

It is visiting hours at the jail, and Debra has taken time off work to go see Chad. I don't see the need, with the chances being good that he will be home soon on bond. Chad is in good spirits and he has a lot of questions concerning his hearing on Monday and whether we have gotten everything taken care of. She assures him that we have been working closely with the attorneys and everything is going along smoothly.

He mentions that he hasn't been able to call the last few nights. He gets a message that he is not using the right PIN. When Debra informs me later, I tell her there is no sense in setting it up - with a little bit of luck, we should have Chad home by Monday night.

Debra tells me, that the other day, when she talked to Gomez, he told her to give him a call as soon as Chad gets home. He will set up an appointment for that Friday to examine Chad and to meet with us to go over recommendations for his treatment.

This is music to our ears. *Chad is finally going to get the treatment he needs.*

Bill calls me at home to discuss Monday's hearing. The focus will be on why Chad is no longer a threat to either himself or those around him and why he wouldn't try to leave. The following points will be presented: (1) his medication has been effective, (2) there will be someone with him at all times, (3) he has lived here for the past six years, (4) he is a graduate of Northumberland High School, (5) even when he robbed the bank he wasn't a real threat because he didn't have a weapon, (6) he will be getting the proper medical attention he needs, and (7) Debra herself is a nurse.

Bill states that he has not yet met with McKenney to go over the bond but will do so before the hearing. Chad has asked me to ask Bill about wearing an ankle bracelet that electronically tracks the person. Bill says you want to use that as a last resort. Anytime you want to leave the house you have to call the Sheriff's Department and tell them you are leaving and then you have to call them when you are back. No thanks!!

I am scheduled to attend a conference on current SEC developments on Monday, Tuesday, and Wednesday in Washington, DC. In order to be at Chad's court hearing, I cancel both my registration at the conference and my hotel reservations.

I get a pleasant surprise when I check the mail. There is a letter from the law firm in Charlottesville that I had contacted earlier concerning filing a libel lawsuit. They may be interested in pursuing the case, but they need additional information. They ask for copies of the articles and they also ask me to prepare a memo that indicates which statements in the articles I consider insulting and defamatory. They also want me to indicate how I would prove the statements are false.

SATURDAY, SEPTEMBER 22ND

I go to my office so I can concentrate on my letter to the attorney in Charlottesville. I present four basic points. The first point deals with the editor's statement that we did not cooperate with the Sheriff's Department. The second point addresses a quote attributed to my wife, which implies that she thought Chad had access to the vehicle and could have used it.

The evidence to support the first point is substantial. The evidence to support the second point would probably come down to Debra's word against the detectives'.

The third point is the amount of coverage given to the counterfeiting charges. The way the article was written they suggest that a counterfeiting operation is being operated out of the house involving more than just Chad.

The fourth point is that the articles dwell on the fact that the officers were instructed to seize any firearms that could have been concealed during the bank robbery. The truth is, of course, that no weapon was used.

I also make the observation that the articles used both Debra's and my names repetitively and left out facts that would have put the incident in a less damning perspective.

My letter contained the following summary: "The viciousness of their attack was unbelievable. By distorting the facts, using small elements of the truth, omitting pertinent facts, and making defamatory statements, they created a sensationalized story that not only painted the wrong picture of Chad but also totally damaged the reputation of the entire family."

It takes me almost five hours to write the letter and to make the necessary photocopies. The letter is not that long, I just want to make sure that I've made a compelling argument.

SUNDAY, SEPTEMBER 23RD

I attend church this morning. First time I've been back since the robbery. I had almost convinced Debra to come. She has been inactive for years. She complains that every time she goes, instead of feeling uplifted, she ends up feeling guilty because she is reminded of all the things she should be doing. We have no paid ministry in our church so it's the members of the congregation that carry the workload. Sometimes it is easy to feel that you are not doing your share, especially in such a small branch as ours.

We start sacrament meeting with an opening song and then a prayer. After the branch announcements are made, we sing a song in preparation of receiving the sacrament. As the sacrament is passed I think of the Lord's sacrifice and the sorrow he felt for his children. I can't help but think of Chad and my feelings for him.

Upon arriving home I decided that my project for the day would be glazing a glass plane window located on the second level of the house. By the time I get the ladder set up and remove the storm windows and the frame, I'm already tired. I force myself to work another hour and then I stop. I am so burned-out and I have absolutely no energy. The adrenaline rush we have been feeding off for so long is definitely gone. I will find that the feeling of exhaustion will last for most of the following week.

Tonight, I have a long phone conversation with Dad. We wonder exactly what will happen at Chad's hearing tomorrow. We also discuss what is the appropriate amount of pressure to put on him while he is home. In other words, should we try to keep him busy or should we back off? We also talk about what should be Chad's continuing treatment.

As I go to sleep that night, I'm excited about the prospect of having Chad home. I think some more about how we should handle him when he's home. I reflect on my fears of what could go wrong. If a bank should be robbed or another crime committed in our neighborhood, I have no doubt who the Sheriff's Department will come looking for. But mainly, I reflect on how excited I am to be able to have him home and out of that jail. Now we can start helping him to get better.

MONDAY, SEPTEMBER 24TH

Debra and I are up early. Debra puts out the steak she purchased in anticipation of Chad's return. We arrive early and wait a few minutes for Glen and his wife to appear. We don't realize it, but they are already in the courthouse waiting for us. Several church friends arrive and we proceed into the courthouse.

I don't see Chuckie or the bailiff I had savagely attacked with my car keys at the previous hearing. I am searched as we go into the courtroom - no one else is. This time, we sit on the left side of the courtroom in the first pew. There are only a few other people besides ourselves.

Sitting on the left side, up towards the front, are several marine patrol officers. Among them is the officer who gave me a ticket for not wearing a life jacket.

We've got too many cops in this county. Indeed, when I go to the county's website I find that Sheriff Middleton has twenty-eight deputies and there are six Virginia State Patrol officers assigned to our county. Who knows how many marine-patrol officers there are. The county has a little more than then twelve thousand men, women, and children. That works out to be 3.4 officers for every one thousand people - not counting the marine patrol officers. New York City has 3.4 officers for every 10,000 people, Chicago has 3.4 for every 9,000 people.

There are only a few cases before Chad's. One is, believe it or not, failure to have a flotation device while operating a boat. That was the same charge that was listed on my ticket. The accused shows up in short pants, but he does have on shoes and socks. The Judge tells him he can be held in contempt of court. Oh, boy!

As the case is finished, I see Bill come out a side door. I can tell by the look on his face and his mannerisms that something is wrong. He leans over the railing and starts to say something, changes his mind, and motions for us to follow him. Once we are in a small conference room, he informs us that he has just met with McKenney and he has not gotten a favorable response from him. McKenney is going to fight the bond. Ah yes - your true colors come shining through! I'm not sure what has happened. I had been led to believe, based on recent prior discussions with Bill, that there was a better than 50-50 chance that they would release Chad on bond.

Bill reviews the points in Chad's favor that we had discussed previously and confirms with me that the total amount of equity in our house is about $70,000. He mentions that the Judge may have several questions for us. Then we go back into the courtroom.

Chad is brought in with shackles on his legs down by his ankles. He looks disheveled and nervous. His acne is breaking out, indicating that they haven't been giving him his medication. He doesn't look up and is sitting in front of our pew. The deputy who had told me to shut up the night of the search escorts him.

The Judge says a few things and then listens to the attorneys' arguments. McKenney argues that the amount of the bond is ridiculously low, given the nature of the crime. He argues that society still needs to be protected from Chad, that he his not only a danger to society but he is a danger to himself. The Judge asks as to whether it has been determined if a weapon was used, and for the first time it comes out in court that Chad did not have a weapon. But McKenney, then uses, of all things, the fact that Chad committed the robbery while he was being treated under the ASAP program. This is akin to saying that Bin Laden still managed to bomb the World Trade Towers even though the terrorists went through airport security!

Bill covers the points we had discussed previously. But the Judge has the look of a man who is concentrating on what he is going to say, not on what the speaker is saying. The Judge indicates to Bill that he is disappointed that we don't have a written report from the psychiatrist and states that we are expecting a decision based on Chad's improvement, but we have nothing to validate his improvement.

It is becoming obvious very quickly that the Judge is not interested in what Bill is saying and could care less that we are willing to put our house on the line. He states that he has a bad feeling about this and he is not prepared to let Chad go. He mentions that he has a brother who has schizophrenia and is well acquainted with what it can do. I think to myself, *then you should know how important it is that Chad receives the proper treatment as soon as possible.* But the Judge reiterates the prosecutor's point that it is safer for everyone that Chad remains locked up. He talks about the dire consequences for Chad and everyone involved if Chad were to do something wrong during this period. He then sets the bail at $100,000 and quickly exits the courtroom.

I look over at Chad and wonder if he fully understands what has happened. I think he does. Debra and I both choke back the tears and are in shock. Chad gets up and extends his hand to the attorney and then is escorted out of the courtroom. We haven't been allowed to say a word to him. So much for our celebration that night and so much for Chad getting the help that he needs.

As far as I'm concerned, the legal system has let Chad down from the get-go. The Sheriff's Department, the jail, and now the courts are robbing Chad of the one thing that can save him - and that is time. The time most precious for treatment is that time immediately following a psychotic episode. Chad has just lost another 30 days.

Our friends try to console us as we leave the courtroom. They talk about the possibility that, if the Judge has been exposed to schizophrenia in his family, maybe he'll show some compassion at the next hearing. Debra and I both know he should have shown it today.

When we meet with Bill for a few minutes, he tells us the next step is for him and Dr. Gomez to get together to discuss Chad's defense and what their recommendation will be to the court. He stresses that the key is still to have the prosecutor accept Dr. Gomez's opinion. He also states that he thinks our things will be returned to us by the end of the week. The next court date is October 22, 2001.

On the way home, Debra reminds me that Chad's birthday is Saturday. She is upset, she thought he would be home. Debra drops me off at the house and heads to Kilmarnock to buy Chad a birthday card and to get a money order for him. In an effort to try to do something useful, I try to concentrate on what, if anything, I can do for Chad. I can't imagine how he must be feeling.

I call and reinstate the inmates phone service by putting down $50. I call the jail to let them know that I've reinstated Chad's phone service and please let him know. I actually talk to a woman who seems pleasant and willing to make an effort to see that Chad gets the message. I can't help but wonder if, women were in charge throughout the Northumberland County legal system, if there wouldn't be a little more compassion shown for Chad and ourselves. I don't know how it could be any worse.

TUESDAY, SEPTEMBER 25TH

It is hard to get up and to go to work this morning, very hard for both of us.

Chad calls us early that night. It is a relief to know that the phone system at the jail is working and that we will be able to talk to him. We discuss the hearing. He tells me that he was so nervous and scared that he couldn't stand it. As we talk about the court proceedings, he is quite lucid. He asks me what does the phrase "innocent until proven guilty' really mean in this country? We joke about how useless the bond laws are in protecting the rights of the accused.

As the night wears on, I can feel myself getting depressed. I now have a better understanding of how someone can fall into a severe depression.

CHAPTER 10

CHAD'S FIRST HEARING: CONFUSION & FRUSTRATION

WEDNESDAY, SEPTEMBER 26TH

I call and leave a message for Dr. Gomez to return my call. Debra and I think that under the circumstances, it is wise to increase Chad's dosage.

At lunchtime, I buy the weekly edition of the *Northern Neck News*. There is no mention of Chad, but there is a large picture of McKenney and Wilkens sitting shoulder to shoulder. They are being praised for starting a new program for the elderly. I think back to what Debra said about them being schoolboy friends. I think of the types of threats I have received every time it even looks like I might be trying to file a complaint against Wilkens.

The day ends without my phone call being returned by Dr. Gomez.

THURSDAY, SEPTEMBER 27TH

I have a dentist appointment today. The dentist and his wife are casual friends of ours. He expresses his concern about what is happening and offers his help if there is anything he can do. I realize after talking to him that most of the community knows very little about what actually happened. All they know is what they read in the papers and what they have heard over the grapevine. It is disheartening to realize that the perception of most of the community is still that Chad is some sort of teen-age thug who endangered the lives of the bank's employees.

We have been invited over to the Dunn's for dinner that night. We are surprised when other members of the church also show up. It is pretty much the same group who has been supporting us at Chad's court appearances. Their support continues to be invaluable, as Debra and I struggle to get through this. Part of our discussion centers around what the possibilities are for Chad once the legal system gets through with him.

FRIDAY, SEPTEMBER 28TH

It is visiting hours today at the jail. Chad's birthday is tomorrow, so I don't want to miss seeing him. Debra and I take separate cars because we will both be going to work after the visit.

The check-in process goes smoother this time. Chad is brought to the window booth about 9:15 and there are fewer visitors than before. He looks good and seems to be in good spirits.

Barry Bonds has always been one Chad's favorite baseball players. He is currently on a pace to break Mark McQuire's homerun record. The Yankees are also playing some good ball, so we spend some time talking baseball. We also discuss Chad's daily routine at the jail. We learn that he has made friends with three other roommates, and they spend a lot of time playing cards together. I don't know quite what to think of that.

During our conversation, we also learn that Chad has not always been taking his medicine. Debra's friend who works at the jail has been on vacation. Chad has been sleeping through the morning pill calls. He is supposed to get his Prozac medicine in the morning. Chad doesn't think it's a big deal, because he has been taking his Zyprexa medicine at night. He thinks that the Prozac is just to help him stay calm. Debra and I both try to stay calm! We remind him that the Prozac he is taking is to help him with his obsessive-compulsive behavior. In other words it's the key towards helping him with his scrotum problem. He seems surprised, I'm sure we have explained this to him before. He promises that he will get up and start taking it. *Can it get any more frustrating!*

Around 10:15, a voice comes over the phone line telling us that our visiting hour time is up and we have to leave. I finally learn that, even though visiting hours are from 9:00 AM to 11:00 AM, you are still only allowed to spend one hour. That's great! Parents of a mentally ill child are allotted one hour a week behind a plate of glass to try to provide care and comfort. Does anyone have any brains in this bureaucracy? If for no other reason you would think they would let you provide the care just to save the taxpayer some money.

112

The day ends with still no phone call from the Sheriff's office saying to come and get your things. It's been six weeks now.

SATURDAY, SEPTEMBER 29TH

It's Chad's birthday. What can I say? A year ago at this time Chad was one of the best and brightest at JMU. He had his whole life to look forward to. It occurs to me that he still does, it's just that his options have been severely limited. Hopefully, he will still be able to find a niche that makes him happy and is worthwhile.

Chad calls around 11:30 AM. We wish him happy birthday and describe his present that Debra had purchased yesterday. It is an Advance Gameboy that is made by Nintendo. It is a hand-held game player that we hope Chad will be allowed to use wherever he ends up. Chad is delighted with the present, and we discuss how it should greatly help in passing the time.

Debra teases him that this is his last year as a teenager. We ask him to describe the birthday cards and letters he has received. In the fifteen minutes we are allotted on the phone, we do our best to make the occasion as joyful as possible. It all feels like a bad dream.

MONDAY, OCTOBER 1ST

Chad calls and wants to talk about what is going to happen next. I tell him that it is my understanding that on the 22nd we will have some sort of resolution to this. Basically, he will either be sent to a mental institution or prison. We are, of course, hoping that it will be the mental hospital where we at least have a chance to salvage as much of Chad's mind as we can. I'm still clinging to what I have read by the experts that if you can treat an individual within six months of a psychotic episode there is a good chance of a full recovery. I try not to think of the fact that we are now well past six months. Thank you, Northumberland County, for your understanding and compassion for the mentally ill.

TUESDAY, OCTOBER 2ND

Bill calls and tells me that he has given Gomez copies of the law pertaining to Chad's situation. Dr. Gomez is going to write up a draft of his findings and forward it to Bill for review. He is hoping that Gomez will have it done by Thursday. Bill also mentions how long the Sheriff has held our car and that it is getting ridiculous. He says he will give McKenney a call and call me right back.

McKenney says he hasn't seen the Sheriff in over three weeks. Apparently, he and Chuckie have been to a training convention. What a waste of taxpayer dollars. McKenney says he will bring the subject up as soon as he sees him. Bill also says that apparently, the Secret Service has gotten involved in the counterfeiting charges and now has possession of our computer equipment. It could be months before we get the equipment back. Dam the Sheriff's Department! Chad was an eighteen-year-old kid who scanned money in the privacy of his bedroom and never and I repeat *never*, tried to pass any of it. To bring this down on our family is outrageous!

WEDNESDAY, OCTOBER 3RD

We receive notice of a certified letter being held for us at the post office. I have no idea what it could be, but the feeling is that it probably is not good.

The bank lets me take an old monitor home that is not being used. I am finally able to turn on the computer I had bought over the Internet the weekend before the robbery. I bought a couple of cheap speakers from Radio Shack. I still don't have a printer. I wonder what are the chances that all of the confiscated equipment will be returned undamaged.

I can't sleep that night.

THURSDAY, OCTOBER 4TH

The certified letter turns out to be a response from the attorney in Charlottesville. I am excited when I see that he must have agreed to take the case. I am sorely disappointed when I open it and read it. The letter is well written and the attorney has taken the time to address all the points I had raised as to why I thought we had enough evidence to support a defamation lawsuit. There are two major reasons that he cites for it being impossible to win under the circumstances I laid out.

The First Amendment gives broad latitude to people who say defamatory things and the laws governing defamation in Virginia give the person even broader latitude! So if someone thinks a statement is false, all the defendant has to do his find someone who is willing to say that they think the statement was a "reasonable interpretation of the facts." The other major reason that I would not win is that the Virginia Constitution and the Virginia Code do not allow for the "right of privacy" in these types of cases. In other words, Debra and I were fair game, because Chad was arrested in our home.

He does agree that the amount of verbiage dedicated to the counterfeiting charges is excessive but again he can't argue that it is not a "reasonable interpretation of the facts." He also makes some interesting points about the butterfly knife. He does think that the references the paper makes to the knife "are rather ridiculous and why they felt the need to report it is of concern." He also makes the observation that "the article states that while the warrant authorized the police to seize concealable pistols if they were found, the only weapon seized was a knife. Hence, by its own terms, the article accurately reports that the police seized something they were not authorized to seize." However, he states there is not enough here to support a charge of defamation.

In closing, he states, "Frequently, accusations and implications are made in newspaper articles which are damaging to the reputations of innocent persons such as yourself, but the law affords them no remedy for defamation." He suggests that we write a letter to the editor "setting forth not only the mistakes and inaccuracies contained in their story, but a detailed account of what really happened to your son so the readers of the paper will appreciate what a tragedy this episode was for the entire family."

FRIDAY, OCTOBER 5ᵀᴴ

I have my hands full at work; Debra goes to visit Chad alone. I tell her to make sure that he knows that Barry Bonds hit his 70th homerun last night.

It has been over seven weeks, and there is still no effort by the Sheriff to return our things. I wonder if this is payback because we made them get a search warrant?

TUESDAY, OCTOBER 9TH

I attend Ali's basketball game, and I'm sorry I did. There is a big crowd, and Ali is tentative and has a bad game. She has a small fracture in her finger, which requires a brace, and she has let it get to her mentally. In addition, she is no longer starting and I know she is not happy with that. She is missing all of her shots badly and starts to sulk during the game. When her coach gets after her she talks back to him. It gets worse when a referee makes a bad call on her, and she lets him know she didn't like it. It is embarrassing to be sitting there and, though this isn't fair to Ali, you can't help but think that other people are once again passing judgment on our family.

As we get home that night, we feel depressed about both Chad and Ali. The weight of Chad's problems seems to beat us all down, one by one.

WEDNESDAY, OCTOBER 10TH

Our computer expert at work gives me a website address that will allow me to gain access to my email messages. I haven't been able to gain access since the Sheriff's Department helped themselves to my equipment. There are 407 messages, most of which are junk mail. There is not a single message that has anything to do with counterfeiting. Looks like Chad was not as active as the boys in blue (okay, brown) thought he was.

I have gotten into the habit of sending Chad current sports scores and updates, almost on a daily basis. Just something to help break up the monotony of his day.

THURSDAY, OCTOBER 11TH

I get a surprise call from Bill. We can go to the Sheriff's office to pick up our car. It has been almost two months since they towed it away, and we informed them that we would not be contesting the fact that Chad robbed the bank. We are both at work now so we will pick up the car tomorrow after we visit Chad.

Bill tells me a little about the strategy they are pursuing. The argument is that Chad acted on an "irresistible impulse" brought on by his mental illness. I don't think anything could be truer. He also states that it is possible that a Judge Taliaferro rather than Judge Hyde may end up deciding this case. Apparently, Judge Taliaferro is ranked higher because he is the Circuit Court Judge, while Hyde is the District Court Judge. Good news or bad news, we had no way of knowing.

FRIDAY, OCTOBER 12TH

The visit with Chad goes smoothly, even though the checking in and waiting for the inmate to come to the window is always a nerve-racking experience. Chad seems to be in good spirits and has a lot of questions. He is still asking about getting out on bond and he also wants to know about the Rockingham court date. The Rockingham case has been postponed pending the outcome of the robbery case. We explain that the Rockingham issues are secondary to what is going on here and that whatever punishment is meted will probably suffice for both cases. He also wants to check with our attorneys to see if they have heard about a case that another inmate told him about - something to do with a guy arrested for robbing a bank but who was able to "walk" on some technicality. Chad's conversations with other inmates are going to be a problem. We know he is gullible and one way he is probably trying to fit in and to protect himself is to act cocky and to show bravado. This will be made all the worse by the effects of the schizophrenia.

On the way back from jail, we hear some startling news over the radio. The Sheriff has shot and killed a teenager who was resisting arrest. He is quoted as saying that he felt he had to do it to protect his men. Apparently, the teenager had aimed a rifle at them and had refused to cooperate with them. The news is unnerving. I feel a quiver go through me. I mention to Debra that thank God we were home when the Sheriff and his deputies showed up on our doorstep, and thank God they didn't catch him before he got home from the robbery. Remembering how confrontational it was at our house, I wouldn't put it past them to have shot Chad if they had caught him. I look over at Debra and she is trembling. We would hear later that after the Sheriff shot him, the kid fled into the woods, and the Sheriff emptied his clip trying to get him. The poor kid would die in the woods from the first shot.

The visit to the Sheriff's office to pick up our car does not go smoothly, of course. Upon arrival, we are told that they cannot

117

release the car because we have to reimburse them for towing charges! We go to gas station and pay the $45.00. After providing evidence that we have paid the towing charges, we have to sign a bunch of papers. Finally, the deputy takes us to the storage area surrounded by a barbwire fence behind the building. As we approach our car, we notice that the plates we had just purchased three months before are gone. He leaves us there to return to the building to check on the plates; and as I inspect the car, I can't believe it. It looks like someone has keyed the passenger side door and someone has rabbit punched the hood, leaving a dent about the size of someone's fist! We confront the deputy as he returns and tells us that the plates have been confiscated and we are going to have to get new ones. He denies knowing anything about the damage to the car and mumbles something about the fact that the car has been back here a long time (No kidding!) and anyone could have climbed the fence and done the damage. He also tells us that we shouldn't drive the car without tags because it is against the law and that we should either go get new tags or have the car towed to our place. With that, he gives me the keys and retreats to the building.

I know it is useless to try to talk to the Sheriff about the damage to the car, and I'll be breaking the attorney's instructions about not making any waves. But I'll be damned if I'm going to leave that car behind because the police have confiscated the plates. Debra protests as I jump in the car and try to start it. It will not start. It is beginning to look as if I'm going to have to tow it, anyway. Finally it starts, and I tell Debra to follow me as I head for home. I dare any deputy to stop me right now in my frame of mind. I can guarantee the whole county will know about the "Merry Christmas" we received the night they were trashing our home and the damage they have done to our car.

No one stops us.

MONDAY, OCTOBER 15TH

Not much happened over the weekend. We are having unseasonably warm days, so I finished painting around the windows I had recently glazed.

The Yankees came back from three games behind to win their series with Oakland. Derek Jeter had a great series. It's a nice way to start the week.

I have been studying to pass the CFA exam. The deadline for registration is today. It is a major undertaking and, frankly, I just don't have the time. I doubt, given Chad's situation, that I'm going to be able to focus on it. But I go ahead and register anyway - I don't want to lose the leverage of the study time I spent this last year.

WEDNESDAY, OCTOBER 17TH

Today is the day the Northumberland papers are published. I buy one to see just how they treat the Sheriff's shooting. He is pretty much painted as being a hero for protecting his men, and there is no mention of the rumor that the sheriff emptied his clip at the young man as he was trying to get away. While the paper was full of details of my son's robbery, where no one is hurt, there are few details about the shooting.

Chad calls that night and tells us that he has run out of spending money. We talk about Monday and what we hope will happen. Chad says he is mentally preparing for the worst. We also talk about the new gaming system that Nintendo is coming out with and about the Yankees.

FRIDAY, OCTOBER 19TH

We visit Chad during regular visiting hours. It is actually an enjoyable experience. There are not that many visitors and we now know the procedures. We will actually talk to him for about an hour and a half. We focus on what we think is going to happen on Monday, and Chad reiterates that he is preparing for the worst. I tell him that I'm optimistic that things are going to go well. We talk about a computer game called Plane Scape Torment that Chad had recently played and that I am now playing. Half the reason I'm playing it is to have something more to talk to Chad about. He also wants to talk about getting bond in case things don't go well on Monday. I tell him I don't think he needs to worry about it as I think there will be some sort of resolution.

I finally get hooked up again to the Internet at home. It has been more than two months since the deputies took my computer. Work is a bear. It is the end-of-quarter reporting period and several employees in our department have taken time off.

SATURDAY, OCTOBER 20TH

I go to work today to get caught up. Even though I'm alone, it is hard to get things done because my mind keeps wandering to what is going to happen on Monday.

SUNDAY, OCTOBER 21ST

I attend church and let everyone know what time Chad's hearing will be. Debra spends most of her day in preparation for Cindy's arrival.

At around five o'clock I get a call from Jim Breeden. I find out that Bill has led me astray. There is not a chance for resolution tomorrow! As a matter of fact, all they are going to do tomorrow is waive the pretrial hearing. He explains to me that at a pretrial hearing is a chance for the defense to discover the facts as presented by the prosecution in order that they might be able to prepare the defense. We aren't going to need the pretrial hearing because we aren't fighting the fact that he did it. Jim states that the press will be disappointed because they will not have much to report.

Well, that's nice that the press will be disappointed, but I know a few other people who are going to be disappointed, as well! How about Chad, Debra, and myself, and not necessarily in that order. I suppress the urge to get confrontational with Jim and to ask him why someone didn't explain this to us earlier. We had been under the impression that at the last hearing, when Chad didn't make bond, he would be brought before Judge Hyde tomorrow for a court trial. Do my lawyers know what they are doing? I suspect they are not telling me the whole story, and it looks like Judge Hyde does not have the authority to decide the case, because Jim now tells me that Judge Taliaferro will hear the case in circuit court.

Jim also tells me that we also don't want to pursue getting Chad out on bond. *I wish like hell that I had not gotten Chad's hopes up.* I know he is probably lying in his bunk right now, trying not to get too excited about tomorrow. It is too late to stop Cindy from coming. She left this morning from Ohio, but I call the members at church to let them know there will be no resolution tomorrow. They tell me they still want to come to show their support - they are better people than I.

We are dumbfounded and Debra is depressed. Cindy shows up with pizza, and we watch the Yankees beat Oakland in the bottom of the ninth with a homerun by Soriano, which tends to lighten the gloom.

MONDAY, OCTOBER 22ND

We arrive early, even though Jim has told us not to show until noon. Debra and I are in court while several cases involving people who are mentally ill are being heard. McKenney and the Judge actually get involved in a discussion involving the merits of institutionalization of the mentally ill. They talk about the current case where the individual has only been accused of a misdemeanor but has refused to come to court because, in his mind, he has been to court once before and the matter was taken care of. A social worker testifies that the guy is relatively harmless and is a schizophrenic. The Judge asks the deputies if any of them are familiar with the accused. One of the deputies, who I saw in action at Chad's arrest, speaks up and says that the guy lives on his street and everyone is afraid of him.

Based on this, the Judge orders the Sheriffs Department to go pick the guy up. Why not! I know the deputies thrive on these types of confrontations. *Come on judges of the world, there has got to be better way of doing this.*

All of the cases have been heard when Chad's case is called at 11:45 AM. Jim hasn't shown up. Everyone waits about ten minutes, and then the bailiff and several others go looking for him. He is nowhere to be found. I'm getting a little frantic that he is not going to show and Chad's case will be further delayed. Judge Hyde recesses the court until 12:15. At 12:30 Jim still hasn't shown and to my surprise everyone just sits around. Jim finally walks through the doors at 12:45. He apologizes to the Judge and then hurries off to meet with Chad for a few minutes. Chad is then brought into the courtroom with chains around his ankles. I can tell by the expression on his face that he is angry.

The whole process only takes a few minutes. Chad and the lawyers sign a few papers and the case has been formally passed on to the Circuit Court. Alarmingly, the next court date is December 18th - almost two months away. Judge Taliaferro will take the case. You would like to think that these judges are good and honorable men. We'll see. Chad is whisked away as soon as he signs and, of course, we have not been allowed to talk to him.

After the court is recessed, we meet with Jim for about 45 minutes. To me, Jim seems a bit shaken. I don't know if Chad told him how he felt or what. I really feel bad for Chad. I know when he left the jail house this morning he was thinking this thing was going to be resolved one way or another. What a shock it must have been for Chad to have his lawyer rush in and tell him that his case was being postponed for another two months.

FRIDAY, OCTOBER 26TH

I taught a class covering budgets today at the bank's operations center. All bank managers were in attendance. We have branches that cover a good part of Eastern Virginia. So there were many in attendance that had not conversed with me since the robbery. It was a bit awkward at first, but I got through it. You can't help but wonder what everybody is thinking.

Debra and Cindy go to visit Chad. They say that Chad has a lot of questions concerning December 18th but he seems to be in pretty good spirits. They are only allowed 45 minutes with him before they are told to leave. Chad calls me later that night, pressing me also for details about December 18th. He also wants to know about the possibilities of getting bail.

SATURDAY, OCTOBER 27TH

We get a two-page letter from Chad today. He mentions that Jim did not go into any details with him on Monday about what was going to happen next. He mentions Debra's birthday, which is coming up, and wants to know if I have bought any new computer games for my new computer.

He goes into detail about how he has talked to several inmates concerning disability pay. They tell him that, because he has been diagnosed with schizophrenia, he should be eligible for it. He talks about saving all his disability payments so he can pay for the plastic surgery needed to correct "his problem." He writes, "I know you guys think I'm crazy with the way I'm obsessed with that problem, but I can't help it. It's so engrossed into my head and I think about it all the time, that I'll never think I'm normal until the problem is fixed...I honestly believe that the symptoms of schizophrenia I have, stemmed from my 'problem'."

He finishes the letter by saying, "I fully intend to go back to school and live a normal life and make good." I just hope that the system lets him.

CHAPTER 11

ALI TAKES CENTER STAGE

MONDAY, OCTOBER 29TH

We attend Ali's basketball game. She plays hard but gets a technical foul called on her. We will find out later that the coaches use this as a reason to get on her case.

TUESDAY, OCTOBER 30TH

Chad calls with some interesting, but what I find to be irritating, news. He found out from another inmate that you are allowed to receive books in jail. The trick is that they have to be sent direct from the publisher. I find that hard to believe, in light of what I was told when I called to ask if we could send him books. I tell him that I will call the jailhouse tomorrow to verify it; and if it's true, we will definitely send him some books.

Ali is upset, because she has had a run in with her coach. Apparently at some team meeting, her coach expressed his displeasure with the effort he had been getting from his team (forget the fact that their record is like 10 & 2 and they are in second place in their district). I don't take Ali's side in the discussion and even admonish her that she needs to learn to hold her tongue when she thinks she is being wronged. Then, Ali informs me that she has been kicked off the team, and refuses to talk to me further. I think it is just a ruse on her part to get the upper hand in the conversation.

I watch the Yankees win their first game of the World Series after having dropped the first two to Arizona. Strong pitching performances by Clemens and Rivera, is the key.

WEDNESDAY, OCTOBER 31ST

I call the jailhouse and, sure enough, we are allowed to send the inmates books if they are sent direct from the publisher. Why I was told at the very beginning that we were not allowed to send them is what I find irritating. Here is a bright kid who now has been in jail for two and a half months and could have been getting constructive reading material and learning something, instead of staring at the walls. I continue to be amazed at just how incompetent and insensitive these law enforcement people are being. Even without being convicted, the accused and the family of the accused are treated as public enemies.

I am surprised when I arrive home from work and Ali is there - she normally either has basketball practice or a game. I realize now that Ali was telling the truth when she said she had been kicked off the team. I feel really bad, because I know Ali's life revolves around basketball. She loves it. She catches every NBA game she can on TV and even serves as a manager on the boy's team, whose season follows the girls.

I ask her to tell me the details. Apparently, the meeting was called because the coaches felt that the girls were slacking off, based on, I guess, that they had lost a game the week before and had a sloppy game Monday night. They singled Ali out because she had missed Friday's practice (her first miss of the season as she had traveled with Debra to Northern Virginia) and had gotten a technical foul in their last game. They coaches said they didn't want any more technical fouls the rest of the season, and then they did a real stupid thing. They told Ali that she needed to apologize to the whole team for missing practice and getting a technical foul. They have been around Ali long enough that they should have known better. Ali will always respond to praise and encouragement, but never to being called on the carpet. She refused to apologize, as she felt she had done nothing wrong, and they kicked her off the team. I don't understand it, she had been working hard for them since the beginning of August and the season was almost at an end.

The coaches are constantly yelling at the girls during games and are quick to yank them if they have done anything wrong. A number of girls who seldom play have quit the team because it just is not worth it. Debra is very upset about the situation and I have to almost physically restrain her from calling the coaches and giving them a piece of her mind. We don't need this. It is also a reminder that it is not just Debra and I who are under a lot of pressure - Ali is too. Didn't one of the experts say that mental illness is often a family disease? I'm beginning to understand what he meant.

THURSDAY, NOVEMBER 1ST

When I get home from work, Ali looks dejected. It's their last game tonight and I know she is feeling bad that she is not there. I believe they go to the District Tournament next to determine the final champion. She tells me she wants to go to the tournament to root for them.

When she gets home, Debra has some bad news. She informs me that the doctor's medical tests have determined that she has what is described as precancerous cells in her uterus. She tells me its not serious, but she might need an operation later. *The thought crosses my mind, what it would be like without Debra.* I don't even want to think about it.

The night; however, ends on a happy note, though only offering a little relief. Scott Brosius hits a two-run homerun in the bottom of the ninth with two outs to pull the Yankees even with Arizona. They go on to win it in the 12th inning. Tino Martinez had done it the night before with a two-run homerun with two outs in the bottom of the ninth to win that game. It had only been done once before in World Series history, and the Yankees did it twice on consecutive nights - unbelievable!

FRIDAY, NOVEMBER 2ND

I visit Chad and it goes fairly well this morning. Debra isn't able to make it; because she has another doctor's appointment in Northern Virginia. We talk about the Yankees and about whether he would qualify for disability pay. As I am leaving, an aunt of one of the other inmates stops me and asks me who my attorneys are and what my opinion is of a court appointed attorney. I told her what little I knew about the pros and cons. She told me her nephew is also mentally ill, and she is hoping that the courts will go easy on him.

I am struck by the thought that these jails and courts are dealing with the mentally ill all the time. You would think they would be better equipped to handle it. Neither the facilities nor the expertise are there to properly treat these people and to give them a chance.

Shortly after I arrive at work, I get a phone call from a family that used to be members of our church here but had recently moved to Arizona. They are a remarkable family that had fled South Africa in the middle of the night on a sailboat to escape the unrest and a government, which would not let them leave legally. They had heard of our troubles and wanted to call to let us know that they were thinking of us and wished us well. They made my day.

SATURDAY, NOVEMBER 3RD

I get on the Internet and order a Stephen King novel from Amazon for Chad. I'm still skeptical as to whether Chad will receive it. So I thought I would try this before I send him any expensive computer training books.

TUESDAY, NOVEMBER 6TH

It's Election Day and I vote. As a couple of the election volunteers check my ID, I see them exchange glances and one of them raises an eyebrow as if to say *Yes, it's him!* or at least that's what I think they may be doing. You can't help but feel paranoid every time you venture out into the public, especially in Northumberland County. Upon leaving the election booth, I'm wondering when Sheriff Middleton is coming up for reelection. The thought has crossed my mind to assist anyone who runs against him.

I get good news tonight. Debra tells me that Ali has been reinstated on the team in time for the district playoffs.

WEDNESDAY, NOVEMBER 7TH

Chad calls and tells us that he got the Stephen King novel. We are both thrilled that we now know that he can receive books. We talk about what should be the next book I send him. He wants to get a computer book that will help him train for something that is called A+ Certificate, which demonstrates proficiency in computer repair. Chad is very excited that he can now be doing something constructive with his time, and so am I.

I call and give Dad the good news and we talk about what inspirational books are available. That night I find the book that Chad wants on AmazonBooks.com and I have it sent directly to the jail.

THURSDAY, NOVEMBER 8TH

The girls win their second district playoff game and Ali has a good game. The championship game will be this Saturday in Fredericksburg. They will be playing James Monroe High School, which was a former Double AA school - Ali's is a Single A.

FRIDAY, NOVEMBER 9TH

Debra goes to see Chad and gets very upset with him. When Debra arrived, Chad had to be awakened, so when they bring him out he is tired and inattentive. He puts his head down into his arms as he is sitting at the window and won't even look up at her. He mumbles to her. Debra says that she was feeling nauseated before they even brought him out, and between Chad's behavior and feeling sick, she just gets up and leaves, after being with Chad for only about ten minutes.

I'm thinking to myself that I hope Debra wasn't so abrupt that she upset Chad. I tell her it was probably the effects of his medicine. She says he was just being rude.

On the way home from the jail she stops and buys him a card and sends him a $50 money order. Go figure!

I also go out and buy a card, but this one is for Debra. It's her birthday tomorrow. I also buy her a gift certificate from Twice Told Tales, a local bookstore. We are planning on celebrating her birthday on Monday. Debra has chosen to work twelve-hour shifts this weekend. I don't think she wants to think about the fact that her son is in jail on her birthday.

SATURDAY, NOVEMBER 10TH

Debra leaves early for work. Ali and I get up and clean the house from top to bottom - sort of a surprise birthday gift for Debra when she gets home. Ali then leaves to catch the team bus to Fredericksburg.

I am saddened by a letter we receive from our family doctor. She announces her retirement, and I know that Debra is really going to miss her. She has been a friend and confidant for Debra, especially since Chad first started exhibiting schizophrenic symptoms. She is that rare breed of doctor who actually takes the time to sit down and listen to you as long as necessary. It would have been nice if she could have been available throughout this ordeal.

I head on up to Fredericksburg to catch what will become one of the most entertaining basketball games I have ever seen. When your child is playing, it just gives it that extra dimension. The gymnasium is packed. Both teams are well coached but I think the Northumberland team has the better talent. However, Ali's team is erratic and they are making some mental errors that are allowing the other team to take the lead early. The erratic start seems to have shaken the confidence of Northumberland, and they are shooting poorly. With about five minutes left in the first half, James Monroe builds up about a twelve-point lead, and it is starting to look like they may get an easy win. Northumberland starts to settle down and as the first half ends manages to cut the lead to about eight points. Ali plays sporadically, playing good defense but only attempts one shot.

The second half starts with both teams shooting well and trading baskets. But, slowly and surely, the Northumberland team starts to chip away at the lead. The crowd is really getting worked into a frenzy and the game is turning into a real dogfight. The girls on both sides are playing their hearts out. Ali only plays a few minutes in the third quarter.

Northumberland is behind by only about three points at the start of the fourth quarter. The fourth quarter is a war. Midway through the quarter Northumberland pulls ahead with a precarious one-point lead, but their star guard is in serious foul trouble, so the coach pulls her out and puts Ali in her spot. With the crowd on its feet and yelling at the top of their lungs, Ali brings the ball down the court and, when the defense collapses on all the other players, Ali calmly shoots a three-pointer from the top of the key and makes it. The Northumberland fans go wild; they now have a four-point lead. After several trips up-and-down the floor, James Monroe hits a basket that cuts the lead back to two, with only a few minutes left in the game. There is absolute pandemonium in the gym. Ali brings the ball up the court and then drives the lane past several defenders and hits a lay-up. Northumberland is back to a four-point lead. James Monroe comes back and misses. As the rebound is fought for Ali grabs the loose ball and heads back up the court. You cannot hear yourself think! She tries to drive the lane again but three defenders collapse on her, she passes the ball

128

back out to her teammate who then makes an uncontested three-point shot, giving them a seven point lead and the District Championship!

Wow! From being kicked off the team to being one of the heroes of the District Championship game! All in a week's work for Ali! I give her the "Thumps-up" as I leave the gym. I'm really happy for her, and I try to savor the moment as I head back to Heathsville and a different kind of reality.

SUNDAY, NOVEMBER 11TH

We have an interesting discussion in our Priesthood meeting this morning. The lesson centers on the principle that we believe in supporting our government as long as the government is governing righteously. The church takes no stance on political parties and encourages its members to seek out those politicians who we feel are honest, highly principled and will work hard in their role as a public servant. If you followed the voting record of the people in Utah, which is predominantly Mormon, you would think this wasn't the case. Utah consistently votes Republican every presidential election and the Republican candidate will always garner his widest margin of victory in Utah. As a matter of fact, I think President Reagan won about 88% of the Utah vote in one election! The leadership of the Church has been very conservative the past forty years, and its membership reflects that.

When I get home I do some research on our local government. Debra and I discuss a report I found on the Internet. A recent U.S. Department of Justice study (1999 Justice Expenditure and Employment Extracts-Bureau of Justice Statistics) reveals that the Northumberland County Sheriff's Department has twice the budget and nearly twice as many deputies as rural counties with similar demographics. A number of our friends have commented that the cops seem to be everywhere in our county. This report helps explain why. What makes this all the more ridiculous is that thirty-five percent of the county's population is over the age of sixty. We discuss the fact that these guys have to justify their existence!

Chad gives us a call and says that Jim paid him a visit. Chad says that he asked Jim what is the worst-case scenario for him. Jim says that the worst-case scenario would be one to two years in prison with time off for good behavior.

MONDAY, NOVEMBER 12TH

We celebrate Debra's birthday today. I take her to lunch at Lee's Restaurant in Kilmarnock. After lunch we walk across the street to Twice Told Tales where Debra picks out several books. I've done the best I can to try and make Debra's birthday as pleasant as possible. I only wish I had a magic wand.

WEDNESDAY, NOVEMBER 14TH

We have a training seminar today for all the supervisors at work. The topic involves doing background checks on prospective employees. In particular, we are looking for any history of incarceration, bankruptcy or mental illness. It is obviously important that when you hire someone in banking that their records be spotless. Nevertheless, I find the seminar to be very depressing. The ramifications of all this for Chad, if we don't get him into a mental hospital soon, are overwhelming.

FRIDAY, NOVEMBER 16TH

Today would have been my mother's 69th birthday. She died almost two years ago after suffering a stroke after heart bypass surgery. At least she was spared this family crisis.

The visit to the jail is a nightmare. It is past 9:00 AM, the lights haven't even been turned on in the foyer, and the visiting rooms are dark. The foyer is full of visitors wondering what is going on and getting angry. No one comes out to tell us what is going on. At about 9:15 AM, the lights come on and everyone scrambles to get in line to request which inmate they are there to see. Finally at about 9:35 AM Chad is brought out.

What he tells me next borders on the absurd. They did not let his computer-training book go through! When I ask him what does he mean, Chad says that he got a message that an unauthorized delivery had arrived for him. They needed instructions on whether to destroy it or store it. Great! Here is a mentally ill teenager who has a chance to improve himself, while incarcerated, and for whatever reason' they deny him the opportunity.

Upon returning to work, I call the jail to inquire why the book was not delivered. I am told that the inmates are not allowed to receive any hardbound books because they can be used as a

130

weapon! Oh boy! How deadly they must be! Certainly more deadly than someone's fist! *And by the way, why didn't you tell me that when I called several weeks ago and asked if it was okay to send books directly to the inmates?* The textbook and the shipping only cost me $65.00.

It's a shame, I know how helpful the book would have been for Chad's mental state.

SUNDAY, NOVEMBER 18TH

I go fishing with several other employees of the bank. One of the employees, a senior vice-president, is an expert fisherman. He takes us out into the Chesapeake Bay, where we troll for rockfish. We have a great time and catch a lot of fish. It's a nice break for me; the fact that my son is sitting in jail for bank robbery doesn't cross my mind for a few hours.

MONDAY, NOVEMBER 19TH

There is a letter in the mail from Sallie Mae. The fact that Chad is not attending school this fall has triggered his student loan repayments. He owes over $7,000. Debra and I don't know what to do. Our mounting medical bills and lawyer fees are swamping us. Chad also has a credit card that I have been making payments on. Do we try and preserve Chad's credit rating, which was fine before he was arrested? Lord knows that the odds are already going to be stacked against him when he gets out of wherever he is going.

I cook some rockfish for Debra tonight, and I must say it was delicious!

TUESDAY, NOVEMBER 20TH

Chad gives us a call. He has been thinking about how he is going to make money, once he gets out of jail. He says he is planning on getting his A+ certification in computer repair and going into business for himself. He also asks me about how I think an arcade business would do in Kilmarnock. I don't have the heart to tell him straight out that I don't think either idea would work. I do tell him that there are a lot of avenues still open for him at the university level, and I think that is still the way to go. I try not to think of the ramifications, if we fail to get Chad admitted to a mental hospital.

I mentioned that Sallie Mae is expecting him to start making loan payments. I agree to give Sallie Mae a call to see if something can be worked out.

FRIDAY, NOVEMBER 23RD

I hate the Northern Neck Regional Jail. They treat the inmate's visitors like they are trash! As I arrive at 9:00 AM, there are a few visitors in line and it seems that they are being processed very slowly. After I've been waiting about five minutes, I get to the front of the line and push the button for assistance. The girl comes on the line and tells me loudly and clearly to wait. I am the only person in the line at the moment. I wait and wait! First, for five minutes, and then ten minutes! Meanwhile, other visitors are coming in and the line behind me is getting long. People are getting impatient. I explain to the people behind me that I was told to wait. I don't know what to do. I don't want to buzz the girl again in fear of agitating her to the point that I am denied a visit. I can't imagine what she is doing. Finally, after fifteen minutes, when the line is almost out the door, I push the button again. She immediately comes on and asks me what I want! What a bitch! She can see all of us through that tinted window! She was content to sit there and do nothing and must have enjoyed watching me take the heat. When I get to the booth, Chad is there and says he has been waiting for me about fifteen minutes. To top it all off, our visit is cut short!

SATURDAY, NOVEMBER 24TH

One of the older nurses that Debra works with, and a good friend, unexpectedly dies. Debra is in tears as she goes to work, and she says it was so touching when she got there. Throughout the day, many of the prisoners, whom her good friend had befriended throughout the years, brought sympathy cards to the nurses' window. They were able to buy the cards through the commissary, and she said many of them had tears in their eyes as they delivered the cards.

TUESDAY, NOVEMBER 27TH

I call Sallie Mae today, and they are unbelievably uncooperative. I try to explain to one girl and then another that my son is incarcerated and I am calling to see if something can be arranged about his school loans. They tell me that they can only discuss the loan with Chad himself. I try to explain to them that Chad can't call them nor will he ever be able to call them until he gets out of jail, and there is certainly no way he can make payments. They tell me there is a "forbearance form" he can fill out and send them that allows him to postpone payments under special circumstance, but interest will still accrue! I get nowhere with them and finally tell them to send me the form and I'll see if I can get it to him somehow.

Chad calls, and I explain to him that Sallie Mae will be sending me a form for him to fill out. He tells me that he did get the soft cover computer book I sent him. I tell him, sarcastically, please don't attack anyone with it, or he might not be able to get any more books at all!

FRIDAY, NOVEMBER 30TH

Debra goes to see Chad today. The visit goes better than her last visit, but she says she did most of the talking and didn't stay long. Chad seemed tired, and she says she was a little alarmed because he would not make eye contact and was constantly picking at his face - an indication that he is either not taking his medicine, or its not working as it should.

We get some good news. Ali has made the honor roll. This is quite an accomplishment given the amount of time she devoted to basketball. We have noticed that Ali has been getting more conscientious about her homework and seems to be applying herself. I wonder if Chad's actions are one of the reasons for this? I think maybe Ali is trying to show those around her that she is not a screw-up. As I take the time to reflect about it, I have every reason to be very proud of Ali right now.

CHAPTER 12

THE JAILHOUSE SNITCH

TUESDAY, DECEMBER 4TH

Bill gave me a call at work. He is very direct and tells me that we need to tell Chad to shut up while he is in jail! Apparently, Chad has been talking to another inmate, who is a stool pigeon. The guy acted like he was Chad's best friend at a time when Chad really needed a friend. The Northern Neck Regional Jail often serves as a temporary holding jail for Federal prisoners until its decided which Federal penitentiary they are going to be sent to. Federal prisoners will get their sentence reduced if they can get information from other inmates that prosecutors can use.

Over a course of several months, this guy had been carefully setting Chad up. He baited Chad by pretending he was really interested in how he did the alleged counterfeiting and the bank robbery. Chad, in an effort to impress this guy, starting bragging about how he did it and once he gets out, they could both successfully operated their own counterfeiting scheme. Once he felt that he had Chad in his pocket, he wore a wire and taped Chad describing how they could do it!

I had to laugh at first! Bill is very serious about the possible damage this could have done. I remind Bill that part of being paranoid schizophrenic is being grandiose and feeling omnipotent. If you add that to the fact that Chad is trying to impress someone he views as a friend, you are going to get this kind of situation. Trying to tell Chad to quit talking is like trying to tell a Republican that Clinton was a good president!

Bill also tells me that Dr. Gomez still hasn't delivered his written psychiatric evaluation to the court. Chad's trial is now only several weeks away. If the report is not delivered soon there will not be enough time for everyone to review and evaluate it. The prosecutor can hold Dr. Gomez in contempt of court if it is not delivered by the court date, but there is a chance that there can be another postponement.

All in all, a pretty depressing phone call from Bill. I realize as I hang up the phone that even though I may find the actions of the stool pigeon and his cohorts as being ridiculous, the reality is that people, such as a jury, don't understand the ramifications of Chad's illness, and they would probably use it against him. Still, I would love to be the defense attorney if the prosecutor tried to use it.

The news about Gomez is even more depressing. Debra is not surprised when I tell her. She is livid and reminds me that it was she that told both our lawyers and me that we needed to rely on another specialist.

Debra has been working long hours lately, not only because we need the money, but also because it is a way for her to keep her mind off our troubles.

WEDNESDAY, DECEMBER 5TH

Chad calls us, and I tell him what Bill had to say about the stool pigeon. It takes a minute for it to sink in, and then Chad says; somewhat exasperated, "Dad, I have been asked hundreds of questions about the bank robbery by dozens of inmates!" "Well, son one of them taped you, and it may be used in court against you," I replied. I then ask him was there one particular prisoner who spent a lot of time with him and then was suddenly transferred from his pod? He replies, "Yes! I think I know who it was!"

I tell him not to talk to anyone else about what he did. I tried to impress upon him especially don't talk to anyone for the next several weeks. We also talk about who it probably was that encouraged the inmate to wear a wire and set Chad up. It had to be either the Sheriff's Department or the Fed.

We finish the phone call with Chad asking me to look into any long-distance college courses he can take while being incarcerated in prison or a mental institution.

TUESDAY, DECEMBER 11TH

Chad calls and we spend most of the time talking about taking college correspondence courses. Chad would like to get an associate degree in business. I am surprised to find that most long-distance college courses that lead to a bachelor's degree are not available to Chad because he is only nineteen. You have to be older than twenty-one, before you can be enrolled. I don't know why.

Neither Chad nor I have heard from Bill since he called last Tuesday. We don't have a clue on what's going on. I tell Chad I will try to get a hold of Jim.

THURSDAY, DECEMBER 13TH

Not surprisingly, the Rappahannock Record newspaper reports that the Sheriff was cleared of any wrong doing when he shot and killed the teenager who had refused to give up his weapon. The article did confirm that the Sheriff had fired a number of rounds from his rifle during the altercation. The special prosecutor who reviewed the case concluded that the "deadly force was justifiable because it was necessary to prevent the escape" of the victim.

Apparently, the whole thing started over the kid trying to see his girl friend, despite a restraining order against him. The boy had told his girl friend that he would rather kill himself than go to jail. As I read the article, I am reminded on how confrontational the deputies were at my home. The kid was probably scared out of his mind.

FRIDAY, DECEMBER 14TH

Jim Breeden calls me and has terrible news! He says that Dr. Gomez's report is too brief and it didn't follow the format that they were hoping it would. They had actually threatened the doctor with a subpoena to get him to respond. Even though it states clearly that Chad has paranoid schizophrenia and could not control his actions on the date of the robbery, there is not enough "meat" to it to satisfy the prosecutor. He has apparently seen the letter and was not impressed.

Jim also mentions that the jail snitch has also done a lot of damage, making it even more important that we have well-substantiated evidence that Chad should be sent to a mental hospital and not a prison.

The attorney's have decided, and it's not clear to me just whose decision it was, that they want to play it safe and get another opinion. They are going to postpone the hearing! Great! Chad's brain will rot for another two months!

I call Debra at work and break the news to her. She becomes very upset and points out to me that a court appointed attorney could have managed just as well to keep Chad in jail this long - without a resolution in sight, and he wouldn't be costing us a fortune. I try to calm Debra down and point out to her that the attorney's know what they are doing and nothing has really changed except the timing. We are still on course to get Chad the help he needs.

I don't tell Debra, but I must admit I am starting to have a few doubts myself. Given the severity of Chad's mental illness, I don't understand the significance of the snitch. The actions of the prosecuting attorney don't seem to be in line with what my attorney's have told me about him. It's as if Chad's illness is a side issue to the questions about what he did. Any reasonable person would recognize that his illness was the cause of all his other troubles.

When I get home, Debra is there. She left work right after I called and doesn't want to talk to anybody. She is very depressed and I'm concerned about her. Poor Chad! He doesn't know anything about the postponement. I don't know what I'm going to say to him when he calls.

SATURDAY, DECEMBER 15TH

I try to work in the yard, but I only last a few minutes. I get very short of breath. I have to go back inside and lie down. I'm thinking it must have something to do with my asthma, though asthma attacks for me are rare.

SUNDAY, DECEMBER 16TH

I call Dad today and we discuss the wisdom of postponing the hearing. We talk about "bravado" within a jailhouse and the impact that the snitch has apparently had. It almost seems like everyone is giving this snitch as much weight as the fact that three separate specialists have tried to convince Chad that nothing is wrong with his scrotum and all of them have failed. Dad mentions that they have had letters from Chad expressing remorse and admitting that he knows he is sick. He wonders can these letters be admitted as evidence! Before we hang up, Dad mentions how proud he is of the way we have been handling things. Some how I don't feel very proud, just frustrated and exhausted.

Cindy calls and says it is not Debra she wants to talk to, it is me. She is very concerned about Debra and wants to know if I realize just how depressed she really is. I know Debra is really depressed and I'm hoping that eventually things will take a turn for the better and we can start getting back to some kind of daily routine. I don't know what else to say. It just seems that you can't give up hope, or there is nothing left.

I get a surprise call from Jim. He wants to meet with Debra and I tomorrow night to go over where we are and what is next.

Ali and I put up the Christmas tree in the hopes that it will cheer Debra up when she gets home from work.

MONDAY, DECEMBER 17TH

Debra meets me after work and we go over to see Jim. He covers what the sentencing guidelines would be if things should go badly. The good news is that the guidelines indicated that Chad would only get about four years, if convicted. This is mainly due to the fact that Chad had no prior record and no weapon was used. The bad news is the fact that Jim finds it necessary to bring this up. I ask him if we aren't still on course to get Chad into a mental institution.

In a way, Jim is setting us up. He stresses the importance of getting another expert opinion from a noted expert in the field. We talk about Dr. Peck. Jim has used him before and says that he makes a very good witness. He would, of course, have to evaluate Chad before we could go any further. He can rely on the physical evidence gathered by Dr. Gomez while Chad was at Tucker's but Dr. Peck will need to do his own psychoanalysis. All of this is going to cost money. Jim wants to know if he should go ahead and proceed in this direction. Debra and I look at each other and tell him, yes.

We talk about Dr. Gomez's report. Jim reiterates that it was short and looked like it was dictated on the fly. Jim also mentioned that it did not incorporate reference to some manual that is often referred to as a guideline in cases such as Chad's. Nevertheless, it will still be used in court to support the fact that what Chad needs is psychiatric care, not incarceration.

We spend some time talking about the snitch. Jim gives us a copy of the "snitch" report. Jim agrees that no one would give it much weight, once they understood the symptoms of paranoid schizophrenia.

Jim also says that the Secret Service is still showing an unusual amount of attention to the counterfeiting aspect. You would think once they understood how mentally ill Chad is, and the fact that he never tried to pass any of it, they would lose interest in the case. But apparently there are some new laws that have been passed to help the Secret Service in their prosecution of anyone using the Internet in any counterfeiting actions. They are eager to try these new laws. Chad's illness apparently carries no weight with the agents of American law enforcement. Jim finishes by telling us not to go to court tomorrow. Chad won't appear. Jim will meet with Chad in the morning and will give us a call to let us know the next court date.

Shortly after we arrive home, Chad gives us a call. He knows nothing about the postponement tomorrow. I have to break the news to him. He is shocked and wants to know why no one told him this earlier. He then becomes angry and says he would rather just go to prison than to stay here! I try to reason with him and to calm him down. I try to explain to him that if he can just hold out for another couple of months, everything is going to be okay. As the one-minute warning comes on, he starts to cry softly. I have an awful feeling when I hang up the phone. Debra and I can only imagine what Chad is going through.

TUESDAY, DECEMBER 18TH

Jim calls to inform us on how it went. The next court date is set for February 26th, which just happens to me my birthday. Maybe it's a good omen. Dr. Peck will need to get his report in ten days prior to the court date. Jim will get in touch with the doctor to get the ball rolling. Jim tells me that the doctor will not only want to schedule several meetings with Chad, but he will want to meet with us, as well.

Chad calls later that afternoon and we are shocked to find out that he did appear in court! He said it was only for a few minutes, but he was there. I tell Chad that Jim told us that he wouldn't appear in court! Debra and I both feel really bad that we weren't there. The thought of him alone in that court, with no supporters, is very painful.

Chad is fit to be tied. He says he can't stand it any longer and that he would rather be in prison where he can at least study. I try to placate him by telling him that if things go well, he could be home by next Christmas. I lay out for him in detail what the next steps are, and Debra and I both tell him to please try and hang in there.

WEDNESDAY, DECEMBER 19TH

I have an 11:15 AM appointment with Dr. Duer to see if she can figure out why I'm running out of breath so easily and feeling so lethargic. After checking a few things, she uses some sort of contraption to check my heart and I see her become alarmed. She tells me that my heart is racing and they need to get me over to the hospital right away! They call the emergency room and tell me to report there immediately. The hospital is just down the street and they are already waiting for me as I come through the door. I sign a few forms and then they have me changed into a hospital garb and have me in a hospital bed within just a few minutes. I'm feeling a little scared and stupid. I should have had this checked out earlier.

A couple of nurses come in and administer an EKG test and take some blood. Debra, who had the day off, shows up. The doctor's office had called her and told her what was going on. I ask her to call work for me to let them know that I won't be coming back today. The doctor comes in and introduces himself and examines me. He tells me that he wants to review the EKG results and then he will tell me what his preliminary diagnosis is.

My boss shows up to check on how I'm doing. It's nice for him to stop by, and I feel a little foolish.

About an hour later, the doctor returns and tells me that he wants to keep me in the hospital for a few days for observation. I have been diagnosed with an atrial fibrillation heart condition. The top part of my heart has been beating extremely fast in an effort to keep the blood circulating properly. The reason I have been feeling lethargic and getting dizzy spells is that I have not been getting enough oxygen. They are going to give me several pills designed to slow my heartbeat and to thin my blood. They want to protect me from a blood clot forming and possibly causing

140

an aneurysm. The blood thinner will also make it possible for them to do cardiac shock treatment down the road, if the medicine does not put my heart back into a normal rhythm. I'm glad Debra is here to interpret all this medical jargon that is being thrown at me.

Great! Now I get to spend a couple days in the hospital, and I've given Debra something else to worry about. Will this downward slide never end?

THURSDAY, DECEMBER 20TH

I had a lousy night's sleep in my new surroundings. Between the IV and the nurses waking me up every two hours to take my vital signs, I just couldn't get any rest. I feel better, though, when I get a full course breakfast served in bed! Even if it is a heart-healthy meal, as they call it.

They perform another EKG on me in the morning and draw some more blood, and then I'm pretty much left to myself. I do have a private room and a TV, but "soaps" are not my thing. Debra comes after lunch to stay with me and we get a very pleasant surprise when at five o'clock everyone from my department shows up! Today, was the Christmas party in our building, where we traditionally exchange gifts at a Christmas luncheon. So everyone dropped by after work to wish me well and to leave a few gifts.

We also get a surprise when I get several phone calls from church members and one church member stops by to wish me well. I was kind of hoping to keep this quiet. One, it's a little embarrassing; two; and I know this is silly, but I don't want anyone in Northumberland County thinking I am in a weakened condition; and three, I know people are going to blame Chad for what has happened. Both sides of our family have a history of heart problems. My grandparents all died of heart attacks, and of course, my mother's death was the result of bypass surgery. But you can't keep a secret in a small town.

FRIDAY, DECEMBER 21ST

Another lousy night. Somehow, I must have caused the IV needle to shift, and my hand where the IV is inserted is causing me so much pain, I can't sleep at all. Over her strong objections, I

141

make the head nurse remove the IV. The nurses also continue to monitor my vital signs throughout the night. When I am awakened at 6:00 AM my hand is swollen, and my skin is black and blue around the area where the needle was inserted.

The doctor drops by early and he promises that he will let me go home today, if the EKG results are favorable. Basically they are looking to make sure that my heart has slowed down to a reasonable level and my blood is thin enough that there is no chance of it clotting. The nurses drop by shortly after and administer the EKG. I don't think I have any hair left on my chest!

The results are favorable and the doctor does release me. I have three different prescriptions to keep my heart in control, and I am to see my doctor once a week for the next few weeks to have blood drawn and to have my heart checked. Once my blood is thin enough, they will perform a cardioversion to see if they can get it back into its normal rhythm. Sounds like fun!

SATURDAY, DECEMBER 22ND

Ali and I go to get Debra a Christmas present. Debra is working the weekend, so today will be a good day. Ali had been with Debra last week at one of the local hardware shops and she had stopped and looked at a compost container, which she really wanted, but decided in the end that we didn't have enough money. I take the truck, and Ali shows me what Debra was looking at, and we get it.

The thing is so big that it is hard to hide when we get it home. By this time, I'm pretty exhausted and I end up sleeping most of the day.

SUNDAY, DECEMBER 23RD

Chad calls. He is still feeling in the "dumps". His postponement and the fact that he won't be home for Christmas are weighing heavily on him. We do our best to cheer him up and encourage him to take his medicine. We also tell him to make sure that he calls us on Christmas day so we can talk to him.

Debra and I both go to Church. It is nice to see some friendly faces and to sing a few Christmas hymns. Afterwards, we go to the movie *The Majestic* starring Jim Carey. It's a great movie and quite uplifting. We needed a movie with a happy ending.

Unfortunately, I make the mistake of stopping and buying the *Northumberland Echo* on the way home. Chad has made the front of the newspaper again. It was almost a good day.

TUESDAY, DECEMBER 25TH

Debra worked Christmas Eve, and we take our time getting up this morning. We exchange gifts and call loved ones. Debra starts preparing a full course meal for this afternoon. She is trying to make the day a pleasant one for Ali and me and at the same time trying to keep her mind off Chad.

Chad calls and we describe a few of the gifts we got for him. He sounds better, and he is looking forward to the Christmas meal that apparently they are going to get this afternoon. It does us good to talk to him, as it seems to make the day more complete. How things have changed in one year's time!

WEDNESDAY, DECEMBER 26TH

As I get home from work, Debra says she has something to tell me, and she wants to tell me before Ali gets home. She says she would have told me last week but she was too afraid of what I would do. This is not like Debra. She really has my attention. On her way home from work one day last week, she stopped at Food Lion in Heathsville. She said it was late, and she was tired; and she just wanted to grab a few things and hurry home. She said that after she grabbed what she wanted, she proceeded to the checkout stand and got into the only line available. She said, after she had been waiting a few minutes, she started to feel uncomfortable and noticed that the man standing next to her seemed to be staring at her. As she looked up, she realized it was Chuck Wilkens and he was staring at her, even though the cashier was busy checking out his purchase. She said that he was only a couple of feet away from her. When the cashier finished Chuckie just moved to the end of the checkout stand and continued staring at Debra the whole time she was checking out. She said as she tried to leave Chuckie was still standing there.

I stop Debra at this point and ask her if he followed her out to the parking lot. She says, "Paul, I don't know I was so scared! I just made sure I had my car keys in my hand and hurried to the car as fast as I could and never looked behind me!" Debra is now visibly shaking, and for some reason I'm strangely feeling very calm and thinking to myself, *"What are we dealing with here? The cop from hell?* I ask Debra was he in uniform? Does she think that the cashier might have noticed the strange behavior? Does she remember who the cashier was? Debra can't remember if he was in uniform and is not even sure if it happened last week or the week before. I am just making her more upset with my questions so I back off. What a jerk!

Debra made the right decision about not telling me when it happened. If she had told me that night, I would have gone directly to the Sheriff's Department and would have very vocally filed a complaint. By doing so, I would have jeopardized Chad's case - sad to say. There is nothing we can do!

THURSDAY, DECEMBER 27TH

I go to see Dr. Duer this morning to get my heart checked and to get some blood drawn. I don't think last night's news is going to help me in the "high-blood pressure" department. Luckily I get out of there without being sent directly to emergency!

FRIDAY, DECEMBER 28TH

Debra gives me a call at work and she is upset. She had gone to see Chad, along with one of his friends who is home from school. What we were hoping would be a great visit for everyone involved, didn't turn out so well. Chad is exhibiting strong schizophrenic symptoms. Debra drills him on whether he has been taking his medicine. Chad actually admits that he has not taken any Prozac in weeks, and he has only been taken his Zyprexa occasionally. Debra is beside herself! What makes matters worse is that she notices that Chad has gotten some kind of small, makeshift tattoo on his hand!

Debra is furious and asks Chad where he got it. Chad says that one of the other inmates does tattoos and Chad bought some stuff for him from the commissary in exchange for the tattoo. Debra doesn't want to make a scene in front of Chad's friend. She asks Chad to please start taking his medicine and tells him how

144

stupid he is for getting a tattoo. She tells him about the risks he took with having someone give it to him with an unsterilized needle.

We both can't believe how incompetent or how unconcerned The Northern Neck Regional Jail is with Chad's care. Without his medicine, Chad's condition is only getting worse which is going to make it all the more impossible for him to fully recuperate him once we can get him some competent care. Another problem is Chad is changing. The influences and company he is keeping are teaching and encouraging him along the criminal path. I can really see the truth in the old saying that a prisoner comes out of incarceration a more hardened criminal than when he went in. All of this, and there is nothing we can do! The criminal justice system and county bureaucracy are slowly but surely changing our son for the worst. *Can anyone imagine how it feels to watch your child forced day by day into an abyss of despair? Can anyone fully appreciate the depths of neglect to which our son is being subjected? Debra, Ali and I must, as normal people, try to retain our poise, but Chad is a sick young man whom society has decided to throw away.*

Debra also tells me that Chad mentioned that he got served with some kind of warrant from Rockingham. I promise Debra I will get in touch with Jim to see if there is anything he can do about Chad's situation and if he knows anything about the warrant. I also want to talk to Jim about getting copies of the search warrants I gave him and to ask him again what the statute of limitations are for filing a complaint against a police officer.

SUNDAY, DECEMBER 30TH

Today is our 21st wedding anniversary. I guess you would understand that we don't feel like celebrating.

I meet Brother Dan Wilson at church. He has ministerial status with the local jails and is allowed to visit and teach the inmates. He has been meeting with Chad, and he tells me that he has enjoyed his visits and finds him to be a very bright kid. They have been reading from the Book of Leviticus and he has been impressed by Chad's ability to pronounce all the names properly.

I like him. More importantly, Chad likes him and has already told me that he has enjoyed his visits with Brother Wilson.

Brother Wilson has a wealth of experience, and he is probably the only good thing that is happening to Chad right now.

MONDAY, DECEMBER 31ST

Chad gives us a call to wish us a happy New Year. I get after Chad about the tattoo and remind him that every time he extends his hand to shake someone else's hand, they will see that tattoo - not great for job interviews. But I don't dwell on it long. It is pretty hard to be mad at someone who has lost his ability to be able to reason and to understand the consequences of their actions.

CHAPTER 13

KIDNAPPING

FRIDAY, JANUARY 4TH, 2002

Debra is going to visit Chad at the jailhouse. The roads are slick, after the snowstorm yesterday. I'm surprised, when she walks into my office shortly after 10 AM. She told me the visit was awful. They hadn't bothered to turn on the lights and were putting everyone in the room where most of the phones didn't work. Debra, after signing in, waited for about ten minutes, when they called her over the intercom to come back to the window. They tell her Chad has been taken to court! She knows nothing about Chad having to go to court and tries to get more information, but they ask her to leave. I don't know what to think of it, and I tell Debra that I will try calling Jim, once again.

I finally get a call from Jim at work. I tell him about the summons Chad has received and he tells me not to be concerned, as they had already taken care of it. I also tell him that Debra tried to visit Chad this morning and they turned her away, saying Chad had been taken to court. He dismisses it as being a clerical error and tells me that they have to notify him if Chad is going to be taken to court.

Jim informs me that they have gotten in touch with Dr. Peck and they are expecting me to call them to set up an appointment. Doctor Peck will usually not take a criminal case for less than $5,000, but because of his association with Jim, agrees to take it for $2,500. I call his office and make an appointment for Monday, January 14th.

I fall asleep that night while reading the autobiography of John Adams written by David McCullough. It's a great book and I'm a new fan of John Adams. Our forefathers were extraordinary men.

Ali awakes me at 1:30 AM and she tells me there is someone on the phone that wants to speak to me. It is Debra's friend who works at the jailhouse. She tells me that Chad is not at the jail! She would have called me earlier, but the phones are all tapped at the jailhouse, so she waited until she got home. She didn't know any of the details, other than the fact that Chad was no longer at the jail. I thank her and find myself wide-awake with panic. What on earth is going on!

Debra hasn't made it home from work yet. She is working the swing shift. I want to call my attorneys, but at 1:30 in the morning I doubt there is anything they can do; and I'm sure they wouldn't appreciate the call. I'm not looking forward to telling Debra; she has already had a stressful day. I am getting angrier by the minute. Are any of these people in the legal system accountable for their actions? My first thought is that somehow the Sheriff's office is involved. I'm thinking that they have decided to get a state psychiatrist to do an examination of Chad before our attorneys even know he is gone. I call the Sheriff's office and ask them if they know anything about my son being transported from the Northern Neck Regional Jail. I am told that they know nothing about it.

Debra has arrived exhausted, and as I tell her the news, she is livid. We can't understand why someone would take Chad without telling anyone the reason and where they were going. We didn't realize how easy it is in this country for the law to do as they pleased. This is not the land of the free it is the land of the naïve! I wonder what John Adams would think about this? The reality is that we have no idea where our son is and what is happening to him.

We debate for about 15 minutes whether there is anything we can do. Debra calls the jailhouse and pleads with the person on duty to give us any information she can. Debra hears whisperings in the background and then the girl tells her that Chad has been released. Debra then says, "What do you mean he has been released? He lives here!" Debra hears more whisperings in the background. She comes back on and tells Debra the U.S. Marshals took him away, and there is absolutely nothing else she can tell us. We thank her and hang up.

The U.S. Marshals! Why in the world would the U.S. Marshals want Chad? All I can think of is it must have something to do with the counterfeiting charge and the Secret Service. They have seemed overly interested in the case, given the facts. Oh, hell, maybe they think Chad has something to do with September 11th, at least that would explain his mysterious disappearance.

We decide to give the U.S Marshals a call and just ask them what they have done with Chad. We call information and get the number for the U.S. Marshal's in Richmond. We call the number and, of course, the answering machine comes on and tells us that office hours are from 8:30 AM to 5:00 PM Monday through Friday.

It is now 3:30 AM. We decide there is nothing we can do now but to try to go to sleep and get some rest. As I lie down, my heart is pounding out of control. I think I have been kidding myself that Chad's situation is not responsible for my recent heart problems. I can't sleep - my emotions are similar to those during the early days of Chad's arrest. I think of the movie, *The Loneliness of the Long Distance Runner*, and I recognize for the first time that Northumberland County has decided that my family and I are not worth any consideration. I wait until 8:30 and try to call Jim at the office and then at home. No luck but I leave a message on his answering machine at home. I was going to use this day to study for the CFA exam, but I am too tired and my nerves are shot. The hours pass by and Jim hasn't returned my call. I wonder if, whoever did this purposely picked Friday to do their kidnapping, knowing how difficult it would be for anyone to track Chad over the weekend. I have visions of the Secret Service interrogating Chad. I try not to think of what Chad must be going through.

At around two o'clock, Debra, who had been resting, says she is going to call the Rockingham Jail. I think it is a waste of time but what harm could it do? Sure enough, they confirm Chad is there!

Debra asks if she can talk to the nurse in medical. She finds that after talking to her, that she is not allowed to give Chad any medicine without a doctor's orders and that the Sheriff's deputies did not bring any of his medicine! In other words, it has been two days since Chad has had any medicine; his last dosage was probably Thursday night. I think the State of Virginia must send

149

all of its sheriff's deputies to the same training school. We are powerless to do anything, of course. Debra explains to the nurse that Chad is paranoid schizophrenic and without his medicine, he turns suicidal. The nurse tells Debra that she will try to see what she can do and to give her a call back tomorrow.

After Debra hangs up, she has a funny look on her face. She looks at me and says she has been praying to herself for the past two hours, asking the Lord to please help her find her son and, out of nowhere an inner voice tells her *Rockingham*. It is good to know that at least one of us is close to the Lord.

We now at least know where he is. The question is why is he there? Our attorneys had assured us that the Rockingham charges were taken care of. I remember that Chad had told me that the warrant had said he was to appear in court Tuesday the 8th. We wait a few more hours hanging around the phone, hoping to hear from Chad or the attorneys. I try Jim's home once again; the answering machine has been turned off. We go to bed that night, still hoping that someone will call and that somehow the nurse has gotten permission to give Chad some medicine.

SUNDAY, JANUARY 6TH

This would prove to be another excruciating day. We wait in vain for the attorneys to call. Debra calls the Rockingham Jail and has found that they are still not giving him his medicine. They do tell her that they have moved him to isolation under observation. Chad must be slowly but surely feeling the effects of being off his medication, and schizophrenia and his obsessive-compulsive disorder are taking over. He must be scared to death.

I call Jim in the evening and leave him a message on the answering machine letting him know that we have located Chad in the Rockingham Jail. Debra has about had it with our attorneys.

MONDAY, JANUARY 7TH

At 8:45 AM I call Jim's secretary and tell her what has happened and that it is imperative that I get a hold of either Jim or Bill. At around 9:30 AM his secretary calls me back and says that Jim is in court, but as soon as he gets out he is going to the Northern Neck Regional Jail to see what has happened. He will give me a call around lunchtime. She tells me that Bill had

150

supposedly worked out something with the Rockingham Commonwealth's Attorney to prevent this from happening.

I call the clerk of the Rockingham District Court, and she is polite enough as I tell her that Chad was not supposed to be there. She tells me that she has nothing in her file to indicate otherwise and that his court hearing is scheduled for Tuesday at 1:00 PM. She also tells me that it was not U.S. Marshals that transported Chad, it was the Sheriff's deputies from Rockingham County. If only the Northern Neck Regional Jail would have told us that.

My friend Jim Spiess calls and says that he told a friend about what had happened on Sunday and his friend said he was going to find out what was going on. He called Jim today and said that Chad had been transported to Rockingham to stand trial for prior charges, and he would be returned home today. He almost got it right, and I'm impressed that he could discover the details while Debra and I could not. The bureaucratic system has no consideration for families of the accused.

I never hear from Jim, and around 4:00 PM his secretary calls and tells me that Jim is still working on it. She leaves me with the impression that he is trying to stop it from happening.

I talk with Dad that night. We both can't get over how this could have happened without either us or our attorneys being notified. We also wonder who dropped the ball in Rockingham. Dad mentions that this is something that the Judge ought to hear when Chad goes to trial here. I find it amazing that the people who I trust the least now are the police and those who make up our court systems.

Still, Jim does not call.

TUESDAY, JANUARY 8TH

I awake with great apprehension. I am hoping that Jim has been successful in stopping the worthless hearing and Chad is on his way back. I keep expecting the attorneys to call me to give me an update. Silly me! Finally, around 11:00 AM, I call and ask to speak with either one of them. Bill comes on the line and sounds angry and tells me that he had it arranged with the ASAP people to stop this from happening and that he called the guy and the guy more or less said that the courts do what they want. In other words, Chad's trial is proceeding as scheduled at 1:00 PM. He will appear in the court surrounded by strangers, with no family, friends, or legal representation. I feel awful, I shut my office door and I want to cry, but the tears won't come.

I call Debra and at the sound of her voice, the tears start to fall as I explain to her what has happened. How could they have done this when he didn't even have any representation?

I call the Rockingham court clerk at about 3:45 PM to see what has happened. She says that she doesn't have the full report on her screen, but it looks like the charges have been dismissed with the possible exception of the marijuana charge, which hasn't been updated yet.

I have to work late and, wouldn't you know it, Chad called from the Rockingham Jail. Debra was at home and took the call. What a relief to finally get to talk to him! Debra said he sounded fine, and he mentioned that the Rockingham Judge was nice to him.

Between what the court clerk told me and Chad's description of the Judge, we go to bed feeling much better.

WEDNESDAY, JANUARY 9TH

Our euphoria doesn't last long. I call the clerk again this morning to get the final outcome of the hearing. She tells me that he was found guilty and that he owes the court $250 for court charges. "What do you mean guilty? You told me yesterday that the charges had been dismissed." She replies that the charge of being intoxicated in public was dismissed, but he was found guilty of being in possession of marijuana! She also says that the failure to comply with ASAP has been dismissed because he was found guilty. The marijuana charge would have been dismissed if he had finished the ASAP program. How could he! Damn it! He was being held in jail without bond. He had been fully compliant with the program until his arrest. I ask her "Do you mean to tell me that he will now have this on his record for the rest of his life?" Her reply is yes. I guess the Judge and his court got their pound of flesh. God help anyone who doesn't appear in your court when scheduled! Right Judge? I guess it doesn't matter that when he did this he was fighting demons and hallucinations that you and I can only imagine!

I give Bill a call as requested to let him know how it turned out. He confirms that the charge will be on Chad's record forever, but he has got more serious things to worry about. Bill says that

152

Jim is writing a letter to both jails complaining that Chad was not given any of his medicine. It is small consolation. The sad thing is that there is no telling how much of a setback this is going to be for Chad, being off his medicine for almost a full week. I hope it is not like we are starting over.

At around lunchtime I call the Rockingham Jail to see if Chad is still there; he is not. Hopefully, that means that he is on his way to the Northern Neck. At 5:00 PM I call the Northern Neck Jail and confirm that Chad is there.

Debra tells me that her friends at work tell her that the Northumberland newspapers have featured Chad on the front page and, once again, the articles are vicious.

FRIDAY, JANUARY 11TH

We both go to visit Chad. It goes smoothly this morning, as it only takes about fifteen minutes to check in and for them to bring Chad. It is not easy conversing with him, as he is now getting used to the medicine again and is pretty much knocked out. He will not establish eye contact, a sure sign that being without his medicine has had a big impact. I tell Chad we are sorry that no one was there for him in Rockingham. He mentions again that the Judge was pretty nice. I ask him does he know what the verdict was and he replies that everything was dismissed. I explain to him that isn't the case. He was found guilty of the marijuana charge and it's on his permanent record. Chad is surprised. He had no idea that was the outcome! He explains to me that he told the Judge that he was in compliance with ASAP until his arrest. Chad had no business being there. As far as I am concerned, the Judge and his cohorts took advantage of a mentally ill teenager. We will find out later that one of the cohorts is Sheriff Middleton, who seems to be doing everything in his power to make Chad look as bad as he can.

As I return to work, I stop and get the newspapers. Sure enough, Chad is on the front page of the *Northumberland Echo*, and it is the fourth time since his arrest. Even the title of the article is misleading as it claims; "Old cases haunt robbery suspect." There is only the one case, but heh why not, let's make it plural so we can sell more newspapers. The beginning of the article is cruel, starting, "Short of being dead, Chad L. Wegkamp probably has the best defense he could ask for to a recent charge

153

of failing to appear in a Rockingham County court. He's been in jail in the Northern Neck." The article is consistent with the others as it sensationalizes the story, leaving out those facts that would show that there is another side.

What is interesting about this article is it now leaves me with no doubt that Sheriff Middleton has been very proactive in keeping this case in the headlines. This newspaper had to go to press by Monday Night. It states that Sheriff Middleton was sent a failure to appear warrant by the Rockingham County the week before, and for the fourth time it sings the praises of the Sheriff's Department for their role in Chad's arrest. The fact that we and our attorney's didn't really even know what was going on for sure until that Monday leaves me to believe that Middleton told the newspapers the whole story while his office told us they didn't know anything about it. My guess is that his plan was to get Chad up there before any of us knew a thing about it.

What is even more astounding is that the newspaper takes credit for the role they played, stating "Wegkamp was due to appear in the Rockingham County court in connection with his treatment....When contacted by the *Echo* Friday, court personnel in Harrisonburg were unaware of Wegkamp's incarceration and indicated the court would make the necessary arrangements to have him transported to the court for the hearing." I thought newspapers were only supposed to report the news, not create it.

I can't help but wonder if it was the actions of Middleton and the *Echo* that circumvented the efforts made by our attorneys to put the Rockingham case on hold and caused Chad to appear before the court without his attorney.

CHAPTER 14

ANOTHER POSTPONEMENT

Debra and I are excited as we travel to Richmond to meet with Dr. Peck, the new psychiatrist that our attorneys have obtained. He is well known in the mental health field, and we are hoping that he will take the time to listen to us. I feel like he probably is the only realistic hope we have in getting Chad back to normal. Debra hates it when I still say it might be possible for Chad to be normal again. She feels we need to face the facts and realize that Chad will never be normal. I keep clinging to those articles that state, if you can treat it early, the chances for almost full recovery are good.

Dr. Peck is a distinguished gentleman. Short in stature. He is very cordial and easy to talk to, and he actually talks to us for almost two hours. It is great therapy for Debra and me; not only does he want to hear everything we have to say, but also he wants to hear it in detail. He is very interested in the time-line of events leading from the first time we suspected something was wrong until the present. He then has us backtrack, using the benefit of hindsight, as to when we think Chad was first struck with a psychotic episode. I tell him I believe it was shortly after he returned to JMU after Christmas break the year before. I had picked him up in Richmond after he had ridden a bus from JMU, and I remember that he had sat with a friend on the bus and they seemed to hit it off pretty well. During the break, Chad was quite helpful around the house and had even done some painting without being asked, just saying that he wanted to do something for us. Little did we know that it would be the last time we would spend with Chad before the illness took over.

Dr. Peck states that the time-line shows that Chad, once stricken, became progressively worse. The fact that he still believes that all of his problems will go away once he takes care of his scrotum shows that the psychosis is still present and certainly can't be treated while he is in jail. He explains that he plans on seeing Chad two or three times before the trial and does tell us that the attorneys and Chad are really his clients. Yea, I know, we just pay the bills. He does confirm; however, that when he is done with his examination he will certainly recommend a course of treatment for Chad. These words mean a lot to Debra and me. I am also pleased because I think Dr. Peck is interested and he is looking forward to meeting Chad.

TUESDAY, JANUARY 15TH

Today, Chad is being transported to meet with Dr. Peck. I wonder throughout the day how it's going. I don't have to wait long to find out. Chad calls that night and tells us all about it. He says he spent over four hours with Dr. Peck. He took a test with over 500 questions and spent a lot of time talking with the doctor. I ask Chad if the deputies were present in the room, and he said they stepped outside shortly after arriving. Chad didn't seem to be too excited about the whole thing, though he does mention that he likes Dr. Peck. He also mentions that Jim Breeden had stopped by the day before and gave him a briefing on what was going on.

It is actually beginning to feel like we are making some progress.

THURSDAY, JANUARY 17TH

I have a checkup today with Dr. Duer. They draw some blood and check my heart and inform me that it is still fibrillating. I mention to Dr. Duer that my allergies have been extremely bad and she prescribes some Allegra and a prescription nose-spray. I haven't mentioned it to anyone, but I have been so stuffed-up at night that between the fibrillating and the allergies I have been short of breath and not getting much sleep. The doctor tells me to go ahead and have Dr. Mann schedule the electrical shock treatment.

Chad gives us a call and wants to talk about the distance-learning programs that are available. It's good to hear him talk in a goal-oriented manner. He is impatient and wants to get started - yesterday. I tell him to be patient and wait and see what happens on February 26th. He wants to know if it is possible for him to receive financial aid while incarcerated. I tell him I will call a few schools to find out.

FRIDAY, JANUARY 18TH

Debra goes alone to visit Chad. She reports that he was alert and that she had a good visit with him.

I call the financial aid office of one of the schools that Chad is interested in. The girl I talked to is very friendly at first, but once I tell her that I'm inquiring on the behalf of my son who is incarcerated, her demeanor changes. She informs me that there is no financial aid available for anyone in prison and quickly hangs up on me.

SATURDAY, JANUARY 19TH

Debra has rented from our local library two videos dealing with schizophrenia. The videos are outdated, but we find them very interesting as they deal directly with individuals who have the illness. It is interesting that all of the individuals are trying desperately to make some sort of meaningful contribution to society. One woman has been successful to the point of having found employment. She is only able to work about five-hour days before it becomes too overwhelming for her. She states that it takes just about everything she has just to get to work. She is only able to concentrate on one thing at a time, so simple things like taking a bath, brushing her teeth, and taking out the garbage often get neglected. She just struggles to get to work.

One of the older gentlemen quotes Shakespeare, summarizing his life as "Sound and fury, signifying absolutely nothing!" Another young man who is featured ends up committing suicide.

The videos don't paint a pleasant picture in relation to Chad's future, but I remind myself that the videos are old and a lot of progress has been made since then.

SUNDAY, JANUARY 20TH

I go to Church this morning but leave immediately after sacrament meeting. I have promised Debra that I would take her to see the movie "A Beautiful Mind" which is based on the life story of John Nash who won a Nobel Prize. He was paranoid schizophrenic. The movie does a great job of portraying the effects the illness has on the human mind and its ramifications for the victim and those close to him. Russell Crowe and Jennifer

Connelly are both excellent. On the way home, Debra and I compare the symptoms portrayed in the movie to the symptoms manifested by Chad. Many of the symptoms are the same, but the movie doesn't show Nash as having some of the more severe symptoms that Chad has shown. Unlike Chad, Nash apparently wasn't obsessed with a bodily function.

Chad calls in the late afternoon and gets upset when I ask him twice if he is taking his medicine. He is further agitated when I tell him that there is no financial aid for someone who is incarcerated. I have to watch myself at times like these, because I feel like yelling at him that maybe he shouldn't have robbed a bank!

We watch the Golden Globes award show. This is not something I would normally watch but I want to see how "A Beautiful Mind" makes out. It wins best picture, best actor, and best supporting actress. On a talk show the next day, Russell Crowe is quoted as saying that it was just entertainment, they were not trying to make a statement, but he hopes that maybe people will show a little more compassion for those who are mentally ill. *Amen to that.* I certainly know that the local sheriff's office needs to see it - not that it would do any good.

MONDAY, JANUARY 21ST

I have the day off because it is Martin Luther King Day. I decide to go for a little canoe ride to see how I make out. There is no breeze in the cool morning air and the river is like a mirror. The ride is peaceful and my heart seems to take the exertion pretty well.

TUESDAY, JANUARY 22ND

Ali is walking between classes at the High School this morning when she recognizes one of the deputies who was in our home the night of the search warrant. He focuses on her and stares at her the whole time it takes her to walk the corridor and to pass him. Once again, I'm impressed by the bravery shown by a member of the Sheriff's Department. I ask Ali to describe him and she replies, "Dad, they all look alike; short, fat, and bald."

FRIDAY, JANUARY 25th

I accompany Debra to see Chad during visitation hours. We haven't talked for almost three days because of the twelve-hour swing shifts Debra has been working. We talk about the Sheriff's Department and I express that I think I am going to file charges. Debra just wants to forget about the whole thing and says that the facts are that Chad robbed the bank and most members of the community consider him dangerous and the deputies courageous. I tell her that the fact Chad robbed the bank did not give them the right to treat us the way they did, and one reason they keep getting away with their bullying is everyone takes the attitude that you are taking. The other thought I have is, *what is going to stop them from harassing Chad and us in the future. Hell! Ali can't even walk down the corridor of her high school without being harassed.*

Chad is pretty much knocked out by his medicine, but physically he looks pretty good. He says that he does 300 pushups every other day. He is now reading the last book I sent him about Abraham Lincoln. We talk about his ability to take college classes in the future and the fact that at least a little more than a month from now, we will finally know what is going to happen.

SATURDAY, JANUARY 26TH

We get the bill from the attorneys today; it is almost $20,000. In addition, we get the bill from the psychiatrist it is over $3,000. It is painful, stressful, and discouraging. There are so many things that need to be repaired on the house. It is all going to have to wait. The billing reflects charges through January 15th. Who knows how much more it's going to be, given that Chad's trial is still coming.

Deana gives us a call, as it is her birthday tomorrow. She thanks me for the card that I sent her and tells me to watch the Utah Jazz and Sacramento Kings play on national TV. Her husband is taking her to the game, and she will be sitting close to the floor behind one of the benches. We watch the game but never do see Deana, as the broadcast shows very little of the fans.

MONDAY, JANUARY 28TH

A funny thing happens on the way to work. Less than a mile from our house, there is a traffic accident. As I pass the accident, Chuckie and one of the other deputies who was in our house is standing on the roadside. As I pass by, Chuckie quickly looks away. I guess I'm a little more intimidating than my wife. I can't wait for the 26th to be over.

Chad calls that night and is excited about the information I've sent him about the distance learning possibilities. I also tell him that I think things are going well for his defense and that seems to lift his spirits.

FRIDAY, FEBRUARY 1ST

Debra goes to see Chad during visiting hours. Chad is in one of his arrogant moods, which soon angers Debra. She leaves upset. We talk at length that night on just how we are going to treat Chad once he gets home and just what we can expect. I think he needs to feel loved while he struggles with his illness, but at the same time there has got to be some ground rules. Our greatest fear is that the illness will consume him, and he will be impossible to handle in a normal home environment. I keep clinging to the articles I've read that claim if you can treat a schizophrenic with medications, they can return to a normal life.

I subscribe to *Sports Illustrated* and one of this week's articles tells about a college basketball star and his mother dealing with a father who is mentally ill. I thought it was going to be a "feel good" story demonstrating how a family has successfully surmounted the odds and maintained a close relationship. It is just the opposite. The mother divorces the physically abusive father, who now "is frequently been spotted riding his bicycle around town looking unkempt and jabbering with voices only he could hear." The article further states that schizophrenics suffer from delusions and hallucinations and become chronically confused, withdrawn and, in some cases, violent. I sincerely hope that this description will not fit my son ten years from now. I will certainly do everything in my power to keep it from happening.

SUNDAY, FEBRUARY 10th

We have a nice phone conversation with Chad today. He is feeling the effects, now that the 26th is fast approaching. He says that on December 18th, when it was determined that his next hearing wouldn't be until February 26th, it seemed like an eternity to him. He finds himself getting anxious now and is eager to get with the attorneys to ask them some questions.

It occurs to me after the phone conversation that it has been six months now since his arrest and the authorities here in Northumberland County still haven't allowed us any physical contact with Chad...I'm sure all of this is harmful for someone who is mentally ill. It is just amazing just how unaccountable everyone is. We couldn't place blame no matter how hard we tried.

TUESDAY, FEBRUARY 12TH

I go to the hospital to under-go some testing of my heart. I am given an EKG and then I'm hooked up to some machine that allows the nurse doing the monitoring to look at my heart. She says I have a beautiful heart! Take that Brad Pitt! The whole thing takes a couple of hours and the doctor tells me they should have all the results within a few days.

FRIDAY, FEBRUARY 15TH

We go see Chad and he looks good. He is preoccupied with what is going to happen on the 26th. He has a lot of questions, many of which we can't answer. I tell him that the Judge may even have some questions for him, so he needs to look his best and to make sure that he has been taking his medicine.

We get a letter from Dad. He tells me that their prayers and thoughts are with us, and they are hoping for the best on the 26th.

TUESDAY, FEBRUARY 19th

Chad calls us tonight and is still asking us the same questions that he was asking during our visit last week. He is afraid that something will go wrong. A number of his questions concern Dr. Peck's report and whether anyone has heard anything.

It is a good question, as we have not heard anything and the trial date is getting closer.

THURSDAY, FEBRUARY 21ST

Jim gives me a call in the afternoon and says he has gotten some feedback from Dr. Peck. He says that Chad is psychotic, delusional, suicidal, and in danger of mutilating himself. The report states that it's a severe case of paranoid schizophrenia. Dr. Peck also says that Chad has been sick for a very long time. While Jim is talking, I find that I can no longer concentrate on what he is saying as I try to fight back the tears. These are not exactly the words a parent likes to hear. I can't get the words, *He is capable of mutilating himself and has been sick for a very long time,* out of my mind. Jim says that he will get us a copy of the report as soon as he receives it.

As I hang up the phone, I have to shut my office door until I can regain my composure. My thoughts start flashing back as I mentally search for clues that maybe Debra and I should have picked up on. Certain memories come flashing back to me, some are even of Chad in early childhood. I'm not sure that I want to tell Debra this. Hindsight is always 20/20.

FRIDAY, FEBRUARY 22ND

I go alone to visit Chad today, and it is a good visit. Chad tells me as far as the 26th is concerned, he is hoping for the best and expecting the worst. Chad says that once he does get out, the first thing he is going to do is kiss the ground, climb a tree, have a milkshake, and watch a movie on TV.

I have written a letter to the Judge in Rockingham County and copied the county clerk. The letter is critical of how the county handled Chad's case and asks for accountability for what happened. I close the letter by asking the following questions:

Is it true that, as the *Northumberland Echo* states, it was their phone call to your court personnel that precipitated the actions that were taken? If so, how could this happen? What jurisdiction do they have?

How can a phone call from another local county's newspaper, which isn't any better than a tabloid, override the efforts made by Chad's attorneys with both the Rockingham County's Commonwealth Attorney and the ASAP offices?

Why do you think the Northumberland County's Sheriff's Department lied to us when we called them and asked them if they knew anything about our son's whereabouts?

Do you realize that when the transfer was made, Chad was taken off his medicine for almost a week and that he has been diagnosed as both suicidal and delusional?

Last question. Do you have any idea how much harder it is going to be for Chad to bounce back, now that his permanent record reflects a misdemeanor?

I conclude the letter by saying; "I'm sorry, but I think that Rockingham County dropped the ball, big time. You were not dealing with a rebellious youth. You were dealing with a family tragedy." I also include in the letter a copy of my diary for the time period covered and a copy of the newspaper article. I don't expect an answer, but I want them to know that Chad was more than just a case file. I don't have any concern that this letter could impact his case in Northumberland, but to be safe, I wait until Friday to mail it.

SUNDAY, FEBRUARY 24TH

Chad gives us a call today and, with the court date two days away, he says he is very nervous. He says that Brother Wilson has paid him a visit and that they're still studying the Old Testament. He says that time is passing by excruciatingly slow. It strikes me how good Chad sounds now. *I wish he could have been on Zyprexa while at JMU.*

MONDAY, FEBRUARY 25TH

I get a big surprise as I arrive to work. In my parking space is a large black tombstone with the wording, "Reserved for the Old Fart." It's my fiftieth birthday tomorrow, and it looks like it's going to be celebrated today! Later on that morning, we have a birthday cake, and the kitchen is decorated with dead limbs and there is a flowerpot full of dead weeds. I am given some pretty funny gag gifts including a Yankee baseball cap with the words "Old Fart" in bright, multicolored letters that have been sewed on to the cap. After we eat our cake, we go and admire my tombstone. Thinking that is the end of it, I go back to my office and find it has been totally papered in black and purple crape. There are black and purple balloons tied to everything, and there is a life-sized grim reaper standing over my desk! It gets kind of weird sitting at my desk trying to work with this grim reaper staring at me throughout the day! It's been a lot of fun. It's a day I won't soon forget.

Jim calls and lets me know that they have received the report from Dr. Peck. The report agrees with Dr. Gomez's report but goes into considerably more analysis. McKenney has been given a copy of the report and Jim says he will be spending the rest of the day preparing for tomorrow. The phone call doesn't last more than a minute.

Debra and I are both pretty nervous right now. It is approaching 9:00 PM and no one has called to say that the trial has been postponed. It actually looks like we are going to have a trial tomorrow!

TUESDAY, FEBRUARY 26TH

We arrive early and find a large number of people from our church are already there. It looks like today is the day! We all file into the courtroom and wait as the court gets started on the docket. Judge Taliaferro does not come across as being a compassionate judge. The judgments he is handing out seem harsh. A boy of about Chad's age is given eight years for stealing a two hundred-dollar lawnmower! The sentence will be suspended provided the boy successfully completes some sort of juvenile "get straight" camp. But still, if he doesn't, he will get eight years!

Chad is announced as the next case on the docket. There is a scurrying of the guards, and Jim comes through the back door and heads straight towards us. I don't like the looks of this. Jim leans over the railing and tells us that he just finished meeting with Chad telling him that the case was being postponed! I can't believe it! I just can't believe it! Jim says that McKenney feels that there was not enough time to study the psychiatric report submitted by Dr. Peck. *I don't give a rat's ass about what McKenney feels, isn't high time for you to start sticking up for my son, who just happens to be your client?* is the first thought that goes through my mind. This is killing us! It has been more than six months since Chad robbed the bank. Six months that are

164

critical to salvaging Chad. As usual though, it appears that Jim is not going to do anything about it. Debra's jaw is clenched and she is staring straight ahead. She doesn't even want to look at Jim.

The next five minutes are perfunctory. Chad is brought out, I can tell by the look on his face that he is not happy. He stands in front of the Judge, as McKenney asks for the postponement explaining that he has not had enough time to review the report. The Judge rubber stamps McKenney's request and Chad is led away. Jim just stands there, barely saying a word. So far I have paid these guys nineteen thousand dollars. The next trial date is set for March 26th.

I am too angry to say anything to Jim and, with all the money we have invested with them, we can only hope they know what the hell they're doing. We meet with Jim for a few minutes after. He downplays the significance of the postponement, saying that things are still going according to plan and that this is a minor glitch. I wonder if Chad feels the same! It's an empty feeling on the ride home. We know no more about what is going to happen to Chad than we did when he was arrested.

We go over to the Dunn's for the birthday party they are giving me. A lot of people from the church are there, including just about everyone who was at the court this morning. What a nice gesture! I know everyone is trying to help Debra and I get our minds off our worries, at least for one night. At one point though, the topic of conversation settles around today's court proceedings. They talk about how harsh the Judge seems and the sentencing for the kid who stole the lawnmower. One member says she can't believe how they can keep doing this to Chad and what a "hard-ass" the Judge seems to be. It is interesting to see how others are viewing the case, and it's nice to know that there are at least a few others who are having the same thoughts I've been having. Just about everyone comments on how good Chad looked. We have a great time and it was a nice break.

CHAPTER 15

SANDBAGGED

I am shocked to get a phone call from Judge John Paul of Rockingham County. He indicates that he has received my letter and asks me if I have time to discuss it. I tell him yes and then he says he would be more than happy to try and address my questions. He states that his office had no idea that Chad had been charged with a bank robbery or that anyone had tried to contact them concerning Chad's case. He said that if I were to investigate the court's actions, I would find that they were pretty routine. When Chad did not show for his December 18th trial, a summons was issued to insure that Chad would be present for the January 8th trial. He also said that the summons was issued to Northumberland County because their records showed the county as being Chad's primary residence. He even gave me the name of the Northumberland County officer who received the summons. So the answer to my question as to whether the Northumberland County Sheriff's office knew where Chad was on January 8th was a resounding *yes*.

He also states that while the drunk in public charges were dropped, he had no choice on the misdemeanor marijuana charge because the condition of his probation was he had to successfully complete the ASAP program.

We then get into a discussion about the events that led to Chad's arrest. How Debra and I knew absolutely nothing about the "free fall" that Chad was in and how nobody at the school or his dorm tried to contact us to let us know that something was seriously wrong with Chad. I told the Judge we didn't even know about his arrest until about two weeks after it happened. The Judge says he serves on several committees in Harrisonburg, where this is a frequent topic. He says he has been trying for years to get JMU more proactive in this area, but they have refused, even arguing that they could be violating privacy laws if they did.

He assures me that, unfortunately, what has happened to Chad happens all too often in this town.

I then ask him about the newspaper claim that they facilitated Chad being transferred up there. The Judge sidesteps me on this one saying that as far as he knew no one had been contacted in his office and the term "court personnel" could be just about anyone in the court system.

The Judge is polite and seems sincere when he wishes us the best for Chad's recovery and tells me "if anyone from your attorney's office had contacted his office directly, Chad would have never been brought up here on these "penny-ante charges."

I can only shake my head after the phone conversation. I still think someone dropped the ball up in Rockingham, but now I suspect that it was probably someone in the ASAP system. I'll probably never know, and as far as my attorney's are concerned, apparently nineteen thousand dollars doesn't buy much.

SATURDAY, MARCH 2ND

I am reading a copy of Peck's report. There is a section where Chad mentions that he was seriously contemplating suicide the day of his examination with Dr. Duck, the urologist he saw last year. I remember Debra telling me that Chad had told Jim something similar at one time. We compare Dr. Peck's notes to what we know and come up the following scenario. Chad had made up his mind prior to his visit with the urologist that he would commit suicide that afternoon if the doctor said there was nothing wrong with his scrotum that morning. Debra was scheduled to work the afternoon shift, and Ali and I would also be out of the house. Chad was going to get in the bathtub and slit his wrists! He wanted to do it in the bathtub because he didn't want to create a mess for us to clean up! Debra remembers she was going to work that afternoon, but at the last minute, she got someone to work it for her. *My God!!*

TUESDAY, MARCH 5TH

I get a call late that night from the Dunn's asking me if I have seen the paper. *Oh, no, not again,* I think to myself." But I'm kind of cavalier about it because I don't think the paper could do much more harm to us than what they have already done. I couldn't have been more mistaken. What Bill describes to me next is not only unbelievable, it is also immoral, if not illegal. Somehow, the *Northumberland Echo* has gotten hold of Chad's psychiatric report, and has published on the front of their newspaper excerpts that they think are the juiciest. Bill starts to read to me parts of the article, I ask him to stop and thank him for calling. I break the news to Debra. She is shocked and just says, "I can't take much more of this." I go to bed that night overwhelmed with how cruel and callous the editor is and wondering how he got his hands on the report. Surely, something that sensitive can't be a public document, and it hadn't even been admitted as evidence. Thoughts of suing the editor's ass occur to me. I don't care if the 1st Amendment fully protects him, maybe I can at least cause him some discomfort and at least force up his insurance premiums. I am also wondering if someone from McKenney's office is responsible.

WEDNESDAY, MARCH 6TH

I get a copy of the newspaper. It is hard to believe, but even after the passage of six months, the article is the lead article and it is one-inch bold type proclaiming "Was alleged bank robber delusional?" The article reveals the most personal problems that Chad has been dealing with. The article goes into great length describing how Chad is obsessed with his scrotum and implies that he has been a heavy drug user for years, which is not true. The article also makes a point that Chad carries himself oddly due to the deformity and tried to operate on himself. The article really make's him sound like a total nut case. While I would agree that someone who has been diagnosed as paranoid schizophrenic fits the public's description as someone who is "nuts," does that mean that their innermost secrets deserve to published and embellished on the front of the newspaper? How humiliating this is for my son, who grew up here and has to return here once this whole ordeal is over.

Debra calls me from work, furious. "How can they get away with this? Did McKenney let this report out or is it all our lawyer's fault." I think the answer is the latter, unfortunately. My guess is they forgot to pull the report out of the court file, making it fully available to anyone who cared to look for it. I remember Bill telling me that he had pulled Dr. Gomez's report from the court file for the expressed purpose of not allowing the media to get access to it.

I place a call to Jim to get his reaction.

Chad calls and asks us if we have seen the article. We tell him, yes. Chad says that several copies of it are circulating in the jail and he has been the brunt of a lot of name-calling and cruel jokes. I can tell he is fighting to keep his composure on the phone. I feel helpless. I wish there was some way I could strike a loved one of the editor's with schizophrenia and place them in that jailhouse. He would get a clue of how it feels and learn about the constant terror a schizophrenic has to deal with and what it is like to have the local newspaper editor feed off the illness of your loved one. Chad asks me how could this happen and comments on how humiliated he is. I try to calm him down and tell him it will blow over before he knows it. I ask him has he been taking his medicine, because I have a fear that he might try to commit suicide.

FRIDAY, MARCH 8TH

Debra and I both go to see Chad. We do our best to try and cheer him up. He seems to be doing okay, and we spend most of the time talking about what is going to happen on the 26th.

Jim has yet to return my call. I will spend Saturday and Sunday studying for the CFA exam. It is somewhat therapeutic for me, because it helps me keep my mind off Chad.

The Andrea Yates's trial is in the news but I purposely try to ignore it. It's too depressing for me.

MONDAY, MARCH 11TH

I try to call Jim again today. I want to talk to him about the newspaper article and stress to him that we can't take much more and that we want the 26th to be it. I also want to ask him for copies of the search warrants, for the umpteenth time, and to stress to him that not once have I heard anyone in court go to bat for Chad, and I'm expecting it on the 26th.

Dad calls me and tells me about an article in *Newsweek*. The topic of schizophrenia has made the cover and it is the lead article. The combination of the Andrea Yates's trial and the movie

"A Beautiful Mind" has made schizophrenia a hot topic. Dad says the article is a good one and strongly encourages me to get a copy.

TUESDAY, MARCH 12TH

Jim finally returns my call. He seems shocked about the newspaper article and says he didn't know anything about it. I don't know quite what to think - the article is now a week old! Jim admits that this is unfortunate and recognizes the harm it has done. He says he will look into it and give me a call back. Please excuse me if I don't hold by breath!

WEDNESDAY, MARCH 13TH

Andrea Yates is found guilty today of murdering her five children. I watch the news that night and I, along with millions of others, are shocked at how quickly the jurors reached their decision.

I receive a copy of a letter that Jim has sent Dr. Peck informing him that portions of his report concerning Chad have been published on the front page of the local newspaper. Jim makes the following remark, "I just found out today that last week the *Northumberland Echo*, the local newspaper (which paper gives real meaning to the term yellow journalism), printed excerpts from your report. The *Echo* loves to sensationalize stories, and, apparently, the article about Chad was no exception. Naturally, the reporter emphasized the bad aspects of Chad's life and focused little on the real mental health issues. I, frankly, have no idea how your report got into the hands of the reporter."

Personally, I think the editor is a bit of a joke and I would be embarrassed if I owned this newspaper.

SATURDAY, MARCH 16TH

I have been watching the news coverage of the Andrea Yates trial for the past few days and I find it difficult to understand how some others feel about the case. One juror is quoted as saying that she knew without a doubt that Andrea Yates could tell right from wrong. She knew this because Andrea made detailed journal entries planning the execution of her children, and she called the police after she had killed them. If I had been on that jury, I would have interpreted these facts totally different.

What sane mother, who dearly loves her children, is going to detail in her journal how she is going to kill them and then call the police immediately after. When loved ones are murdered by other loved ones, it is always a crime of passion or insanity. I believe that Andrea carefully and methodically killed her children for the very reason she said she did, to save their souls. Is this someone who can clearly tell the difference between right and wrong?

Some of the ultraconservative "talking heads' and their guests applauded the decision, saying that Andrea got what she deserved. Is the world really this "black and white?"

I also find it disturbing that the jurors were not allowed to know that if they found Andrea not guilty, she would be sent to a mental hospital. They were under the impression that if they found Andrea not guilty, she would be set free!

The ramifications of this for Chad scare me. Virginia has the same insanity defense laws as Texas. I am also afraid that many of the people in Heathsville would be as harsh and unforgiving as some in Texas, especially if they believe everything they have been reading in the *Northumberland Echo*. How, in the United States of America in the year 2002 can the most defenseless, the mentally ill, be treated without compassion, fairness, or justice?

SUNDAY, MARCH 24TH

I attend church this morning. A number of the members who usually come to support Chad when he appears in court are not there. The Spaulding's youngest son has a life threatening brain tumor and they will not be able to make it as they attend to his care. I do not see the Dunns today either. The stake authorities are here as it is Branch Conference. Everyone is pretty busy, but Talmage catches me as I'm about to leave and gives us a beautiful framed photograph taken by his brother. It is a picture of an old sawmill located in the countryside. It is so serene and beautiful. Why can't life be a little more like that picture?

Later that afternoon I get a call from the Georgetown University Hospital. It is Bill Dunn. He tells me they are going to cut him open tomorrow. His cancer is apparently back. He actually apologizes for not being able to make Chad's trial. *God, I hope he is all right.*

Chad calls soon after Bill and is anxious to know if we have heard anything from the attorneys. We haven't which, I suppose, is good news. We talk about his chances on Tuesday. All of us are getting excited that this portion of the process may be coming to an end. I tell him to call us tomorrow night in case we hear anything from the attorneys.

MONDAY, MARCH 25TH

At 4:30 in the afternoon I get a call from Jim. The news is not good to say the least, but why am I not surprised. Basically Jim has been sandbagged by his good buddy McKenney and, in the process, so have we. McKenney has, all of sudden, decided to go after Chad showing no mercy whatsoever. He will ask for a postponement of the trial so he can get his own psychiatric evaluation done. Gone are all the promises about how he would rely on the expert opinions of Dr. Peck and Dr. Gomez. Remember, it was McKenney who asked for a postponement of the last trial because he didn't have enough time to evaluate the psychiatric report, and now he is asking for another two months. *Think about it Mr. Prosecutor, you are directly responsible in making sure that Chad has yet again been denied proper treatment. Why don't you just keep postponing and denying him bail until this illness rots his entire brain!* I am surprised to hear Jim actually say during the conversation that he had been sandbagged. He tells me that the Judge will certainly grant McKenney the extension - no surprise! He tells me that he is concerned how Chad will take this - its getting funnier all the time - and he will suggest to the court that he gets counseling while he sits there for another two months. He mentions that the Andrea Yates's case and the last newspaper article have had a big impact on what has just happened. He tells me that Chad's case is at one o'clock tomorrow, and he will try to arrange it so we can meet with Chad. He will plan on meeting with us at 12:00. I have a lot of questions, but I'll wait until tomorrow.

When I hang up the phone, the realization that I've got to break this news to both Debra and Chad hits me. Debra reacts angrily and reiterates once again what a poor job our attorneys have been doing and how we should have gotten attorneys from Richmond who could have cared less about their relationships with the "good ol'boy" network here in Northumberland County.

172

We talk about what, if anything, can we do now. We also discuss how several of our friends have told us that McKenney has a reputation for being two-faced. It is well deserved.

Chad calls, and I am the one who has to break it to him. He is silent for a few seconds and then says, "I knew this was going to happen. Dad, I just want to get this over with." I try to explain to Chad that I know this is tough, but you got to keep hanging in there - the last thing you need is a felony record. Chad then asks how do I know that this next psychiatric report doesn't show up on the front of the newspapers. I tell him I know what he means and the thought has even crossed my mind that I wouldn't put it past McKenney to ask for another postponement because he hasn't had time to review the psychiatric report once he gets it! But we both agree that even the Judge must be getting tired of these delays, and it would be surprising if he let it happen again. Chad comes back to me again though and says that the end result is going to be the same and we might as well get it over. I tell Chad that it can't be much longer now and there is no guarantee how much prison time he will get. We keep talking about four years, but it could be more. That point does seem to cause Chad to pause, and then Debra gets on the phone and pleads with him not to tell Jim tomorrow that he wants it over. We know Jim would keep Chad from doing anything stupid, but it would be nice to have Chad on board while we fight this battle. Chad promises his mother that he'll do what we want him to do.

I have a good talk with Dad tonight. The fact that the prosecuting attorney has pulled a fast one on us means that all bets are off!

TUESDAY, MARCH 26TH

Debra, Ali, and I are all going to the trial and we stop to pick up a friend along the way. We are looking forward to seeing Chad and watching while McKenney explains why it is necessary to postpone the trial once again. We have a slew of questions for Jim.

We arrive at the appointed hour and don't have to wait long for Jim to appear. He takes us to a side office and starts discussing the case. After a few minutes of listening, I realize that Chad has already been brought out in court this morning! Jim acts like it is no big deal, apparently the court got through it's docket early, so they might as well take care of Chad's case now - never mind, that we and the rest of Chad's supporters are not there. Apparently they brought him out, quickly gave McKenney his extension, and then hauled Chad off. So much for Debra and me being able to see him. I look over at Debra, and see the surprise written on her face and decide not to say anything, because I'm too angry.

I do ask Jim why is so much attention being paid to what McKenney wants? Doesn't Jim carry the same weight as the prosecutor? Isn't the Judge supposed to be neutral? I also mention that if I was Chad's attorney, I would have very forcefully made the point that Chad's chances for full recovery are slipping away and why does the prosecution wait until now to call their own expert? They've had seven months!

Jim says that playing "hardball" at this point is not a wise decision. He explains that both the defense and the prosecution have the right to a jury trial. McKenney could insist on a jury trial and the chances of getting a sympathetic jury in the ultraconservative town of Heathsville would be "slim-to-none." Jim also states that juries are unpredictable, they tend not to consider medical evidence, because they don't understand it. Certainly the Andrea Yates's case and the O.J. Simpson case bear him out. The point is also made that if we were to go to a jury trial now, the case would be postponed even longer. In addition, the point system is not applicable to juries. They could sentence Chad anywhere from five years to life.

The next trial date has been set for May 21st. Jim mentions that maybe if a decision is not made on that date, he could try to get Chad out on bail. I look at Debra, and we both sadly shake our heads because there is no equity left in the house. Jim says maybe we can get a reduced bail. I ask Jim what he thinks our chances are now. He says that he is still cautiously optimistic and points out that we do have two psychiatrists who will both testify that Chad could not comprehend the consequences of his actions and couldn't tell the difference between right and wrong.

While we are talking, a deputy sticks his head in and says that there are a number of people out in lobby who are our friends inquiring about what is going on. I go out in the foyer and see that there has been another good turnout from our friends at church. I explain to them what has happened and thank them for coming.

As we return home, Debra and I both have an "empty" feeling and a better appreciation of how important it is to the bureaucracy that Chad is punished to the fullest extent of the law. Why are Christians in the "Bible belt" so unforgiving and so quick to judge?

CHAPTER 16

SHOCKED & BEWILDERED: YET ANOTHER POSTPONEMENT

THURSDAY, MARCH 28TH

For the past few days I've been wondering what to do next? I am so busy at work and trying to study for the exam, but I feel like maybe I don't have my priorities right. Shouldn't my number one priority be Chad? Is there anything that I can do now that will help his case? With McKenney having betrayed us, I do have a number of options available that I didn't have before.

I actually talked to a few people at the *Washington Post* but I don't get anywhere. Their answer is basically that they don't have enough circulation in this area to justifying running a local story. I do make the point that I think this could be a national story of great interest. One person seems interested but says let me talk to the editor, and I'll get back to you. They never get back to me. I am also surprised when I call the various national nonprofit organizations that deal with mental health. None of them offer much of anything. One organization says they don't get involved with criminal cases and another says you need to get a lawyer. Please don't ask me for any contributions!

I notice on the Internet that they are having a contest asking participants to vote on what they think is the best photograph of the year for 2001. One of the pictures is a thought-provoking photo of an eighteen year-old Indian girl being chained to a post outside a Muslim Tomb in India. The girl is mentally ill and her parents believe that by chaining her there, the healing powers of the tomb may eventually cure her, even if it takes years! The girl is begging for scraps of food as people pass. As uncivilized as this is, it does raise the question of whether we treat our mentally ill much better.

I saw Chad this morning. The lack of communication in the procedure is typical. They don't tell you which room to go to. I try the room where they normally bring the prisoners, where all of the phones actually work. I wait about fifteen minutes, but no Chad. I hear something over the speaker to the effect that Chad is in the other room. Sure enough, Chad is there waiting for me. I can barely hear him over the phone. I do get to visit with him for about forty-five minutes. Chad tells me some surprising things about what went on in court that Tuesday morning. Apparently, McKenney is really "out-for-blood" now; making noises about getting a jury trial. Chad even thought he had been successful, but I told him that Jim told us that the trial would still be held in front of the Judge.

Chad also mentioned that there were two dates being considered, May 7th and May 21st. To Chad's dismay, Jim pushed for the 21st date. I told him that Jim probably pushed for that date so McKenney wouldn't be able to ask for yet another delay. I am still irritated by the fact that all this was done prior to the appointed court time and before any of us who supported Chad were there. It almost makes you wonder if it was by design.

I get a call from Dr. Duer. My blood is thin enough now. I will be getting a call from Dr. Mann next week to setup the cardioversion.

Later that day I call some statewide family support groups and mental health groups trying to find anyone who would be able to help us. People are sympathetic but no luck.

MONDAY, APRIL 1ST

It is quarter-end at the bank, and we can barely keep our heads above water. The Bank's annual meeting is this Friday and the Board meeting is the following Monday. We have to close out the books and produce financial statements and management reports for the Bank and its affiliates, a total of six companies, by Friday.

I give Jim another call to see if I can get some feedback from him on what the U.S. Marshall's summons means. They put me through to his voice mail as always.

I am also waiting for the doctor to call and schedule my cardioversion.

TUESDAY, APRIL 2ND

Jim finally calls me and says that he has obtained a copy of the U.S. Marshall's summons and it is basically just them "staking-their-claim." They are not taking over the robbery case. This is what we thought was happening, but, still it's nice to finally get some confirmation. However, the way things are going, we still have that fear that the Marshall's could show up any minute and take Chad away.

Jim also mentions that I am not being "paranoid" about our phones being tapped. It is no coincidence that we started hearing the "clicking" noises around the same time that Chad was served his summons. He tells me that he thinks one of the reasons they are pursuing this is the fact that I am a banker. It would make for nice headlines for them. Oh brother! What grown men will do to further their own careers. You would think that "The Fed" would have bigger fish to fry. Jim gives me the name of someone who I can contact who can scan our phone lines to see if they are tapped.

WEDNESDAY, APRIL 3RD

I get a call from Dr. Mann today. They want to do the cardioversion tomorrow. I go to the hospital to do some blood work and give Debra a call.

THURSDAY, APRIL 4TH

We report to the hospital at 6:30 AM. They are very efficient and by 7:45 AM I'm hooked up to several machines with monitors taped all over my chest, back, and even my legs. They put something in my IV and the next thing I know it is about 8:10 AM, and they are all done with the procedure. They tell me it took two attempts, raising the dosage on the second try, but it was successful! My heart is now beating with the proper sinus rhythm - whatever that means.

I am to come back in a week for a checkup to make sure that my heart has maintained the proper rhythm. When I get home, my chest feels like it has been sunburned and I can see the outlines of where they had placed the pads when they delivered the shock treatment. I vowed that I would never drink another caffeine drink for as long as I live.

On the way home, I hear on the radio that funding has been cut for the state program that assists prisoners in making the transition back to society. Only in Virginia - sorry Texas!

MONDAY, APRIL 8TH

Monday comes to an end without a phone call from Chad. He also didn't call over the weekend. It has been almost a week since I have talked to him. I'm getting a little nervous, and I'm hoping that everything is okay.

TUESDAY, APRIL 9TH

Today's issue of *The Wall Street Journal* has an article that discusses the success of the drug Zyprexa for schizophrenia medication. The company that produces the drug, Eli Lilly & Co., remains "king of the hill" despite the best efforts of rival drug companies. The article focuses on the fact that even though the drug is more costly then its rivals and causes moderate to serious weight gain for most of its users, it is the leader by a wide margin. Zyprexa's total sales in 2001 were over $3 billion. Risperdal, the second leading schizophrenia drug, had sales of less than $2 billion in 2001.

The articles states that many doctors believe that Zyprexa has the least side effects and it has a reputation of being very good, especially for those individuals with moderate to severe schizophrenia. All of this makes me feel good that Chad is using Zyprexa, and we can certainly vouch for the weight-gain side effect. However, the makers of Risperdal claim that users are less inclined to suffer relapses and it is much cheaper. The article also states that the newest drug on the market, Geodon, claims to be as effective as Zyprexa without the weight gain. It is nice to know that there are some options out there.

Another encouraging fact is that all three of the producers of Zyprexa, Risperdal, and Geodon will be coming out on the market soon with injectable forms for long-term use. This appeals to me because I can envision Chad forgetting or purposely not taking his pills every day.

FRIDAY, APRIL 12TH

I visit Chad alone today. We have a good talk, mostly about sports. We discuss the Jazz's chances in the playoffs and Barry Bonds fast start.

I drove the CRV today for the purpose of getting an estimate on how much it is going to cost to fix the damage that happened while in the Northumberland Sheriff's custody. The damage is $402. Come to find out, the owners of the repair shop live within a mile of us. They are both very nice and quite cordial - I think they know who I am. Driving home, it dawns on me that the Sheriff will argue that, given the date of the estimate, that the damage could have happened after we regained possession of the car. I should have gotten the estimate done immediately after. I do not feel we are dealing with honorable men.

I get the addresses of 60 Minutes and the Virginia Chapter of the American Civil Liberties Union (ACLU) off the Internet and give them a call, asking for information. I am feeling guilty that I haven't been doing enough to help Chad.

SATURDAY, APRIL 13TH

I am surprised to find a reply already from the ACLU in the mailbox. The reply lists the criteria they have established for accepting a case. They state that they generally take cases that affect the civil liberties of large numbers of people by challenging unconstitutional government laws and government policies. They ask themselves three basic questions when they are considering a case: (1) is it a significant civil liberties issue? (2) what impact will it not only have on the client but other people as well? (3) how is the Virginia government involved? They also state that they normally only take cases where there are no serious factual disputes because they want to concentrate on the law itself.

They list five major categories of civil rights they seek to protect. I feel that Chad's rights and our own have been violated under two of the categories, the right to privacy and the due process of the law. The right to privacy is described as a guaranteed zone of personal privacy and autonomy, which cannot be penetrated by the government or by other institutions. The due process of law is the right to be treated fairly when facing criminal charges or other serious accusations. I can remember that the one attorney told us that Virginia has some of the worst privacy laws in the country, and the fact that Chad was arrested in our home made us all "fair-game" - so I don't have much hope of succeeding under this right. However, I feel the due process of law is another matter and that we would have a very compelling case, especially given Chad's mental illness.

The next part of the ACLU's reply is not very encouraging. They state "There are many cases and problems of unfairness and injustice which the ACLU of Virginia is simply unable to handle. With a staff of three people and more than five hundred requests for help every month, we cannot accept many of the cases the fall within our guidelines." I'm floored! I thought the ACLU had far more resources. They only have a staff of three people for the entire state of Virginia? Nevertheless, I will try to solicit their help in the near future. I will probably emphasize Chad's treatment (or lack thereof) while he has been in jail.

SUNDAY, APRIL 14TH

I have been entertaining an idea for the past few weeks and decide to act upon it. We have made no attempt to try to tell our side of the story or, more importantly, Chad's. We have stood by, based on the advice of our lawyers, as the local media has viciously attacked our son and ourselves. But with McKenney's actions of the past few months, I think it is fair to say that all bets are off - and anything we do now couldn't possibly hurt Chad anymore than he has already been hurt.

I'm seriously thinking of doing a mass mailing within the county of a carefully worded letter that tells our side of the story. The more I think about it, the more excited I get! To actually do something constructive that could help Chad and defend ourselves energizes me. There are about twelve thousand total people in the county. We could reach many of them for about six hundred dollars worth of postage and let the "grape vine" take care of the rest. Sending a letter to the editor would be a very risky proposition. I can almost guarantee that it would be editorialize to the point that it would do us more harm than good.

My biggest concern would be that I don't want to do anything that would compromise our bank in anyway. So, before I would let the letter go, I would make sure its okay with our CEO and then, maybe, run it by our attorneys. I spend a good part of the day writing the letter.

I call Dad that night and we discuss the letter at length. He is impressed by its originality but voices concerns as to what the repercussions could be. We do talk about the fact that the attorneys have indicated that it is now okay to defend Chad as we see fit, provided we don't attack the Sheriff's Department. I am trying to be patient, but all we have to show for it, after exercising a great deal of patience, is a situation that is getting progressively worse for Chad legally and even worst for his chances of achieving a complete recovery. You can even say that it has been a disaster so far, given that Chad has already received a misdemeanor charge while he was just supposed to be awaiting trial and has had his very personal psychiatric report printed on the front of the newspaper. *Just who is it in this whole mess that we can count on!*

MONDAY, APRIL 15TH

I meet with the CEO of the bank and discuss the letter with him. He expresses reservations about the letter, and though he doesn't tell me no – saying, "You need to do what you need to do." I can tell that he would prefer that I didn't send it. He also makes a point that the fact the letter is coming from me would probably create a bias that I would say anything to make Chad and myself look better. He also can't believe that I would consider sending it out without consulting the attorneys. Based on this conversation, I will not send the letter.

WEDNESDAY, APRIL 17TH

We finally get a call from Chad. We haven't talked to him since Friday. He seems to be getting more and more institutionalized. He says he is spending most of his time playing cards with other inmates. He did say he tried to call us the night before, but he couldn't get through. The phone is clicking away as we talk; it wouldn't surprise me if every phone call an inmate places is being recorded.

Debra goes to visit Chad. We receive a letter from the attorney containing a copy of the criminal complaint filed by the U.S. Secret Service against Chad. The complaint alleges that Chad "knowingly and with intent to defraud, manufactured counterfeited obligations of the United States in violation of Title 18 USC 471." Nowhere is he charged with trying to distribute the money and, of course, no mention is made of the facts that Chad was a severely mentally ill eighteen year-old.

The affidavit contains some details that I was unaware of. Whereas, the paper had proclaimed that a large sack of counterfeit bills had been found, the truth is, only fifty-four bills had been recovered. They had been discovered before Chad robbed the bank, apparently in the driveway of the oyster house located just down the hill from us. The person who found them was an acquaintance of ours! I wish he or the Sheriff's office would have said something to us. If they had, chances are pretty good that it would have been the tip-off for Debra and me on just how serious things had become, and the bank robbery would have been avoided.

And guess who was the lead detective on the case and provided the Secret Service with the evidence? Mr. James Bruce, the same detective who had been rough with Chad while taking his fingerprints. What an idiot! *Mr. Bruce if you had been smart enough to have knocked on our door to inform us that some counterfeit money had been found next to our property two weeks before the bank robbery, there would have been no bank robbery.* It's nice to know our tax dollars are supporting such incompetence.

SUNDAY, APRIL 21ST

We have a shallow well, which we depend on for all our water needs. Yesterday Debra heard the pump struggling and, instead of turning off the pump, she turned off the water valve. The pump burned itself out. We have no water, and to get a competent, reliable plumber to respond quickly to a service call is usually just about impossible around here. I am amazed this morning when a licensed plumber agrees to respond within the hour to install a new pump. He does a good job and I'm relieved that this is not something else I have to deal with for a good part of a week.

FRIDAY, APRIL 26TH

I go visit Chad alone. We mainly talk a lot about basketball. How well Toronto has done without Vince Carter and how poorly the Wizards are doing without Michael Jordan. Chad tells me that his pod has not been allowed to go outside since November. I ask him why and he just shrugs his shoulders and says he doesn't know. I can't imagine what it must be like not to go outside for six months straight. Sure sounds like great therapy for someone who is severely mentally ill!

MONDAY, APRIL 29TH

Chad calls tonight and brings up a point that I hadn't even thought about. What happens with the counterfeiting charge if he should win his case? Does he have to stay at the jail until that is cleared? I have no idea and I'm surprised that the same question hasn't occurred to me. It's a good question for Jim.

MONDAY, MAY 6TH

Dad gives me a call tonight. He is intrigued about a program he watched on *60 Minutes* the day before. It is about a psychiatrist named Dr. Torrey who has strong ideas about the efforts of those in his profession to find a cure for the severely mentally ill - namely paranoid schizophrenics. Dad says that the doctor apparently practices in northern Virginia and has some radical ideas that might be of some use for us. I tell Dad I will call *60 Minutes* and see if I can get a copy of the program.

Dad also reads a letter that he and Linda have received from Chad that was coherent and well written. He tells them not to worry about him and tells them once he gets out of jail his goal is to return to school to get a degree. If only he had been on the higher dosage of Zyprexa sooner!

FRIDAY, MAY 10TH

I have a good visit with Chad. We talk at length about the coming court case. We are concerned that Dr. Jarnecke hasn't made any attempt to see Chad yet. It is hard to believe they would allow this thing to be postponed again. We are afraid the same scenario will play out as it did for the prior postponements. The psychiatrist's report will arrive just a few days before trial, and once again McKenney will say that he hasn't had enough time to study the report. Chad says he doesn't know if he can take another two months. He seems dejected and humble, which tells me that he is taking his medicine, though he is fidgeting more than I would like and there is very little eye contact. I remember that Dr. Peck said that Chad had not been properly medicated.

SATURDAY, MAY 11TH

Ali's high school track team went to the district championship today. Ali runs on several of their relay teams and is their 300-meter hurdles representative. She wins the 300 meters hurdle event and their relay teams finish second and fourth - not bad for a junior!

SUNDAY, MAY 12TH

It is Mother's Day and I feel bad for Debra. Though I don't say anything to her, I know she is thinking about Chad and the present circumstances – man, life can be tough! Ali and I clean the house and cook dinner for her and give her a nice card. For a Mother's Day present she had purchased a number of things for her garden earlier in the week. Debra spends most of her free time now in her gardens. It is her stress reliever.

WEDNESDAY, MAY 15TH

Chad calls and says that Dr. Jarnecke actually came and saw him today. When I press Chad for details, he doesn't remember much. I ask him if he asked a lot of questions, and Chad says yes - but he can't seem to remember any of them. Talking to Chad can be frustrating at times. I ask him how long was Jarnecke there, and Chad says maybe an hour or an hour-and-a-half. Sure doesn't seem to be enough time to refute the opinions of the other psychiatrists.

This is good news - if Jarnecke can produce his report quickly, maybe this will finally be over on the 21st. Debra and I discuss this point after Chad's call and Debra feels there is no way it will be over. Jarnecke was also supposed to have interviewed Debra, but it hasn't happened yet.

FRIDAY, MAY 17TH

Debra says she had a good visit with Chad. He is getting excited about Tuesday but Debra does tell him that she thinks it will be postponed. Chad says to please tell Jim, if it does get postponed, to do everything he can to get it rescheduled right away.

Debra tells me that it looks like Chad has actually lost a little weight and she is afraid that he is not taking his medicine. He seemed nervous and kept trying to clean off the tabletop in front of him, and there was no eye contact. I don't quite know how to react to this - it is not good news - but when Chad is on his medicine, he seems normal and I don't know how that will play in court!

I put in a call to Jim to find out what is going on. He does not call us back.

SATURDAY, MAY 18TH

Chad calls and we have to tell him we haven't heard from Jim and don't know anything more than what we knew yesterday. We also remind Chad that it was our understanding that Debra was supposed to talk to the psychiatrist. I think we are now all resigned to the fact that on Tuesday we will be dealing with the fourth postponement of Chad's trial. We get a call from several of our friends at church asking about the time, but we tell them we are pretty sure it will be postponed, so don't worry about coming.

MONDAY, MAY 20TH

Jim calls me at work and wants to know if Chad has seen the psychiatrist - not a good sign. I tell him yes and I ask him if the trial is going to be postponed once again. He tells me that he is going to see Chad and make a few phone calls and get back to me latter in the day. He never calls.

I get a call from a friend asking about the time of the trial tomorrow. She says that she called the court and they don't show Chad as even being on the docket!

Chad calls us around dinnertime and wants to know what is going on. I tell him I'm sorry but I still don't know anything and I ask him if he saw Jim today. The answer is no, he hasn't heard a thing from anybody. I'm sure Chad must feel like no one is on his side. I ask him if he knows for sure that he is being transported to the courthouse? He says, "As far as I know, I am." I tell him that, "No matter what, your mother and I will be there tomorrow, in case they do bring you out."

Debra and I are at a lost as to what to do, but we have been burned once before on false information that he was not appearing in court.

TUESDAY, MAY 21ST

I don't know why, but as Debra and I are driving to the courthouse, I'm feeling nervous, even though I know that it is almost a sure thing there will be no trial today. Debra looks at me incredulously and says; "You are feeling nervous! I feel like I have been going to throw-up for the past two days!"

We never did hear from Jim, and I have no idea if he is even going to be there.

Upon arriving we are surprised to see that the Rasmussen's from church have showed up. They are such a great couple. They are a retired couple from Alberta, Canada that are on a mission for our church. They are very likable, and he is presently our Branch President. It is nice to have their support today.

As the court cases get underway, there is no sign of Jim, or any indication that Chad is on the docket. To further add to our anxiety, Debra thinks she hears one of the officers say that Chad is not here. But just a few minutes later, as someone passes through a door in the back of the courtroom, we see Chad. He smiles at us and gives a short wave - it made our day.

They bring him out a few minutes later, and I am shocked by the amount of weight he has put on and the puffiness of his face - these are all side effects of the Zyprexa. My guess is that Chad weighed about a hundred and fifty pounds when they arrested him and he now weighs about two hundred and twenty pounds. He is in prison garb, his hands are handcuffed, and he is pale - he looks every bit the prisoner.

McKenney asks the Judge for a postponement of the case, stating that he had talked to Jim Breeden the night before and he was in agreement. The psychiatrist's report has not been received. The court does issue an order that the psychiatrist will have to appear in court in person if the report is not produced by the next appointed court date. That magical date has now been set for June 25th. It is quite obvious that no one in this system cares about Chad's welfare, and the primary concern is that everyone gets their pound of his flesh. Justice will prevail; mercy has no place here.

Chad is escorted quickly from the court. He gives a backward glance and tries to wave his hands in good-by, but the officer has a hold of his arm.

We leave the courtroom and thank the Rasmussen's for coming. When we get home, there is a message on the answering machine from Jim stating that he tried to get a hold of us the night before and that we should give him a call on his car phone. Neither Debra nor I are in the mood to talk to him.

I call Dad and let him know what has happened. His first question was, did anyone speak up for Chad. The answer is, of course, no.

FRIDAY, MAY 24TH

I go see Chad alone. We discuss last Tuesday. I asked him had he seen Jim at all - the answer is no. Chad seems to be okay with it. The fact that the postponement was for five weeks instead of two months helps. We also agree that, with the court order, there shouldn't be the problem with getting the report so late that McKenney claims he hasn't had enough time to review it, which would postpone the trial once again. I am almost certain now that one of the strategies that McKenney is pursuing is to delay the case as long as he can, so if he loses, he can state that at least Chad was in jail for a year - it's called CYA. But we don't see how he can postpone it again - we have high hopes for June 25th.

SATURDAY, JUNE 1ST

I took the CFA exam today; and it was a bear, and I'm exhausted. On the drive home, I already start thinking of what more I can do to help Chad, now that for at least the next couple of months I don't have to worry about studying.

CHAPTER 17

RIGHT FROM WRONG

THURSDAY, JUNE 6TH

I get a pleasant surprise at work. Deana gives me a call from Salt Lake to see how everyone is doing. She is really enjoying her job and she has been training for and running in 5K races the past few months. She said that Grandpa stopped by the other day at her work and they went out in the mall and got an ice cream cone and had a good chat. I'm glad that Deana is not here right now and dealing with all this crap - though I'm sure she would be a real asset for us if she were. It makes me appreciate all the more how well Ali has been handling herself.

I also get a call from Debra, who says that Dr. Jarnecke's secretary called her and set up a time for Debra to talk with Dr. Jarnecke by phone tomorrow. She asks me to call Jim and let him know and to see if he has any advice. I leave a message for Jim, but once again, he doesn't call.

Debra has been trying for over a month to get in touch with Dr. Jarnecke. It is encouraging news from the standpoint that maybe, just maybe, there will be an actual trial on June 25th.

There is an article this week in the *Wall Street Journal* entitled, "A Tamer Schizophrenia Drug?" It's about to be put out on the market by Bristol-Myers. It will be called Aripiprazole and they claim it's the next-generation drug for schizophrenia because it works by modifying the levels of a key chemical in the brain. They claim that the drug has none of the serious side effects of the other antipsychotic drugs. As a matter of fact, they claim based on a recent study that users tend to lose a little weight, not gain it.

FRIDAY, JUNE 7TH

Debra has the day off work, but it is going to be a full day with a lot of stress. She goes and sees Chad at the jail, runs some errands, and then hurries home to call Dr. Jarnecke at the appointed time. She says they talked about twenty-five minutes, but she had trouble composing herself and cried off and on during the call. She was so upset that she can't remember much about what they talked about, but she did say she tried to stress just how obsessed Chad was with his scrotum. She says Dr. Jarnecke seemed nice, but she did not get the feeling that the phone call had gone well. I told her not to worry about it and that I'm sure she did a good job - which I am.

SATURDAY, JUNE 8TH

I have a long telephone conversation with Dad today. We get caught up on family news but our main topic of conversation is about the police finding the counterfeit money right next to our home and not informing us. Why? Did they consider us suspects - I doubt it. Not one of us had even so much as a misdemeanor charge. Was it because I'm a banker? Did they think that somehow because of my background that I would try to pull a stunt like that? Who knows, but the unmistakable fact is that, if they had told us about the counterfeit money, I know it would have been the trigger for me to investigate Chad's room to see what I could find. After all, it was at this point that we knew Chad was mentally ill and had an obsession to get four thousand dollars to get the scrotum surgery he thought he needed. This would have been the sign we needed to know that Chad would go to any length to get that money. I can just feel Dad shaking his head at the end of the line, thinking, as I did, that chances are very good that the bank robbery wouldn't have happened if someone had told us what was found next to our property. That doesn't seem too complicated, does it? If someone broke into the home next door and robbed it, wouldn't you expect the neighbor/police to let you know about it?

SUNDAY, JUNE 9TH

I was discussing Chad's case with a friend today at church, and he told me some alarming news. He couldn't tell me his sources, but he was told that McKenney is doing everything in his power to prolong the case until he can't prolong it anymore. He will then ask for a jury trial. He is getting a lot of heat from Chad's victims and the Sheriff's Department, and they want their day in court. He says that there is absolutely no way that Chad's trial will occur on the 25th, because McKenney is bound and determined to have a jury trial.

I am stunned to hear this. It was said with such conviction, that even though its second-hand information, I believe it's true. It also occurs to me that the county attorney's office is an elected office, which means that McKenney is going to do whatever is best for himself, the extenuating circumstances behind why Chad did what he did be damned. I have also wondered why hardly anyone is ever there when Chad is brought out in court - it's probably because they will be told when the actual trial will be held. I also feel that Jim is holding back on us and is not telling us the full story on what is going on.

It is very depressing news. If a jury trial is called, it could be months before we have a resolution. I try not to think of what the ramifications are for Chad's recovery. How does the greatest country in the world allow this to happen! Why don't we just take all the mentally ill people in this country out somewhere and shoot them? It really shouldn't matter if they have a potential for recovery or not! Just think of what a nicer place this would be to live in, no street people and the tax savings would be tremendous!

I have promised Ali that I was going to take her to the movies today, and I'm determined that I'm not going to let this news spoil the day. We stop at Hardees and have some lunch, and then go see the movie the "Sum of all Fears," featuring Ben Afflick and Morgan Freeman. The critics have generally not been kind to the movie, but we enjoyed it. I especially enjoyed the scene in the football stadium; it was well done. Morgan Freeman has always been one of my favorite actors.

Ali and I talk about Chad on the way home and she told me something that I didn't know about the day he was arrested. The two detectives that had followed Debra into the yard when she arrived home with Chad had knocked on the door and quizzed Ali about an hour before. They had asked her a bunch of personal questions about where Debra and I worked, who were all the members of the household including their ages. She said they especially perked up when she mentioned Chad. Ali answered all their questions and didn't have a chance to tell us, because the detectives were there when we arrived. Once again, if we had known that Ali had been questioned like that, we would have realized that we were definitely being watched and we would have

191

no doubt put two and two together. We would not have gone through that whole brutal scene that night. It irritates me that the detectives would question Ali like that outside of our presence, but then again, as we all know, just about everything the Sheriff's Department does irritates me.

Chad calls that night, and I do tell him about the information I received. He expresses surprise and says that would postpone my trial for months. Before we have time to talk about it further, there is a pill call. If Chad doesn't respond, he will not get his pills. He frantically says he has got to go to get his pills, and I tell him give us a call in a few days to see if we have heard anything more. I am surprised at the urgency in Chad's voice to respond to the pill call. It is a good sign that Chad has been taking his medicine regularly - though Debra would say later that maybe he is just selling the pills to other prisoners! Thanks a lot Deb!

MONDAY, JUNE 10TH

The thought that anyone would expect Chad to spend another three months in jail waiting for his trial is too much for me. The thought of him lying in his bunk at night trying to deal with his demons, in that atmosphere, with no hope of seeing the light of day anytime soon is sobering. I call a bail-bondsman to see how that works. They charge a fee of eight to ten percent depending on the size of the bond. He says they try to work with you. You can even make monthly payments, if your credit is good. Some arrangements can also be made using your house as collateral, even if the equity in the house doesn't cover the full bond amount. The bail money is returned to the bondsman upon resolution of the case. He says it is not uncommon for the bail money to be outstanding for a year or more. It is basically a loan arrangement, though a very lucrative one for the bondsman if the case is settled quickly. He says to give him a call a few days before the bail hearing and he could have it ready for me.

I tell Debra about what the bondsman told me. She thinks that maybe it would be better if Chad stayed there until trial. He is accustomed to it now, and the time served will count against his sentence. It would be a moot point if the Judge doesn't reduce the bail significantly. If we could get the bail set at something below $40,000, we could probably handle it.

We then get into another discussion about whether we should file complaints against the Sheriff's office and his band of rednecks. I'm concerned that if we don't do something soon, it will be too late because of some statute of limitation we are all unaware of. We are closing, very quickly, on a year since Chad's arrest. Debra doesn't have the heart for it. All she wants is peace. As far as she is concerned, they are all a bunch of ignorant men that don't deserve the time of day.

I tell her I'm sorry, but I can't pretend this didn't happen – someone has to try to stop it from happening again. I'm not going to stand still and watch these people take my son down.

TUESDAY, JUNE 11TH

Before I go to work, I go to the Sheriff's office to pick up the complaint form. I know I'm taking a risk by going alone - I wouldn't put it past these guys to make up a story that I threatened them like they did when I called previously and asked what the procedures were. I know Debra doesn't have the stomach for it, and I certainly don't want to put any of my friends in harm's way. Of course they won't just give you the form when you get there. They make you wait until an officer brings the form out to you. And guess who brings it out? Chuckie, himself. For some reason he is all polite! After he makes a few points about filling out the form, he informs me that I need to bring it back and turn it into the Sheriff's office. Oh that's great! I have to turn this form in to the very people I'm lodging the complaint against. There has got to be another way.

WEDNESDAY, JUNE 12TH

Chad calls and says that he didn't sleep that night, after I told him about the jury trial. I feel bad and I tell him to remember that it was second-hand information. We talk about the ramifications, and I promise Chad that I will try to reach Jim to see what I can find out.

Chad also mentions that we don't need to come and see him every Friday. He is fine and will be able to sleep if we don't come.

Neither one of us goes to see Chad, which will make it only the second time since his arrest that we have missed seeing him during regular visiting hours.

I make a few phone calls to see if there is any alternative to filing the complaint form with someone besides the people I'm filing the complaint against. Unbelievably, there is not a good alternative. I inquire with our state delegate's office and find that the Sheriff is considered to be a constitutional officer, someone who is elected by the people. He only reports to the people and about the only thing they can do, if they don't like the way he does his job, is not elect him to office the next time. Great! If we feel he is in violation of a state law, we can contact the state police. One person recommended that when we file our complaint, to also lodge it with the appropriate commonwealth's attorney. He also warns us to tell as many people as possible about what we are doing, because you may need them as witnesses if anyone in the Sheriff's office seeks retribution. Amen.

I have a doctor's appointment today and I get bad news. My heart has slipped out of equilibrium and it is fibrillating again. It is frustrating, because I have been taking my medicine as instructed and have even avoided caffeine drinks since the cardioversion. They want to make me an appointment with a doctor in Richmond.

I tried getting hold of Jim yesterday and give it another try today. I am surprised when he actually picks up the phone. I think he thought I was going to be someone else. I ask Jim the questions I told Chad I was going to ask him. It becomes a frustrating phone call, because, for some reason, Jim seems to be talking in circles and doesn't give a straight answer to any of my questions. I tell him that someone who is well connected heard that McKenney would be asking for a jury trial, once he can no longer keep postponing it. Jim says he doubts that and says that if the third psychiatrist comes to the same conclusion as the first two, we will probably start wrapping things up on the 25th! I ask him, does he really think that the psychiatrist would do that - isn't he working for the prosecution? Jim seems to think there is a strong possibility that he could.

I ask Jim would it be possible to get Chad out on reduced bail if things don't go well. He says that it is a great idea and is so enthusiastic about it that it seems to contradict what he told me about the 25th. I also tell him that I did pick up the complaint form from the Sheriff's Department. He says that I can only hurt Chad by filing it. He actually says that, if I do this, the Sheriff and his deputies will put pressure on McKenney to "fry" Chad. Boy! What a sad commentary. I tell Jim that every source I've looked at says the statute of limitations runs out after a year, and in some cases just six months - yet you told me I had two years. Then Jim says something about his having talked only about filing a civil case. *I see, in other words you haven't been straight up with me* I think to myself. After hanging up, I have further concerns when I look up several civil cases that have been filed against the police, and without fail, every one of them was decided in favor of the police. There is even one where the police and prosecutor jail an innocent victim, and they win their case when the victim tries to sue them for unlawful arrest, excessive force and illegal search and seizure! The local government was protected by the doctrine of sovereign immunity, and the plaintiff failed to establish a specific link between the police chief's indifference to the specific conduct of the police department and the plaintiff's actual injury. It will be very tough to win a civil case, and Jim knows that. I am just about convinced now that one of Jim's goals in this whole process is to help McKenney protect his friend, Chuckie.

SUNDAY, JUNE 16TH

Chad calls and wishes me a happy Father's Day. It is nice to hear. *Hang in there son.*

I tell him that I talked to Jim about the questions we had but that I didn't get a straight answer. I basically don't know anything more then I did before the phone call. I tell Chad that Jim seems to think that the third psychiatrist may actually support the previous psychiatric findings. I also tell Chad that if it does go to jury trial, we may try to get him out on a reduced bail. I ask him what he thinks about that - with the caveat that the bail would have to be reduced substantially before we could afford it. He says that if the trial is just weeks away instead of months, just leave him where he is, if not, then he would like us to try to get him out.

Debra cooks breakfast and dinner for me, and Ali gives me a big hug. It's been a nice Father's Day. I can't help but wonder if Chad will be home for the next one.

WEDNESDAY, JUNE 19TH

I get a call from Dr. Sperry, who practices in Richmond. He is the heart specialist referred by Dr. Duer. He asks me a few questions and tells me to keep taking the Coumadin for another three weeks. He will have his secretary call me to set up another cardioversion. I'm not sure why they think another cardioversion is going to help, but I will do as I'm told. I hope doctors are better at what they are doing than lawyers.

Chad calls and wants to know what is going on and have we heard from Jim. The answers are nothing and no. We talk about what we think might happen on Tuesday. Chad raises another good question about whether the Federal retainer filed on him would negate a bond hearing. I tell Chad that I will call and leave a message for Jim tomorrow to call me and that maybe I'll have some answers when I visit him on Friday. It is ironic that just about an hour before Chad called, Debra asked me if I have heard anything from Jim.

We watch a show on TV called "State VS". It is an actual murder trial where the media is allowed to film both the prosecutor and the criminal lawyer as they prepare for trial, select jurors and argue their cases. It also shows the jury during their deliberations. It is scary to see the jurors deliberate and watch them take sides totally opposite from each other. I am also surprised how some of the jurors are eager to put a man in jail for twenty-two years on evidence that I don't think gets over the hurdle of reasonable doubt. I can see why Jim wants to avoid a jury trial. I am also struck by how hard the criminal defense lawyer works to do all he can for his client - he shows a lot passion, something we have not seen in our own attorneys. I keep hoping they will surprise me, when we actually get down to having some sort of a trial.

FRIDAY, JUNE 21ST

I go to visit Chad alone. Debra has to work a twelve-hour shift. Jim never called, so I don't have any news for him. I am alarmed by the visit. It is obvious now that Chad is deteriorating. I don't know how else to put it. He is sullen and mumbling, when I try to get him to speak, and he will not look at me the whole forty-five minutes I'm there. I have to carry the whole conversation. He didn't sound that bad when I talked to him on the phone Wednesday night. He looks bad physically, and he is showing absolutely no emotion. Usually, I can get him to laugh just a little when I'm there - not today. *My son is losing his fight against mental illness, he's helpless!* I'm afraid we have reached that point where any potential for a full recovery is gone. *This system is killing my son. My God! Won't someone please help us!!!*

As I drive to Kilmarnock, I try to work out in my mind why Chad has deteriorated as much as he has in such a short period of time. My guess is that Debra's suspicions that Chad is not taking his medicine, especially the Prozac, are true. Chad has already admitted that he has missed some pill calls in the morning because he sleeps in. My guess is that he has probably missed them all for the past few months. Because of his weight gain, I feel more confident that he has been taking the Zyprexa at night. I wonder if maybe he has recently decided because of the weight gain to stop taking the Zyprexa and because he knows now that there is a possibility of a jury trial. I remember that I still have the phone number of the person that is in charge of the health treatment of prison inmates.

When I get back to the office, I find that Jim has called. It takes several tries, but I finally get hold of him late afternoon. His news is exactly what I expected, and it is exactly what my friend at Church told me was going to happen. The psychiatrist has found that Chad is paranoid schizophrenic, but that he could tell the difference between right and wrong at the time of the bank robbery. What is bothersome to me is that Jim finds it necessary to bring up once again how the Sheriff's Department doesn't like the fact that I have been critical of them. Then he tells me that the Sheriff has told McKenney to throw the book at Chad. What a coincidence, that we are having this conversation just a few days after I have picked up the complaint form. Then Jim takes it one step further and suggests that the reason this is happening is because of my threats against the police department. Boy! That speaks highly of everyone involved. First of all, what threats? I guess now, I'm supposed to be chastened/intimidated to the point that I will promise not to file the complaint. I am on to this little sideshow. I don't make any comment, and wait for Jim to get back to explaining what will happen on Tuesday. We will enter a not guilty, at which time McKenney will ask for jury trial. Incredibly,

Jim gets back to how my refusal to kiss the Sheriff's ass is hurting this case. It is not very comforting to know that your own attorneys are just as much a part of this "good-ol boy" network as anyone else. In the final analysis, if I conclude that Jim's and Bill's apparent promise to McKenney to protect his friend, Chuckie, has hurt their effectiveness in their defense of Chad, I will probably file a malpractice suit against them.

The psychiatrist's report is interesting to read. Strangely enough, there is a lot in the report that can be used to substantiate Chad's defense. He describes Chad this way, "His affect was flat and he exhibited little energy during the interview. His mood appears to be depressed. He expressed ideas of helplessness and hopelessness and reports that he has experienced suicidal ideation in the past, though not at the time of the interview. He states that he has considered slitting his wrist, but denies that he has taken any steps in that direction. His depression appears to be secondary to his belief about his bodily deformities."

The psychiatrist concludes his report by saying: "1) Mr. Wegkamp was suffering from a major mental disease or defect at the time of the offense, that being Schizophrenia, Paranoid type. 2.) Mr.Wegkamp was aware of the wrongfulness of his actions at the time of the offense. His actions and his descriptions of his actions reveal that he was thinking in terms of the categories of "right and wrong" throughout his planning of the offense. 3.) Mr. Wegkamp was able to direct and control his actions at the time of the offense."

Yes, I'm sure that a boy who goes around the house pulling up on the front part of his pants to give his scrotum more support, has tried to operate on himself, and is constantly talking with imaginary voices, knew exactly what he was doing when he walked into that bank! How blessed we are that doctors, lawyers, and jurors know exactly what paranoid schizophrenics are thinking. I wonder how I can have totally lost my faith in the people who control this case – it is a terrible feeling.

Concerning Chad's treatment, the doctor says, "Regardless of the outcome of the legal proceedings, treatment is warranted. This should involve a combination of psychotropic medication, which he is currently receiving, and psychotherapy, which he is not. His past compliance with psychological treatment has been poor, which is a reflection of his specific disorder. He has expressed a willingness to cooperate with physical treatment, but he has been less cooperative with psychiatric treatment. He continues to report that he misses doses of medication. His lack of insight into the nature of his illness, common in the diagnostic category of Paranoid Schizophrenia, leads him away from effective treatment. Based on my review of the records and my interview with Mr. Wegkamp, it is my opinion that, with effective treatment, he is unlikely to repeat (the) type of actions that bring him to the Court's attention at this time."

When I get home I get an unpleasant surprise in the mail. Jim has forwarded a bill from Dr. Peck to me. It includes almost forty dollars of interest/finance charges on a call made back in August 2001 that Dr. Peck had with Jim. The charge for the phone call is one hundred and thirty-eight dollars. But that is nothing, on March 26th there is a charge for $1,200 for lost time - that was the day that Dr. Peck was supposed to testify in the trial that was postponed on short notice by Jim's good friend, McKenney. But no problem, we'll just stick the Wegkamp's with the bill. The total bill is $1,725, which brings the total amount to $4,800 that we have paid Dr. Peck to date, which is almost twice the amount that Jim said his services would cost us. Even our hired consultants are combining against us.

I give Dad a call and we discuss the day's events. We discuss the merits of dismissing Breeden & Company and conclude it is too late in the game to do that. I don't even know where to begin to do something like that; will the court even allow me to do it at this point I don't know. All of the psychiatrists that have been used, have all been Jim's contacts. Besides, I've already invested too much in Breeden - there is no money left to pay anyone else.

I read to Dad those parts of the psychiatric report that are favorable to Chad. Dad just can't believe that here we have three separate psychiatric reports, all stressing that Chad needs proper care as soon as possible, yet he is still tied up in a system that seems determined to destroy him. Where is the humanity? Where is the common sense? Why can't both sides get together to work something out that could possibly save Chad? All I can tell Dad is that I think the other side is insisting that they get their day in court. They don't buy the fact that Chad is severely mentally ill, or they just don't care.

It is about 10:00 PM, I have waited till now to call Debra at work to break the news to her. I know the news will upset her, to say the least, and I think her twelve-hour shift is over at 11:00 PM. I'm afraid if I wait until tomorrow, I will get chewed out for not telling her sooner. I give her a quick summary of what has happened, and she quickly cuts me off and says she has got to go. I go to sleep around 12:00 PM, Debra hasn't made it home yet; but that's not uncommon.

SATURDAY, JUNE 22ND

Debra tells me this morning to please never call her at work and give her news like that again. She says she can't handle it. I can tell she hasn't gotten much sleep and has been crying most of the night. I will find that I won't be able to talk to her about the case for the entire weekend.

Chad calls and I'm surprised that he sounds as good as he does after what I saw yesterday. He wants to know what is going to happen on Tuesday, and I pretty much repeat what I told him yesterday. He asks me if I remembered to ask Jim what impact this would have on the Fed's retainer. I have to tell him no. I do tell him that Monday is going to be a pretty important day for him. He needs to pay close attention to everything that Jim is telling him. There are serious ramifications, no matter what he chooses. He asks me what he should do. I tell him that if it were I, I would plead not guilty. Even if he gets some sort of plea bargain, he will end up with a felony record that will haunt him the rest of his life. I also tell him that the chances of him getting a sympathetic jury in Heathsville are slim to none and it is easy for me to say plead not guilty - I don't have to do the time if he loses. It's a sad commentary that because his attorney's have proven so unreliable to this point Chad is seeking guidance from me. I also remind him that there are two psychiatrist's that say you couldn't tell the difference between right from wrong and didn't understand the ramifications of what you were about to do.

Debra is withdrawn and doesn't want to talk about Chad. She is really low. I try to remain upbeat, just so I don't pull her down any lower. However, sometimes I feel I'm the only one who's fighting the fight for Chad legally and politically. I don't think I'm ever going to see the "best efforts" from our attorneys, given their obvious desire to maintain a good relationship with McKenney.

SUNDAY, JUNE 23RD

Several members at Church tell me they will be there on Tuesday. Their support continues to be a source of strength for Debra and me. I tell one member that it looks like McKenney is going to insist on a jury trial if things don't go his way. The member just shakes his head in disbelief - he knows how sick Chad is.

Dad calls me and says he has been "stewing" since my last call. He asks me if I can get with the attorney and see if some sort of plea bargain can be arranged in which Chad will plead guilty on the condition that they agree he will be sent to a medical facility where he can get the help he needs. Sounds pretty simple and almost fair, but I'm afraid it doesn't satisfy the other side's desire for "justice!" It is hard for me to accept that Chad should plead guilty - its not like he has any control of the mental illness that engulfs him. However, I am starting to come to the realization that "what is fair" is not going to happen. I tell Dad that I will try to get hold of Jim tomorrow and ask him that question.

MONDAY, JUNE 24TH

I have a rough night. I kept having strange dreams concerning Chad. In one, he is put in prison for life, and in another, he commits suicide.

I get a call from Cindy. She is very concerned about Debra. She said she called her yesterday and Debra didn't want to talk; she can tell that her sister is really depressed. She asks me if I think she needs to come to help Deb. I tell her that Debra has gotten another prescription for Prozac, and I think it will do the trick - but I take Cindy's phone number in case it doesn't.

I do leave a phone call for Jim to please give me a call. I leave a message that I have a question and I would like an update on what is going on. I leave him both my work number and home number.

Jim had told me that he was going to visit the jail and meet with Chad today to get him prepared for tomorrow. I told Chad that on Saturday. I hope Jim doesn't let him down. I also told Chad to give us a call Monday night, if Chad does see Jim.

Chad does call and says that he met with Jim. Chad says that though they talked about what was going to happen, he really didn't know what exactly was going on. Welcome to the club, kid! He says that all he got out of it was that he was going to plead not guilty. I can't really get too upset with Jim; my guess is that Jim told him more, but that Chad wasn't able to assimilate it all. Chad expressed dismay because he forgot to ask Jim about bail and the impact of the Federal restraining order. I tell him that if Jim should call latter or if we see him before the trial tomorrow, I'll ask him. I tell Chad to make sure he asks Jim, if he sees him before we do.

We go to bed that night without hearing from Jim and expecting the worst tomorrow.

TUESDAY, JUNE 25TH

Just when you think things are going to get worse, they get better. I had just about given up on Jim; but today, he does surprise me! He seemed to be in control today.

We have another nice turnout from our friends at church, and Chad is one of the first cases on the docket. Chad is brought out with chains on his feet and he does look huge. I wonder if any of the court personnel remembered what he looked like ten months ago.

Jim comes over and says he has some good news. There was a mistake on the point system used to guide the Judge in Chad's sentencing, if he were to be found guilty. The mid-range for Chad's sentencing has been reduced to three-and-a-half years from four-and-a-half years. He gives me a copy on the new guidelines.

As usual, I don't know what is going on. Jim and McKenney are bantering with the Judge on what is to transpire next, and we learn that the case has been delayed another two weeks - there will be a deposition on July 9th. McKenney mentions that he will be moving for a jury trial on that date, and Jim looks up from his papers and says he will make a motion to dismiss it! The Judge sort of chuckles. So does Jim, and I get the impression that McKenney is doing some sort of posturing and that it is really Jim that controls what is going to happen next.

Apparently, there was never any chance for a jury trial unless we wanted it! Why Jim told me something different earlier when I asked why he wasn't opposing McKenney getting a third psychiatrist, I don't know. I get the feeling that we don't know half of what is going on.

Just like that, we are done for the day - it took all of five minutes. After leaving the courtroom, we meet with Jim and ask what just happened. Jim explains that at the deposition, the attorneys will present the facts of the cases as they see them. The Judge wants the three psychiatrists to get together to reach a conclusion on what would be the best treatment for Chad and that the Judge will meet with the psychiatrists to ask them questions. I realize after we talk with Jim that I'm not sure when this is supposed to happen. I got the impression it would be sometime after the deposition. In the end, as I understand it, the Judge will make a ruling on exactly what Chad's punishment will be and the subsequent treatment. One such scenario would be that Chad could get another six months in prison and then another year at a mental institution. Jim says one of the problems of coming up with a suitable treatment program for Chad is that a lot of the options that used to be available are being taken away as a result of the large budget deficit in Virginia. The bulk of the treatment would coincide with the last part of his incarceration so he would be better equipped to reenter society.

I can't believe it! It is like out of nowhere common sense and fairness have entered the picture. Jim also mentions that the Judge had commented to him earlier about the impressive showing of support that shows up for Chad each court date. I think how lost we would be without our friends.

After Jim leaves, we discuss with our friends what has just happened. Someone comments that McKenney has definitely been playing the political scene lately - apparently elections are not that far away.

CHAPTER 18

WHAT JUST HAPPENED!?

FRIDAY, JUNE 28TH

Debra goes to see Chad today. She was upset by her visit. She said that Chad was exhibiting some peculiar behavior and that he will never listen to anything she tries to tell him. She didn't stay long. Chad told her that Jim told him that he could still get a jury trial.

I try to get Chad removed from our car insurance. Our premium is $2,400 a year and Chad is a big part of that. They won't take him off unless we can show he has insurance with someone else. I finally explain that he is incarcerated and they tell me that I will need to show them proof of his sentencing before they can remove him.

I feel weak today and I'm exhausted by the time I get home. It's been pretty much like this all week. Dr. Sperry's secretary does call and schedules another cardioversion on July 22nd. I've got to get this heart thing fixed!

When I get home, I tell Debra the date of the cardioversion. She is disappointed, because she was planning on taking a vacation that week to visit Cindy and her newborn nephew. I feel bad because I know it would really help her if she could get away from here for a while.

SATURDAY, JUNE 29TH

I start reading a book by Dr. Xavier Amador entitled, *I Am Not Sick, I Don't Need Help!* The book addresses why so many seriously mentally ill patients refuse to get help and to take their medicine. He is the Director of Psychology at the New York State Psychiatric Institute. He has concluded, based on his studies and studies of others, that someone who is schizophrenic has poor insight into their illness; not because they are being stubborn or uncooperative, but as the result of brain dysfunction. The brain circuitry responsible for a person's self-concept is not working as it should, literally stranding a person in time. Schizophrenics believe that they have the same capabilities that they enjoyed prior to being stricken with the illness. They truly believe that there is absolutely nothing wrong with them mentally. This is why most of them have such unrealistic plans for the future.

He also explains why it is so important that a schizophrenic receive proper treatment early and often. Every time a person suffers a psychotic episode, brain cells are altered or die during and immediately following the episode. Psychosis is toxic to the brain.

Another disturbing fact for me is that anytime a schizophrenic experiences hallucinations, delusions, or even has a short period of extremely disorganized thoughts, they are having a psychotic episode. I'm afraid that Chad has had dozens and dozens of psychotic episodes over the past year and a half.

WEDNESDAY, JULY 3RD

We watch the television program "State VS" and are appalled when the film crew shows a prosecuting attorney walk into the jail and request to listen to all the telephone conversations an inmate has had since being incarcerated. She gives the correctional officer the inmate's name and she then proceeds to listen to all of the "private" taped phone conversations.

THURSDAY, JULY 4TH

Even though I've got the day off, we don't do anything special. Debra has to work and Ali went out the night before with her friends. We have heard absolutely nothing from Jim & Company since the last hearing - I can only assume that the reason for this is that they aren't doing much or they just don't think it's important to keep us in the loop.

Chad calls and wants to know if we have heard anything. I ask him if they are doing anything special at the jailhouse, and he says they were served fried chicken for dinner. When darkness falls, Ali and I go outside to watch the fireworks being set-off up and down the river by the homeowners who live on its banks. It is a beautiful sight - it puts me in a melancholy mood. I wish I could turn the clock back to a year ago - there would have still been enough time to keep this nightmare from ever happening.

FRIDAY, JULY 5TH

Neither one of us goes to see Chad today. This is only the third Friday we have missed since his arrest.

On the way to work, I catch the tail end of a news item on the radio regarding some research that has just been concluded. Apparently, someone is claiming to have identified the gene that causes schizophrenia. I'm not sure what this means or what the ramifications are. I search the Internet, and watch the news, but I don't hear anything more about it. It strikes me, as I was searching the huge "Health" section on the website, that there is nothing regarding mental health.

MONDAY, JULY 8TH

I don't know why, but today I feel impressed to write the complaint letter against "Chuckie." At lunchtime I sit down to write, and it only takes a few minutes to complete the cover page. I guess I've had the letter formed in my subconscious for some time now. The cover page is about the basic charge. I am attaching excerpts from this journal to provide the details. I include the days of Chad's arrest, the day after, the day we retrieved our car, and the day Chuckie played his intimidation game with Debra at the supermarket.

I also include a paragraph citing who I will contact if I feel there is any retribution from the Sheriff's Department for filing the complaint or if I am not satisfied with resolution. Sad to say, I think the odds are pretty good that I will be contacting these people.

Even though it's Chad's deposition tomorrow, I really don't expect to hear from Jim - it would be out of character for him if I did. I am hoping that he at least sees Chad and that Chad calls us after. I will get my wish, though I am shocked by what I am told!

At 8:30 PM, Chad calls and says he has just seen Jim. We can tell that something is up by the excitement in his voice. Jim has advised Chad to plead guilty tomorrow!! Where in the hell did this come from? Jim thinks that a jury trial is just too risky, and by pleading guilty the Judge will decide the outcome. I can only assume that Jim feels that Chad will receive more equitable treatment from the Judge. But I wouldn't know. Apparently Jim also feels that we don't need to be included in this decision! I was also under the impression, based on the last hearing, that a jury trial was up to *us* not McKenney. *What the hell is going on!*

Talking to Chad, I try not to sound upset. I don't want to upset him and I think he wants reassurance from us that he is doing the right thing. Chad focuses on the fact that if it were to go to jury trial and he loses, and even if the jury takes pity on him, he could still get five to ten years. Under the point system, the Judge would be dealing with sentencing guidelines of three to six years. Jim told Chad that, because of the circumstances, he feels that the sentence could be the minimum, and he already has served almost a year. I wonder to myself what are the chances of my son having a full recovery or even a partial recovery. Debra and I are only too well aware of the lack of treatment schizophrenics receive in prison. The Chad we once knew is going to be gone forever.

I ask Chad if Jim said anything about what kind of treatment he would get while being incarcerated, or would he serve any of his time in a medical facility. Chad says that Jim did briefly say something about it; but, he couldn't remember what. He did remember Jim saying something to the effect that by pleading guilty we would have some control about where he would end up. I tell Chad that he is doing the right thing by following the advice of his attorney and tell him we'll see him in court tomorrow. Then the mechanical voice comes on and tells us our time is up. I say good-bye to my son on the last day of his life when he is not a convicted felon.

I call Dad after and relay what Chad has told me. Dad also is confused about what has happened and has many of the same questions I have. He is perplexed as to why we have been left out of the loop and says we need to try to get a hold of Jim before tomorrow. I am frustrated. I have no better chance of getting hold of Jim tonight as I do of getting hold of the Man in the Moon. Dad can't believe that, with the mountain of psychiatric evidence we have concerning how seriously ill Chad is, that it has come down to this. He can't believe it can be pushed aside and not even considered. He speculates that if Jim wants Chad to plead guilty, he has worked out some kind of deal that would allow Chad to receive some treatment.

Dad also mentions that it is unbelievable that our legal system finds it necessary to incarcerate a severe mentally ill nineteen year-old boy who is incapable of understanding the ramifications of what he was doing; while Fortune 100 executives and directors, who have defrauded investors and employees of millions and millions of dollars will never spend a day in jail. The phone conversation does not last long. I am lost in my own thoughts, and I tell Dad that I will call him tomorrow.

TUESDAY, JULY 9TH

Neither one of us sleeps well. I get up at 4:30 AM and go to the computer to work on the dairy. I am anxious for the time to pass quickly, so we can get to the court and talk to Jim to see what his version of the events are. It is not a pleasant experience to get up one morning and to prepare yourself to endure the pain of watching your son plead guilty to a felony. Once again, I think back to the day he was born. When I held him in my arms and looked into his eyes, I promised him that no one was ever going to harm him. How did this happen - it is so surreal - can I please wake up now!

We arrive twenty-five minutes before the scheduled court time, hoping that Jim will be there. Several of our friends from Church show up, but at 9:00 AM there is no sign of Jim. We go in and wait for the court proceedings to get underway. After about an hour, Jim shows up. Eventually, as court proceedings are going on, Jim leans over the railing to tell me what is happening. As far as I'm concerned, this is not going to work, and I quickly tell him that Chad called us last night and said you told him to plead guilty. This gets Jim's attention, and he tells me let's go find a room to talk about this. I motion for Debra to follow us. Jim starts off by telling us about his conversation with Chad, and it's pretty much the same as what Chad told us. He then states that he is perfectly willing to take this to trial, and he is prepared to do so; but he says that the risks are great. If Chad pleads guilty today, the sentencing range would be between three to six years. If he pleads not guilty and loses, the minimum sentence he would get is five years and the maximum is life.

I want to ask Jim how did we get from what was supposed to be a deposition today to Chad pleading guilty! But instead I ask, "What happened? From the very beginning we have been preparing ourselves to plead not guilty by reason of insanity." Jim says two things; 1) McKenney didn't live up to his word and 2) you threatening the Sheriff's Department. That did it for me! I finally decide to let Jim know how I feel about the quality of their representation to date. "Jim, have I ever filed a complaint against the Sheriff's Department? Don't try to blame me for the fact that you and your firm have done a lousy job! I have spent thousand and thousand of dollars on you guys and your psychiatrists, and what do we have to show for it! Based on the results to date, Chad has a misdemeanor on his record, he will become a convicted felon today and has had his psychiatric report splashed on the front of the local newspaper." Jim lashes back, "I resent that, I have worked very, very hard on this case!" I reply, "It is not only that, Jim, it is also the fact that you never communicate with us! We never know what is going on!" Jim replies, "I have gone out my way to communicate with you, I have sent you copies of everything as I have gotten them. I don't need this! I want off this case! I will make sure that whoever you get will get everything in my files!" Debra is crying and says softly, "Please stop." Jim says to me, "You don't seem to understand the significance of what Chad did. A bank robbery is a very serious offense. It is not a misdemeanor." Jim is physically trembling and says again that we are not dealing with a misdemeanor. Jim obviously had not understood that when I mentioned misdemeanor I was referring to the marijuana conviction.

I have gone too far. Debra is sobbing and Jim is still shaking. It strikes me that Jim has taken my criticism pretty hard, he is not an attorney who is accustomed to failure, and I can tell that we are not the only ones that have been under a lot of pressure. I take a deep breath and say; "Jim, Chad will never be able to fully recover if he spends an extended time in prison. We both know that." Jim settles down. I think we both realize that what is done is done - the best thing we can do now is to concentrate on what is best for Chad going forward. I tell Jim I realize that, given where we are now, the best thing for Chad is to plead guilty. We discuss more calmly how we got to where we are now, and Jim says the Andrea Yates trial had a big impact on this case. He has been successful in a number of insanity cases prior to this one, but he wonders if he will ever be able to win another one after the dreadful Andrea Yates decision. We conclude that the most likely outcome of a jury trial, given the extreme conservative nature of the county's citizens, is that Chad will be found guilty, and the jury will feel they are being kind by just giving him ten to fifteen years, instead of life.

We start talking about what can we do now for Chad. Jim discusses the merits of moving Chad to the Saluda Regional Jail. It has a much better reputation than the Northern Neck Jail. We both know the Superintendent and feel that as long as Chad continues to be a model prisoner, he will be able to participate in work release programs and be allowed to have physical visits. Jim comments that all attorneys in this area hate dealing with the Northern Neck Jail. They are usually made to wait a half hour or more when they go to visit their clients, and Jim says they once made him remove a small paper clip from the papers he was carrying.

Debra has composed herself and is starting to come around to the discussion, now that we are being constructive. I ask, is it possible to request that, as part as of his guilty plea, he will get proper psychiatric care and maybe even spend part of his sentence in a medical facility? Jim says we can ask, but the courts really have very little control over these things, once an inmate is handed over to the correctional authorities. I then ask is there anything we can do now in getting him some treatment? Debra and I both comment on Chad's unbelievable weight gain and the fact that Chad has not received any treatment since his visit to Tuckers over nine months ago. Jim exclaims that there is certainly something we can do about that! He says that he can request the court to allow treatment before his sentencing date and that he can get a court order today to allow Chad to be transported to see Dr. Gomez to get his medication reevaluated. This makes us all feel a little better. Then the discussion turns to what we can do to keep Chad's sentence at a minimum.

Jim says that he will subpoena Dr. Jarnecke to attend the sentencing and to testify how important it is that Chad receives the proper treatment while incarcerated and how detrimental an extended sentence would be for Chad. He says, given that Dr. Jarnecke is the State's own psychologist, his recommendations would carry more weight and it wouldn't cost us anything. He says he has already talked to Dr. Jarnecke about this, and that he is more then willing to cooperate.

Jim also says that both Debra and I will probably be called to testify. Debra's testimony is more crucial because she is the mother and has an extensive background in the medical field. Jim also points out that having a good turnout on the sentencing date certainly wouldn't hurt.

As our discussion is coming to an end, Jim mentions the one thing that has been bothering him the last two days. He is not sure that Chad has the mental capacity right now to fully understand the ramifications of what pleading guilty will mean to him. Jim says he feels he has a good relationship with Chad (something that Chad has confirmed), but he doesn't want to unduly influence Chad's decision. Jim says that he wants to reaffirm with Chad that this is truly what he wants to do and that Chad understands he will be a convicted felon by pleading guilty. With that, we break up and return to the courtroom.

We have been meeting with Jim for about forty-five minutes. Apparently, the court has finished with everyone else, as all the court personnel and our friends are waiting for us and all the other visitors are gone. Jim goes to meet with Chad, and about ten minutes later Jim and Chad enter the courtroom. The next ten minutes are a blur to me. For some reason, McKenney finds it necessary to give a detailed account of what Chad did when he went into the bank. After McKenney finishes, Jim says, and I think I detect a little irritation in his voice, "Your honor we have never disputed the facts of the robbery, it has been our contention all along that Chad didn't know what he was doing by reason of insanity."

Chad then actually enters a not guilty plea, but he pleads guilty on the grounds that there is such a disparity between punishments if he was to be found guilty by a jury that he doesn't dare take the risk. This is some nuance that Jim didn't tell us about, but it is somewhat comforting to know that on the record Chad does not accept the prosecution's assertion that he could understand the ramifications of what he was doing. Regardless, Chad is now a convicted felon. I hope that the prosecution, the Sheriff's Department, the Judge, and Chad's victims are all content now. But they still will have another opportunity to extract more flesh on September 24th, the day of Chad's sentencing. It is hard to describe what I am feeling; the best I can come up with is *numb*. At one stage, I do fight back a few tears, but I'll be damned if I am going to let any of these court personnel and the deputies see me cry.

A couple of small things happen after Chad enters his plea that I think embody the impersonal nature of the whole process. The sentencing date had originally been set for September tenth, but Jim has a conflict; and just like that, it gets pushed back two weeks. It means nothing to everyone involved, except of course Chad, who now has to wait another two weeks to know his fate. In addition, Jim makes the point to the Judge that Chad has received almost no treatment for almost a year and he would like the court to allow Chad to visit his psychiatrist before the sentencing. The Judge has no problem with it, but McKenney voices concern that it is asking too much of the Sheriff's Department to escort Chad to Richmond for the appointment because it will interfere with the deputies summer vacation time! Can you believe it!

As we file out of the courtroom, Jim approaches me and reiterates how important it is that we have a good turnout on September 24th. Needless to say, the drive home is like a dream. I'm second-guessing myself as to whether we have done the right thing. There is no way Chad can recover while in prison. I think of the woman who was found not guilty of murdering her husband because she was experiencing post partum depression. Chad illness is much more severe, and he didn't hurt anyone; but, here he is, going to prison at age nineteen. I also wonder if this would have occurred in a more liberal state, such as Massachusetts. Maybe Chad would have already been admitted to a medical facility where he would be getting some help, and criminal charges would not have been pursued.

I give Dad a call and he is perplexed that more wasn't made of the psychiatrist's findings. I tell Dad that fairness and reason have long since given way to local politics. I tell Dad about my quarrel with Jim and the details of the proceedings. He says that it is probably a good thing that Jim now knows how unhappy we are about the job they have done - maybe that will get their attention and they'll do a better job of wrapping this up.

We talk about the fact that today's results have no bearing on the Federal counterfeiting charge and how the prosecution showed no mercy. I tell Dad that at least I'm free now to file a complaint against the Sheriff's office without them threatening me that it will impact the outcome of Chad's trial. Dad is alarmed that I would consider doing this, given the fact that Chad hasn't been sentenced. He pleads with me not to do this given the nature of what we are dealing with. I can't believe it. The one-year anniversary of Chad's arrest is a little more than a month away and Chad's sentencing is six weeks after August 14th. I'm afraid that the statute of limitations will have expired by then. Don't tell me that the Sheriff's Department has gotten away with their actions and that this county has gotten away with nailing my son to the cross! Damn it! I thought I lived in America! How unfair the law is, that the statute of limitations can run out before a case is resolved. I firmly believe now that one of the reasons for McKenney's constant delaying actions was to insure that this case wouldn't be resolved until his buddy was out of harms way. No one cares about Chad.

Dad reminds me that Jim said that I had up to two years to file a civil suit, and we both believe that I need to quickly get to a civil rights attorney that can gives us the facts and could care less about his relationship with McKenney. I don't have much faith in a civil suit and, based on case results that I find on the Internet, the old adage that you can't fight city hall is very true. I have a sinking feeling that about the only chance I have of obtaining some justice and maybe some reimbursement for property damage is by filing the complaint. I tell Dad that there is a chance that by filing the complaint, I will encourage the Sheriff's office to actually want things to go well for Chad at the sentencing. They got their conviction - I'm sure they think that helps in some way to validate their actions. By filing this complaint they will learn for the first time that I am keeping a detailed dairy of events as they occur, that I have pictures and witnesses that can verify the property damage, and that it can be very embarrassing for them if it were to become public knowledge. I also mention the fact that by filing the complaint, we will have on record Chuckie's threats and abuse, and chances are that he will never bother us again.

Dad brings up a good point about how maybe Chuckie's harassment of Debra at the supermarket four months after Chad's arrest has extended the statute of limitations. We both agree that the best thing to do now is to find a lawyer who can answer some of these questions.

It is ironic that about a half-hour after finishing our discussion, Ali comes up to my study and drops a newspaper in my lap, and I can tell she is upset. On the front page is the original picture of Chad being escorted to the courthouse that appeared in the same newspaper almost a year ago. The bold headline declares that, "Alleged robber schizophrenic but not legally insane." While I had been talking to Dad, Debra and Ali had gone to the local convenience store to get some milk and the newspaper.

The article follows the usual trend of sensationalizing the story by distorting the facts and by leaving out those items that would put Chad in a better light. The article states that the strength of the state's psychiatrist report apparently convinced Chad and his defense team to plead guilty. There is no mention of the fact that there were two other opinions both filed by experts with stronger credentials than that of the State's and that both opined that Chad should not be held accountable. There is no reference to the potential life term that could be handed down by the good ultra-conservative Christians of Heathsville - the real reason Chad pleaded guilty. The article actually prints the reasoning behind Jarnecke's conclusion why Chad could tell the difference between right and wrong. Of course, the reasoning of the other two experts as to why Chad could not tell the difference between right and wrong is not mentioned.

The article paints McKenney in a very positive light, implying that he is a hard-charging, no-nonsense guy, who gets the job done. One quote reads, "McKenney said that there was no plea agreement in the case, but he would drop state counterfeiting charges against the 19-year-old Wegkamp since the federal government has charged Wegkamp with counterfeiting." I remember being told that the Sheriff and McKenney sometimes actually write the articles that appear in the paper, all Editor Newton does is to correct them for grammatical errors and print them.

I go downstairs to talk with Debra about the article. She is in tears. "I just can't take this anymore! I just can't take it!" She then tells me she saw McKenney yesterday when she was driving through Heathsville. He was standing outside of the *Northumberland Echo*'s offices. She was hoping it didn't mean anything, and now she knows it did. Sure enough, not only did McKenney and the newspaper know that Chad was going to plead guilty before we did - they even knew it before Chad did. Thanks Jim! I can only take solace in the fact that I know McKenney one day will have to face the only Judge that really matters.

WEDNESDAY, JULY 10TH

I can't and don't want to get out of bed and go to work. I feel like a heavy dark cloud surrounds me and a piece of me has died. I don't ever remember it ever being harder to get up and go about the day's business - but I do. In many respects, this day is harder than the day after Chad was arrested. Debra called in the day before, knowing she wouldn't be able to make it today. She is taking Prozac, but she is not doing well; and I worry about her. Her two-week vacation is supposed to start this weekend. It will come none too soon. As a husband and a father, I still feel helpless.

FRIDAY, JULY 12TH

Debra and I ride together to go see Chad. Debra tells me that for the past two nights she has found Ali awake, crying. Poor Ali, she hardly ever gets any attention from me, and I keep thinking by her rough exterior that she has made it through all of this quite well. Chad and Ali did everything together growing up - this has had to have some effect on her. *Hang in there kid. Hopefully, this will soon be over.* Ali is going with Debra to Ohio - it will also be a good for her to get away.

We talk with Chad about the court proceedings. Chad says he was disappointed that no plea agreement had been entered into and that his sentencing got postponed by two weeks. He states that he doesn't understand it - usually when you agree to plead guilty, there are some concessions from the other side. He tells us that he doesn't think the attorneys did a very good job. I tell him, don't get me started. We also talk about the Saluda Jail and how he will probably like it there. Hopefully, he does get transferred there before the sentencing so the delay won't matter.

215

CHAPTER 19

THE LONG WAIT

SUNDAY, JULY 14TH

Debra and Ali leave for Ohio. I'm now the protector of the dog and cats.

Dad calls me in the afternoon. We talk more about whether McKenney is going to give us a break at Chad's sentencing. Dad is hoping that McKenney is satisfied with the guilty conviction and won't press for the maximum sentence. I tell Dad that Debra thinks we are both nuts, if we think that is really going to happen. Chad is the best thing that could have possibly happened for McKenney's political career.

Dad says that he is hoping he is advising us correctly. He strongly urges me to keep trying to get a "second opinion" from a qualified attorney, and he offers to pay for it.

MONDAY, JULY 15TH

None of the lawyers I had called last week have returned my calls. I call another local law firm to see whom they would recommend for a civil case. They give me a strong recommendation of a civil rights attorney in Richmond. They say he has had extensive experience in lawsuits involving police brutality and corruption. I leave a voice-mail message for him to call me.

I get a phone call from Chad that night, but I screw up in answering the call. Usually the computerized voice comes on and says you have a call from the Northern Neck Regional Jail, press one if you want to accept the call. I realize just as I am pressing one, that the voice message said I had a collect call from the Northern Neck Regional Jail. Out of habit I had pressed one, without really paying attention to the message. It cuts the caller off. I'm confused because I have just recently made a prepayment and I don't know why Chad would call collect. I wait by the phone hoping that Chad will try to call back - he doesn't.

TUESDAY, JULY 16TH

I have not heard from the civil rights attorney, so I try calling his office again. This time I get his secretary, and she actually sets an initial consultation for July 30th! I wish we could have set up the appointment for an earlier date; but beggars can't be choosers. I am now anxious and can't wait. I'm hoping that nothing happens that would cause him to postpone. We are getting very close to the anniversary of Chad's arrest.

WEDNESDAY, JULY 17TH

Debra calls to see how I'm doing. I tell her about the phone call on Monday and the fact that I have not heard from Chad since our visit last week. She wants to know if I'm planning on visiting Chad on Friday. I tell her I will, if I haven't heard from him by then.

Debra then says she forgot to tell me something. Just a few days before she left for Ohio, someone from personnel at her job called her and wanted to know the outcome of Chad's case. They wanted to know what the verdict was (like they didn't know), how long Chad was going to be incarcerated, and where. I didn't know this was any of their business. Debra and I both wonder if it is possible that they can fire her, now that Chad is a convicted felon. One more thing to worry about!

I call and cancel my cardioversion scheduled for Monday. They are adamant that they will not perform the procedure without someone being there who can drive me home. I thought about asking several of my friends to accompany me, but it is in Richmond, and someone would have to sacrifice their whole day - it is asking too much.

THURSDAY, JULY 18TH

I am wondering if the reason we haven't heard from Chad is that he has been transferred to the Saluda Regional Jail. I call the Northern Neck Regional Jail and they inform me that Chad is still there. I tell my boss that I will be visiting Chad tomorrow morning, if I don't hear from him tonight.

FRIDAY, JULY 19TH

I drive the forty miles to Warsaw to see Chad. Prison guards are waiting at the entrance to the parking lot. They are telling all the visitors to turn around and leave. One guard approaches me and asks me if I'm here for a certain meeting or am I a visitor. When I tell him I'm a visitor, he tells me I have to leave. No explanation, no apologies, just leave. Do these people have any idea that they are playing with people's lives, or are they just stupid! My vote is on stupid! It is a reminder to me just how important it is that I don't give up on the diary - this story needs to get out.

Debra calls me that afternoon to see how Chad is doing. I have to tell her that I wasn't allowed to visit him and that it has now been over a week since we have heard from him. I don't want this to upset Debra's vacation, and I tell her that I will call the phone company today to make sure the line is all right. I remind her to enjoy her vacation; she will not get another break for a long time.

I think to myself that if anything has happened to Chad and no one has told us - all hell is going to break loose. I really need to write that letter to the American Civil Liberties Union.

I do get some good news. I passed level one of the CFA exam. I still am going to have to deal with the time constraints of trying to study for the next level of the CFA exam and writing in the dairy. Both tasks are exhausting.

SUNDAY, JULY 21ST

I finally get a phone call from Chad today. It's a good thing I called the phone company and asked them to check the phone line, because Chad said his phone calls had been blocked. He was getting a message that the residents at this phone number had refused to accept any phone calls from the inmate. Brother!

I remind him that he will be going to see Dr. Gomez tomorrow for treatment and to get his medication reevaluated. He wants to know why he is going! I tell him that one of the things we are hoping the doctor will do is get him off the Zyprexa and onto Geodon or Risperdal, neither of which have weight gain as a side effect. I remind Chad that, though he has undergone several psychiatric evaluations, he hasn't received any treatment for almost a year - courtesy of the Northumberland County judicial system and the Northern Neck Regional Jail.

I don't say anything about my fear that the Sheriff's Department will come up with some excuse as to why they can't transport him. Debra and I are both praying that this happens without a hitch tomorrow. I make Chad promise that he will call Tuesday night to let me know how it went.

TUESDAY, JULY 23rd

Chad calls and says that everything went according to plan. He visited with Dr. Gomez for about forty-five minutes. Chad said that Dr. Gomez was changing his medication and that he said he would phone in the prescription to the jail. What a relief! I ask Chad what kind of questions did Dr. Gomez ask him, and Chad said he really couldn't remember. I also ask him if the Sheriff's deputies gave him any trouble and he says, no. I emphasize to Chad how important it is to take this new medicine as prescribed - it is the only way he is going to get better. He says he will, but I'm not convinced he means it.

After talking to Chad, I give Debra a call and give her the good news - I want her to enjoy her vacation as much as she can.

SATURDAY, JULY 27TH

Debra and Ali arrive home from vacation. It is late in the afternoon and they are tired from their drive from Ohio. It is good to see them, and they said they really had a good time. Debra loves her new nephew and says he is so cute! Her sister is mad at her because Debra would cuddle him every time he would start to act up and now he is spoiled! Ali went to a Six-Flags theme park and got to see a professional baseball game for the first time. It was the Cleveland Indians versus the front-running Minnesota Twins. It was the game where a batter for Minnesota, after being hit by a pitch, picked the ball up and nailed the pitcher, causing both benches to clear. She said it was great and I had to laugh. I've seen the replay on ESPN a number of times, so I know exactly what she is talking about. I am so glad they were able to get away for a few weeks.

TUESDAY, JULY 30TH

I drive to Richmond to visit with the civil rights attorney. I pay him a flat $250.00 fee for the opportunity to discuss my case with him and to see if it is worth pursuing. I also want to get responses to some of the same questions I have been asking for almost a year now and have never seemed to be able to get a straight answer.

After explaining the details of Chad's arrest and the treatment we had received from the Sheriff's Department, I ask him about the statute of limitations. He says that we have a year to file a defamatory lawsuit and two years to file a civil lawsuit based on whether our constitutional rights have been violated. He then surprises me by saying that the defamatory lawsuit would be tougher to prove and that we might have a very good case based on our constitutional rights being violated. Despite the crudeness exhibited by Wilkins, the fact that he was directing his remarks to us as a group rather than anyone of us specifically will protect him, and the law gives these guys so much leeway in a search warrant situation, we probably would not win a defamatory suit.

He does say that it looks like a good case can be made about our constitutional rights. The fact that they treated every member of the family as criminals is the basis. He wants me to get him a copy of the search warrants and wants me to find out if any male officers were present while Debra and Ali were being stripped searched.

I then ask the attorney what are the ramifications if I start writing letters and mentioning names. He gives me the same advice that Jim gave me about filing a complaint directly with the Sheriff's Department. The complaint will get me nothing, and they have already made it quite clear that Chad will suffer because of it. He advises me to wait until after the sentencing before I do anything. As far as mentioning names, he says, "The truth is a very powerful defense." But, he warns me that chances are good they would file a defamatory lawsuit against me, especially if it had an impact on their careers. He also says that defamatory lawsuits are easier to win if the plaintiff can show that it affected their livelihood. In any case, I would probably spend a small fortune in attorney's fees protecting myself. Isn't it funny, no matter what avenue you try to pursue, the odds are always strongly in their favor.

220

The attorney can tell that I'm frustrated. He tells me, "Look I know where you are coming from. You are dealing with a bunch of cowboys, as you so adequately put it, that probably all played together on the local football team as teenagers and got away with breaking a few laws themselves but were lucky enough not to get caught. Now they work as deputies. It is a problem in every rural area of the country. The amount of money that they are being paid can only attract the bottom-of-the barrel. How much do these guys make - maybe if their lucky, $25,000 a year! You got a bunch of guys whose IQ's are registered by two digits and stick with the job because they get to ride around town with guns on their hips and they can tell everyone how important they are."

His remarks make me realize that he has dealt with my type of situation many times.

I then ask him about the odd behavior of Debra's employer in asking her to give them the details of Chad's conviction. I ask him if she were to suddenly be let go, would we have any recourse. He doesn't miss a beat and tells me, yes, absolutely. He explains that the actions of the court have already established that Chad is severely mentally handicapped. This handicapped protection is extended to members of the immediate family. If they were to discharge Debra based on Chad's conviction, it would leave them wide open to a discrimination lawsuit and would put them under the radar of the Equal Opportunity Commission. He assures me that there is no way that they are going to dismiss Debra.

Well, I can certainly put my mind at ease on this one. It was worth the trip for that reason alone.

SUNDAY, AUGUST 4TH

I bear my testimony in Sacrament meeting at Church. The first Sunday of every month is set aside for a fast-and-testimony meeting. The testimony meeting is a time to bear witness of your faith in Christ and the principles and ordinances that he established. I have not spoken in Church since Chad robbed the bank and I'm careful not to approach the subject, knowing that I am not emotionally stable enough to talk about it in that kind of a setting. I do mention the recent corporate scandals as I touch on the facts that honesty and integrity are still the backbone of our economic system, no matter how many laws and regulations we pass to try to stop abuses. As I am bearing my testimony, I am thinking about the honesty and integrity of the individuals that Debra and I have been forced to deal with within the Northumberland County legal system.

The dictionary defines integrity as an unimpaired state, uprightness and honesty. The people we have had to deal with fall far short of this description. But what makes this fact so sad and sobering is the power these men wield in our county. What troubles me even more is that I know many of Northumberland's residents have no clue as to the "good-ol boy" network that controls their county.

A weird thing happens that afternoon. I am upstairs walking in our bedroom when I almost pass out. I am dizzy in a manner I have never felt before, I grab hold of a chair, and it isn't long before the feeling passes. As far as I can remember, I have never passed out in my entire life.

FRIDAY, AUGUST 9TH

We go to Richmond to have my cardioversion done. We talked with Chad the night before and I told him that we wouldn't be able to visit him. He is okay with that and wishes me luck.

After arriving at the hospital, it isn't long before I am shaved and prepared for the shock treatment. The nurses are nervous as they watch the heart monitor, as my heart is beating extremely slow, a result of the medicine I've taken for so long. The Head Nurse comes in and asks if I have been getting dizzy spells or have passed out recently. When I answer in the affirmative, she doesn't say anything and leaves. I don't think they ever intended to slow my heart down that much, and I now understand why I have been feeling so tired lately.

The doctor then comes in and introduces himself. He seems to be a very likable fellow, and he has some surprising news for me. My heart is not out of rhythm but given the severity of the slow heartbeat he wants to do a stress test and wants to keep me overnight for observation. I have had it with this. This has been so time consuming and the medical bills are piling up. I have a feeling that if I had not been put on all this medication I would probably be doing fine right now, given that my heart is back in its normal rhythm. I tell him, no. He asks me to take the stress test right now, if he can arrange it, which I agree to. I am put on a treadmill and manage to get my heart rate up to the point where the doctor feels comfortable enough to let me go home. He does want me to be fitted with a heart monitor for twenty-four hours next week and he puts me on some different kind of medicine. I am supposed to go back and see him next month. What a hassle!

SUNDAY, AUGUST 11TH

This weekend has been tough for me. The anniversary of Chad's arrest will be on Wednesday. I only have a few days left, before the statute of limitations expire, to file a complaint against the Sheriff or Wilkins. I have a strong feeling that I could be faced with a situation where it is now or never. Certainly, the Sheriff's Department and all the players involved deserve to be held accountable. But the risk that McKenney will go for the maximum sentence, as a way to get back at us, is just too great!

TUESDAY, AUGUST 13TH

Today is the anniversary of the bank robbery. The day doesn't mean that much to us because Chad was arrested on the fourteenth. However, I am sure that Chad's victims have marked this date and they are well aware of it. It still pains us to think that our son could have done this to such nice people. Words just can't express the feelings that Debra and I have about the terror our son put them through. I can only hope that one day they realize just how sick Chad was and is. I hope they can appreciate the fact that Chad gets no respite from the voices and hallucinations that haunt him every minute of the day and will probably do so for the rest of his life.

The "good-ol" boys are at it again. There is a picture on the front of this week's paper of Chuckie showing off their brand new fingerprinting equipment to Newton, the editor. The description below the photo indicates that Middleton took it. To see that picture of Chuckie, in full uniform, being glorified by his buddies is just about enough to make me change my mind about filing that complaint. I have one day left - technically, Chad was arrested on the fifteenth at 12:30 AM.

Dale calls us tonight and asks if we would like to meet them at Lowery's in Tappahannock for dinner tomorrow night. They are passing through on their way back to Budapest.

WEDNESDAY, AUGUST 14TH

We don't tell Dale and Lisa that today is the anniversary of Chad's arrest. Towards the end of the evening, the talk does turn to Chad and where we are with the proceedings. It is difficult to talk about it without getting choked up. I think both Debra and I are surprised at how close to the surface our emotions still are.

At one time Debra jokes with Dale that since he is in the business of training police officers, he needs to make a stop in Northumberland County. Dale just smiles, and shakes his head and says, "I'm in the business of training foreign police officers; thank you just the same."

We drove separate cars to the restaurant. On the long ride home my thoughts are of Chad. I just hope and pray that Chad will be able to find some peace and happiness in this life - everyone deserves that, even convicted felons.

THURSDAY, AUGUST 15TH

Ali has been elected captain (she is the only starting senior) on the girl's basketball team and they have all their starters back from the District championship team of last year. They have high hopes of being a contender for the state title and they get off to a good start tonight by easily winning their first scrimmage game. Ali had fourteen points and played a good all-around game.

FRIDAY, AUGUST 16TH

I go to see Chad alone and we end up having a good visit. He is very depressed and down. He tells me he can't take much more of this place. I ask him what is wrong and he tells me that a number of things have happened this week. Apparently, three of the guys that he has been playing cards with for months got busted for smoking. They were all transferred to another pod and Chad will probably not see them again. In addition, he went to sleep early one night and left his laundry bag out, and someone stole it! He has been wearing the same underwear for a week now. He went to the laundry people to ask for help and they told him to get lost. He has ordered underwear from the commissary, but he won't get those until Monday. I tell him I can't believe that someone would stoop so low as to steal another inmate's laundry. He also says that he gets no respect around here. When he goes to lunch, everyone sneers at him. Chad actually fights back the tears as he is telling me this.

I really don't know what to say to comfort Chad. You can only say "hang in there" so many times, and I've been saying that to Chad for over a year now. I think of McKenney postponing Chad's trial at every opportunity and denying him bail or proper medical treatment. He gets to go home at night and be with his family, while my teenage son is left to wrestle with his own private demons behind bars and within the midst of criminals.

Chad is so down, and I'm afraid of the consequences, so I do my best to give him something to look forward to. I suspect that part of his problem is his paranoia, but I don't mention that. I do remind him that his stay here should be cut short soon and that the Saluda Jail is supposed to be a much better place to serve time. Both Jim and I know the Superintendent at Saluda and he is a good man, who I think will keep an eye out for Chad's well being. I also remind him that the time he is serving now does count towards his sentence and, who knows, but maybe we will catch a break at his sentencing.

Chad seems to perk up, and asks me if I could give Jim a call and ask him a few questions. I tell him sure and that the next time Chad calls maybe I'll have some answers for him. Chad wants me to see if Jim has gotten any feedback from the pre-sentencing evaluation he underwent; when he thinks Chad will be transferred to Saluda; and what is being done about resolving the counterfeiting charge with the Fed.

As I leave, Chad is in a better state-of-mind and I make a mental note to make sure I call Jim as soon as I get to work. If I could give Chad some positive feedback on any one of the three questions, I know it could go a long ways towards helping Chad bear the stress of the next six weeks.

SUNDAY, AUGUST 18TH

I go to Church and ask the Branch President to remind everyone that Chad's sentencing is September 24th and we/Chad could sure use their support.

Chad calls that afternoon and I have to tell him that I haven't talked with Jim yet, but I will try him again on Monday. He sounds like he is doing okay.

225

I do some research on the Internet regarding outcomes of recent court cases in Virginia involving insanity defenses. What I find just makes it all the harder to accept what has happened to Chad. There was the Lorena Bobbitt case that had attracted national attention. She cut off her husband's penis one night. Her lawyer would argue that she acted on an irresistible impulse, and she was found innocent and won her temporary insanity case.

There is another case that just floors me when you compare the result of that case to Chad's. It was the mother and school teacher in Fairfax County that murdered her husband while she was experiencing postpartum depression. She had no prior record and she won her temporary insanity case and never spent a day in jail! What can I say? Chad was an eighteen-year-old, severely mentally ill teenager, who didn't physically harm anyone, and he gets three-and-a-half years in prison that will make it impossible for him to make a full recovery for the rest of his life. Where is the justice in that?

MONDAY, AUGUST 19TH

Jim does return my call from Friday. Unfortunately, he has not received the pre-sentencing evaluation, and he has tried to call the contact at the Fed but they have not returned his call. He does say however, that he has just got about everything in place to transfer Chad to Saluda!

Jim surprises me by making a comment that maybe Chad going in front of the Fed would be a good thing, because they have much better facilities than the state. I can't help but remember that a year ago at this time, Jim was telling us that we did not want to go the Fed route. Of course, that was before his good buddy double-crossed him and Chad.

Chad calls again that night and I give him the good news about Saluda. Chad is ecstatic and I spend the rest of the phone call trying to settle him down (I'm thinking in the back of my mind that something could still go wrong).

TUESDAY, AUGUST 20TH

Upon arriving home after a rough day at work, Debra tells me she has also had a stressful day. At 6:30 PM we get a call from Chad and he says that he has really been sick for almost two days now and hasn't been able to keep anything down. He says that the nurses will not do anything for him. He went to see them last night and they gave him some liquid to drink and he immediately vomited that up. When he went back to see them, they told him there was nothing more than could do and not to bother them anymore. Chad says he feels so nauseated right now he doesn't even dare to drink a cup of water. Debra tells Chad, "It doesn't matter what the nurses told you, you march right back there and tell them that you are really sick. If that doesn't work, complain to the guard on duty and keep complaining until someone does something about it!"

I feel bad now for both Chad and Debra. The competency of the Northern Neck Regional Jail has been in question in our minds for a long time and now Debra is visibly upset that no one seems to be lifting a finger to help Chad. She also tells me I hope he isn't hallucinating and tries to hurt himself! Now I'm upset!

A couple of hours pass, and we don't hear anything more from Chad. Its now 9:30 PM and the TV program "American Idol" is about to start. We have been watching the show together for five weeks now, rooting for our favorite singer, Kelly Clarkson. Just then, the phone rings and Ali tells Debra that she has hurt her knee and she needs us to bring the other car to come and get her. Ali had a scrimmage game tonight and has taken Debra's car. Debra, who is now exhausted, and already stressed to the max, tells Ali that her knee can't be that bad, she has managed to get to the phone so she can manage to get the car back and hangs up on Ali. A minute latter the phone rings; it is a friend of Debra's, who has attended the scrimmage game, and confirms that Ali has hurt her knee. Debra asks her if Ali is playing the "drama queen" or is she really hurt that badly. Her friend replies that she isn't sure and Debra tells her to have Ali drive our car home now and then hangs up. Debra and I will both regret not going to Ali's aid immediately. We will find out in the days ahead that Ali's injury is serious.

Ali will not get home until 11:30 PM and her knee has swollen up like a balloon.

WEDNESDAY, AUGUST 21ST

Ali actually wants to go to school even though it hurts her to put any weight on her right leg. Debra makes her stay home and packs her knee in ice and goes to the store to get some ace bandages and some painkiller.

THURSDAY, AUGUST 22ND

This is another stressful day for Debra. She goes to the doctor to get a cyst removed from the back of her neck. She gets a local anesthesia and it takes eight stitches to close it up after the doctor is done. After that, she takes Ali to the doctor. Ali's knee is still swollen badly, and the doctor makes an appointment for a MRI to be done next week.

FRIDAY, AUGUST 23RD

Debra goes to visit Chad before going to work. He wants to know why he hasn't been transferred after what we told him on Monday. All Debra can do is to tell him that she doesn't know. Chad still seems to be pretty despondent, though he is not acting as paranoid as he was last Friday. Debra gives me call at work and we discuss why Jim would tell us that Chad's transfer is imminent if it wasn't true. I tell Debra that I have to believe it is going to happen any day now.

TUESDAY, AUGUST 27TH

Jim calls with great news! The court order has gone through for Chad's transfer!

It is kind of ironic, because today is the day I send a letter to the American Civil Liberties Union protesting the treatment, or lack thereof, that Chad has received at the Northern Neck Regional Jail. I have little hope that they will take Chad's case given the amount of requests they get and their limited staff. However, I do think that the case meets the definition of what they will consider based on the rights of the mentally ill and the ramifications for them if the suit was successful.

Ali goes to the hospital to have a MRI done on her knee. We won't get the results until next week.

THURSDAY, AUGUST 29TH

We receive a copy of the court order for Chad's transfer. The Judge, Jim, and McKenney sign the court order. I wonder if the delay was because McKenney was slow to sign it, but I'll have to give him credit, at least he signed it.

FRIDAY, AUGUST 30TH

For some reason, Chad is still at the Northern Neck Regional Jail. Debra calls ahead to make sure he is there and then goes to see Chad and shows him the court order through the window. Debra says that he gets very excited and during the rest of their visit has a big smile on his face.

SUNDAY, SEPTEMBER 1ST

We get a call from Chad and he is at the Saluda Jail! The transfer was made just a few hours after Debra had seen him on Friday. I asked him if they let him know about it ahead of time. He says not really, one of the guards came and took him to a holding cell. He thought he was in some kind of trouble. They then told him that he was being transferred, and they let him go back to the pod to get some of his things. I asked him how the other inmates reacted, and he said they loved it - Chad wasn't allowed to take any of his commissary purchases with him so he passed out his junk food and radio to them. He had been held there for over a year.

He says that he loves the Saluda Jail. There is more for the inmates to do, and they are allowed to go outside in the yard every day and play basketball. He says that the commissary is more like a small grocery store. He got to eat some Doritos for the first time since his incarceration. He says that he is in a smaller pod with only fifteen other inmates. He is also excited about the fact that they have two cable TVs in the pod. He also says that they are required to do their laundry three times a week - the Northern Neck Regional Jail had no laundry requirements. Chad says they could have cared less if they were filthy or not.

What a relief! I'm so happy that Chad likes his new surroundings. I am hoping that the guards and nurses will be more conscientious of making sure Chad takes his medicine. The best we can hope for now is that Chad will not spend much more than a year here and that the deterioration of his mental state will stabilize until he is released and we can get him some psychotherapy.

TUESDAY, SEPTEMBER 3RD

I have not heard back from the civil rights attorney since I've sent him copies of the search warrant. I suspect it is a bad sign that he hasn't called. I give him a call and sure enough, he says that we are all mentioned in the search warrant so again, no matter how crude they were, they still had the legal authority to search all of us. He says that we will probably be wasting our time pursuing it. *Is that all it takes in this country to be stripped searched in your own home? A judge or a magistrate, who doesn't know the first thing about what is going on, who puts your name and all of your family's names on a piece of paper, because the sheriff wants him to, and then sanctifies it by calling it a search warrant!*

I knew this was going to happen. The civil case is going to amount to nothing, and the statute of limitations has expired for filing a complaint. I mention this to the attorney and then ask does this mean they got away with everything? The taunting? The threats? The whooping and hollering like a bunch of savages as they closed in for the kill? The physical damage to our home and car? Their chest thumping and media glorification in the months ahead?

He says I still want you to call me after the 24th. I hope he has got something planned and whatever it is, I hope it will work.

THURSDAY, SEPTEMBER 5TH

Chad surprises us by calling us first thing in the morning. He needs addresses of the people who have been writing him. He left all that information behind when he was transferred. He sounds agitated, and when I ask him what is wrong he starts complaining about the jail. After he complains for a few minutes, I stop him and ask does this mean you wish you were back at the Northern Neck Jail? He says no, and as I hang up the phone, I wonder what it will take to get Chad to mellow out.

Debra takes Ali to an orthopedic surgeon to go over her MRI results. The news is somewhat encouraging. The MRI indicates that Ali has torn her ACL (anterior cruciate ligament), but the doctor says that the x-rays contain shadows and it is hard to determine exactly what the damage is. He is encouraged about how stable Ali's knee is and the fact that the swelling has gone down considerably. He thinks there is good chance that Ali hasn't torn her ACL but has damaged her meniscus. He says he can fix that with arthroscopy surgery and Ali can be back to playing ball within a week! He says he just won't know the extent of the damage for sure until he can gets inside with the arthroscope. They scheduled surgery for next Wednesday.

In the afternoon, Debra goes to see Chad for the first time at the Middle Peninsula Regional Security Center, otherwise known as the Saluda Jail. Our first clue that this is a better jail is the fact that visiting hours are all day Thursday. The hours are from 9:00 AM to 11:00 AM on Fridays for the Northern Neck Jail. Debra says that there is a receptionist who greets you when you come in. You give her the name of the inmate you want to see, and she explains to you how to get to the visitor's room. The setup is still the same. You talk by telephone through a glass plate window. She also says they did get to talk for over an hour.

Unfortunately, she says that Chad is not doing well. She says he looks awful and seemed to be totally psychotic. She says that he was hyper, and kept tracing the window with his finger and wiping the counter top with his sleeve. He seemed very depressed. But the worst news is that Chad says the voices are back and, instead of speaking to him in fragments, they are using full sentences! Debra says Chad starts to cry as he tells her this, and then says, "Mom I'm scared. I really think I need to go to a mental hospital - what is wrong with me?"

Debra is distraught as she leaves the jail and immediately tries to call both Dr. Gomez and Jim. She leaves messages that something is wrong with Chad and to please call her. She also calls the jail and asks to speak to the nurse. She explains what has happened, and the nurse says she will leave a message for their psychologist to see Chad. Debra then becomes further distraught when the nurse tells her the name of the psychologist. She knows who he is and doesn't think much of his work.

When I get home that night, Debra and I talk at length about what we think has gone wrong. We discuss whether Chad is still missing pill calls at this jail or if the new medicine that has been prescribed for him is not doing the job. I do tell Debra that I have fears that maybe her actions today may result in Chad being put back on Zyprexa. That is the last thing I want - the side effects were terrible for Chad. Debra tells me that she did leave in her message a request to Dr. Gomez not to put Chad back on the Zyprexa unless there was no alternative.

FRIDAY, SEPTEMBER 6TH

By the end of the day I am pleased that both Dr. Gomez and Jim have not only returned Debra's calls but they have also arranged a court-ordered visit for Chad to see Dr. Gomez on the 18th. They must have realized the urgency behind Debra's call, and for that I'm grateful.

SUNDAY, SEPTEMBER 8TH

Chad calls and he sounds fine to me. There is no indication in his tone that there is anything wrong, and we have a pleasant conversation. I ask him if he is still hearing voices and he says, no. After I hang up the phone, I don't know quite what to think, other than that the roller coaster ride continues.

TUESDAY, SEPTEMBER 10TH

We get a thank-you card from Chad today in the mail. It means a lot to me and I'm thinking maybe we are making some progress. The fact that Chad showed some insight into his illness last week and his thanking us for our help this week is a good sign to me. I mention to Debra again that I hope Dr. Gomez doesn't put Chad back on the Zyprexa. I also tell her that maybe the fact that Chad was still transitioning to his new surroundings had a lot to do with his behavior last week.

WEDNESDAY, SEPTEMBER 11TH

Ali is having her arthroscopic surgery this morning, and I have taken the morning off to be with her. The doctor tells us that the entire procedure takes about forty-five minutes to an hour depending on the extent of the damage. We squeeze Ali's hand and wish here good luck as they roll her off to the operating room. She has never had an operation before.

An hour passes and there is no sign that they have finished. I mentioned to Debra that something must have gone wrong. About a half-hour later the doctor comes out and tells us that unfortunately Ali's ACL was totally severed and that she will need a major operation in the near future. Just like that, Ali's high school athletic career is over.

I have to go back to work. Debra will break the news to Ali after she wakes up. I feel really bad now that I didn't rush to Ali the night she called and said she hurt her knee.

THURSDAY, SEPTEMBER 12TH

Both Ali and Debra go to see Chad. Ali has never visited Chad since he has been incarcerated. She has gone to most of his hearings, but she has never wanted to see him behind bars. Debra says that when Chad sees Ali, his face lights up with a grin from ear-to-ear and he never stops smiling the whole time they are there! Ali and Chad will talk with each other for over an hour and Debra says she was perfectly content to watch them chat away.

Chad tells them that he saw Jim yesterday and that Jim said he was going to put Chad on the stand to testify.

FRIDAY, SEPTEMBER 13TH

Jim leaves us a message that he has received the pre-sentencing evaluation and he has left us a copy. I go and get it and read it that night. It is basically a summary of Chad's history and a summary of three psychiatric reports that have been filed with the court. When you get to the last page, there is supposed to be a sentencing recommendation. The box is checked no recommendation. So what's the point? There is nothing in this report that the Judge doesn't already know. The only possible value of it is that it is a short synopsis of all the facts. Jim will tell me later that the reports used to make recommendations as to what part of the sentencing range the judges should be in when they pass their sentence. Apparently, problems arose when a judge's sentence was not in the range recommended and left either side open to questioning - so they just stop making recommendations. Seems to me then that maybe some taxpayer dollars could be put to better use.

TUESDAY, SEPTEMBER 17TH

I am surprised this morning when I awake. The first thought that hits me is that Chad's sentencing is now just a week away. I am already feeling nervous and stressed. What am I going to be feeling like seven days from now! Debra started feeling like this about a week ago. Luckily Cindy will be arriving with her newborn babe on the 20th! That should work wonders in helping Debra keep her mind off things, and Cindy will be a source of strength.

WEDNESDAY, SEPTEMBER 18TH

I get a call from Jim while at work, and he wonders if Debra and I can meet him tonight to cover a few items and to go over what he will be asking Debra.

I meet Debra at Arbys' for a quick bite, and I tell her some unbelievable news that I have just heard from a friend. Sheriff's Middleton's daughter is being charged with negligent homicide in King William County. Apparently, she had run a stop sign and hit a motorcycle, killing one of the riders and severely injuring the other! I can't help it, a small part of me of which I am not proud wishes that the Middleton's are given the same treatment at the hands of the law enforcement authorities in King William County as Middleton and his staff gave my family. I know it's not likely. Considering Middleton's position, I'm sure they will be granted special favors. But still, to get a taste of his own medicine the King William deputies need to approach Middleton in his home exchanging high five's and yelling and hollering like a bunch of hyenas and then wishing him a Merry Christmas as they arrest his daughter. They then need to approach his wife and children, strip-search them, and tell them that they are now all going to jail. But before they leave they need to do about $2,000 worth of property damage to his home and then make sure that in the weeks ahead the local newspaper applauds their great police work and that the King William Sheriff is quoted as saying that the Middleton's did not cooperate. And God help Middleton if he tries to file a complaint - because if he does - rest assured that things will get worse for his daughter.

I also wonder if any of this will even appear in the *Northumberland Echo* next week. You can bet your bottom dollar, if the circumstances were exactly the same except my daughter was involved, it would be the lead story next week.

We can only hope that she and her family are treated with understanding and compassion.

We have a good visit with Jim. He tells us about his visit with Chad and what was discussed. He tells us that Dave Harmon is taking an active interest in Chad and that he and Jim talked about the possibility of Chad being able to take some college courses while incarcerated and being allowed some "work release" privileges if he shows improvement.

We discuss at length Chad's present condition, and I do get an appreciation for the fact the Jim is one of but a handful of people who truly understand just how sick Chad really is. We discuss Chad's continuing obsession with his perceived scrotum problem. I make the point that Chad is convinced that if he can just get his scrotum fixed, all of his problems will go away and he'll be back to normal. Jim says he knows exactly what I mean. He mentions that you can be having an interesting discussion with Chad about his symptoms, but at the same time you know that Chad is convinced that his problems are not mental but physical. Jim mentions that, as you are talking to Chad, you can't help but like him and you want to so much just take him by the arms and shake him and say, "Listen to me, Chad! There is absolutely nothing physically wrong with you; there is nothing to worry about; you are going to be okay!" He says he realizes that if he has the urge to do this, that he can imagine how often we have wanted to do it. But you can't. It will only make Chad even more convinced that you don't understand his problem. All of us discuss whether Chad will ever be able to overcome this.

When Jim starts to go over Debra's testimony, she starts crying. She apologizes and then tells Jim she is afraid that she is going to cry the whole time she is up there! Jim tells her not to worry - if Chad were his son, he would be crying too. I think to myself that if Debra starts crying I'm not going to be able to hold the tears back. This is going to be rough. I just hope that Debra can compose herself enough to get through it. No one understands Chad's past history and its impact on him better than Debra does.

Jim gives us some copies of letters addressed to the court, written by three of the bank employees who were present when Chad robbed them. Any hope that there might be any forgiveness in their hearts is soon put to rest. The letters are venomous, and all three of them want Chad to fry! The tone of the letters would certainly be understandable, if they had been written shortly after the robbery occurred, but all three of them have been written in the past few days, more than a year after the robbery. I am fully aware that all three of these ladies actually feared for their safety for those few minutes that Chad was in their bank, but as far as I'm concerned their letters make them sound pretty "small-minded." Surely there must have been enough rumors going around that made them realize that there might be another side to this story.

One of the writers hints at there being another side. She says, "But I feel this young man had planned this robbery and did it without regard for anyone (incredibly, she says this after stating in the prior sentence that she thought she was safe because the Sheriff's office was right across the street)." She had obviously read Jarnecke's conclusion in the paper as to why he thought Chad could tell the difference between right and wrong and that Chad's defense was his mental illness. I guess she thinks that we were just making the whole thing up in order to get Chad off. She also shows her ignorance about a basic fact of paranoid schizophrenia. The illness has it most devastating impact on the frontal lobe area of the brain, which is the part of the brain that allows a person to rationalize and understand the impact of their actions upon themselves and others.

One of the bank tellers concludes her letter by saying, "I think the robber should be made aware of how he hurt others!" See above.

One of the other tellers waxes philosophical and concludes: "It was my 'wake up call' to how the world really is and not how I wish it was." I don't think she is referring to the fact that Chad has been struck down by paranoid schizophrenia in the prime of his life.

One of the things I find interesting about the letters is that none of them refer to Chad by name. They know full well what his name is. I guess it would personalize him too much if they were to use it. Well ladies "the robber" you are trying to put behind bars for years happens to be my son. I think about our decision not to trust Chad's fate to the whims of a local jury, and it's beginning to look like the right decision.

Debra "baits" Jim a bit by asking him has this thing already been decided and the outcome will be on the front of *the Northumberland Echo* and in the stores before we even get out of the courtroom (referring to what happen to us on the last court

236

date)? Jim doesn't bite, but he does tell us some interesting facts we never knew. Colston Newton, the editor who has been responsible for all the vicious articles on Chad is a convicted felon himself! He is actually the former prosecuting attorney for Westmoreland County, who had opened a private practice and had tried to cover his wife's spending habits (or so he says) by stealing funds from the trust accounts that he was the fiduciary over. The responsibility of fiduciary is to protect and watch over the funds that he has been entrusted with. After serving time, he could never work as a lawyer again, so the *Northumberland Echo* hired him as an editor for his writing skills. And to think that this man is free to destroy our reputations and that of our son.

Jim observes that all this it makes it all the more unbelievable that he would attack Chad in the manner he has. Jim would also tell us that he knows Colston and speaks to him from time to time. He told him how low he thought the paper had sunk by publishing the most personal parts of Chad's psychiatric evaluation and misrepresenting the extent of Chad's alcohol and drug abuse. He asked Colston what purpose was he trying to serve and did he have any idea just how damaging and detrimental this was to this young man. Debra and I would discuss later whether Colston is consciously or unconsciously trying to pull people down to his level.

After we arrive home, Debra discovers that she has lost her purse. She thinks she left it at Jim's office. Debra is a basket case. This is the last thing we need right now.

What a day!

THURSDAY, SEPTEMBER 19TH

We make several phone calls to Jim's office and then Arby's and find that she had left her purse at Arby's. I go to pick it up and everything is still in her purse. Thanks to Arby's and to whomever turned it in.

I take a long lunch hour and drive to Saluda to see Chad. I had actually been taken on a tour of the Saluda Jail several years earlier. Little did I know at the time that my son would one day take up residence here. The experience is such a contrast to that of the Northern Neck Regional Jail. The facilities are much cleaner and to have a receptionist/guard greet you with a smile when you walk in seems like a small miracle.

It is great to see Chad. He looks good physically. He has lost over thirty-five pounds since they took him off the Zyprexa. The combination of the Risperdal, and Geodon are doing the job. He seems to be in a good spirits and is obviously happy that he will soon learn his fate. We talk about the sentencing and how we are both hoping and praying that the sentence is close to the low end of the range. We also talk about what the possibilities are going to be for his employment, once he is released. I tell him that I think the trade areas are a possibility - people don't care if you have done time and are mentally ill if you can fix their car. Chad says he still wants to go to school and eventually try to open his own business. He is afraid that no one will hire him, and the only way he is going to be able to make it is if he works for himself. I don't disagree.

FRIDAY, SEPTEMBER 20TH

Jim gives me a call at work. He says that he has just had a long phone conversation with Dave Harmon. Dave says that his goal for every inmate they receive is to make them a better person before they leave. He says that he has taken Chad's file home with him and has noticed that one of the recurring themes throughout all the reports is that Chad has not always been taking his medication. He tells Jim that his nursing staff is instructed to visit all the inmates during pill call. The nurses carry water with them and they are instructed to not leave the inmates until they see them put the pills in their mouth and watch them swallow as they drink their water. If the inmates are asleep, they are instructed to wake them up. No one is to miss a pill call. This is like music to my ears.

Jim says that one of the worst things that could happen to us on Tuesday is to have the Judge order that Chad serves his sentence somewhere other than Saluda. Jim has talked to Dr. Jarnecke about trying to keep Chad in Saluda and the doctor, after hearing about the pill procedures, says that we wouldn't be able to do better anywhere else in Virginia.

Jim then makes a request to see if I can get someone from church, in addition to President Rasmussen, to testify on Chad's behalf, preferably someone who knows Chad well. This will turn out to be more of a problem than I imagine. As I call around, I find that the two members who would be the best are both out of town on the 24th. I can't get a hold of several others. Even though we are a small branch, not everyone knew Chad well. I leave a message on the answering machine for one of the members who I know will be at the sentencing, but she will be out of town until Monday night. I'm afraid I'm going to spring this on her at the last second.

Cindy arrives from Ohio at almost midnight. Her, newborn son is one cute kid. Debra is very excited to see them. I know this is going to be a big help for Debra.

SUNDAY, SEPTEMBER 22ND

Chad calls and says that Dave Harmon talked with him again today and said there is no way he can let Chad out on work release given his condition. I'm hoping that isn't true for the whole time he is there.

We have been letting Ali have free use of the car, and she has taken full advantage of it. She has struck a deer on her way home tonight, probably causing around $800.00 damage to the front end of the car. She is distraught and is crying as she comes into the house. She feels really bad about hitting the deer and has aggravated the pain in her knee. Needless to say, none of this helps anyone's stress level.

MONDAY, SEPTEMBER 23RD

It's tough going to work, but once I get started, I'm okay and it helps me get through the day. I make a few phone calls to be sure Jim has hooked up with the witnesses from Church. Debra takes Chad's court clothes to the jail. She has picked him out a pair of Dockers and a polo dress shirt. If nothing else, at least Chad will be the best-dressed inmate in court.

There is no getting away from the tension tonight. Debra and I both know that the length of Chad's sentence will determine what success, if any, we will have in salvaging him. Debra is a bundle of nerves and has felt sick all day. Jim calls and goes over Debra's testimony with her. After she hangs up, she shrugs her shoulders as if to say, that wasn't much help.

Chad calls. He is upset and wants to know if I can call Jim for him. He wants to let Jim know that if his sentence exceeds two years he wants to go to a regular prison. He stills has this notion that a prison is so much better than a jail. There is no use arguing. The best argument for Chad staying in Saluda is the medical treatment he will receive, which is something he doesn't even think he needs.

CHAPTER 20

THE SENTENCING

If thou art called to pass through tribulation; if thou art in perils among false brethren; If thou art accused with all manner of false accusations; If thine enemies fall upon thee; if they tear thee from the society of thy father and mother and brethren and sisters; and if thou shouldst be cast into the pit; know thou, my son, that all these things shall give thee experience, and shall be for thy good. Therefore, fear not what man can do, for God shall be with you forever and ever.

Joseph Smith
Liberty Jail
Liberty, Missouri, March 1839

TUESDAY, SEPTEMBER 24ᵀᴴ

We are getting so used to this now - we actually get a decent night's sleep. We are a little wary about not reporting until 10:15 AM per Jim's instructions. We remember all too well the time they swept Chad through the proceedings in the morning session when he wasn't supposed to appear until the afternoon session. The fact that Debra is testifying and that Jim wants to meet with several of the witnesses beforehand should prevent this from happening. We leave Cindy's son with one of the members in our church, who has agreed to watch him during the trial.

We arrive at the appointed time, and President Rasmussen and his wife are already there. The President is one of the witnesses for Chad. He will testify as to the support that Chad and we will receive from the church as Chad struggles with his illness. As we are chatting with the Rasmussens, other friends from the Church arrive, and so does Jim. He tells us that he wants to see how Chad is doing and how things are going in the courtroom and he'll get back to us.

We introduce Cindy to those church members who don't know her. We start to visit out in the foyer and Jim comes back and says that Chad's will be the last case presented, and right now they are only on case ten of twenty-two cases. It's about 10:30 AM. There are about ten of us and we remain in the foyer and continue to visit to pass the time away. At 11:30 Jim comes to get Debra to go over her testimony once again. At around 12:00 Debra returns and says she was never in the courtroom, so she doesn't have any idea how things are going. I'm hoping that Jim will come out and give us an update.

At around 12:30, everyone is wondering what is going on, and I feel bad that I told everyone to come at 11:00 AM. I'm afraid that now the court will break for lunch and our friends will have to wait a few hours more. That is exactly what happens. At 12:45 PM everyone comes streaming out of the courtroom. The guard at the door tells us that court has been recessed until 2:00 PM. That's okay, we have waited thirteen months now, what is a few more hours.

I'm a little perturbed that Jim has kind of left all of us hanging out there. He is still nowhere to be seen. We decide we might as well go get some lunch. As we drive to the convenience store, Debra tells us that she got more out of going over her testimony with Jim today, then she had the night before. It made more sense to her today about where he was going with it.

After arriving back at the courthouse, I am relieved to see that everyone was able to return. We debate whether we should go into the court room now or wait. Jim comes out and says there are four cases remaining until Chad's case and that we should all file into the courtroom now.

There is nothing that occurs with those four cases that changes my mind about what we are facing. If anything, they make us realize all the more what a pompous ass McKenney is. When one defense attorney says that he wants to call a character witness to the stand - after both he and McKenney had been discussing the merits of the case with the Judge, McKenney tosses his papers on his desk and throws his hands up in the air, indicating that to do so would be a complete waste of time, and he says sarcastically, "It's your case! Do what you want!"

The case involves a black couple that are divorced. The defendant is being held for driving a car without a license and it's his second offense after having a prior juvenile record. The defense attorney has called the defendant's former wife to the stand. The defense attorney is trying to show that the man is a responsible father who still visits his children and pays his child support. The wife is dignified and you can tell she is sincere as she testifies for her ex-husband.

When it comes time for cross-examination, McKenney pounces on her, calling her by name, and exclaiming something to the effect of, "Come on, what is really going on here? How far in arrears is your ex-husband in his child support payments?" McKenney tells the Judge that the defendant is $15,000 in arrears. His wife tries to explain that the debt has accrued over a long period of time, when either the defendant was incarcerated or unemployed and was incapable of sending her child support. McKenney quickly cuts her off and says in a loud voice, "How many children has your ex-husband fathered!" At this point, Debra nudges me and I can see her shaking her head in disgust. "Do you know that, as far as this court can determine, he has fathered at least nine children! You can bet he doesn't pay child support for all of them!" McKenney gets his desired reaction. The woman is flustered and looks confused. I can't hear her reply. McKenney proclaims that he has no further questions. I am surprised that during this line of questioning the defense attorney does nothing.

The Judge does exactly what McKenney requests and orders the defendant to be returned to jail with an extended sentence. The defendant and his attorney never had a chance. I question the old adage that I have often heard, that the burden-of-proof lies with the prosecution. Not in this court. Thank God he didn't steal a loaf of bread, i.e. *Les Misérables*! I wonder if I can be held in contempt-of-court for thinking these thoughts! I also gain a better appreciation why it is so important for a local defense attorney to stay on the good side of McKenney. What a sad state of affairs for anyone who is accused of a crime in Northumberland County.

As Chad's case approaches, I recall that Judge Taliaferro and McKenney used to practice together in the same law firm. Even if I was to give the Judge the benefit of a doubt and assume that he would be fair and would not allow his personal relationships with McKenney and Middleton to influence his decision, I'm not sure he as what it takes to stand up to public opinion that has been worked up to a frenzy against Chad by the Sheriff's Department, the victims, and the *Northumberland Echo*. You add to this formula that he is a newly appointed judge, whom I'm sure doesn't want to rock the boat, and he seems to want to have a reputation of being tough on criminals. It doesn't bode well for Chad. What he needs now is a judge with tremendous courage, who leans towards compassion. I don't think he is going to get it.

I mention none of this to Debra. She is tense and is wringing her fingers. I know she is feeling tremendous pressure, hoping that at least a few of the things that she will say on the witness stand will convey that Chad needs to be treated with mercy. He has already been convicted as a felon. My heart goes out to her. She is such a good mother. It hurts me to think of her pain and that public perception is so cruel.

I have a mixed feeling of being useless and frustrated. Jim has not asked me to testify. I think he feels that I will show anger on the witness stand and hurt Chad's chances. Even now I'm not allowed to defend my son.

The time has finally arrived. It is now 3:00 PM. All of our friends are still with us. Chad is brought out. He has been allowed to change into his court clothes. He is wearing leg irons. I guess they don't want him to appear too civilized. He gives us a short wave. Because Chad is the last case, the courtroom only consists of court personnel, our friends, some news reporters, Dr. Jarnecke, and a surprising number of Sheriff's deputies, and the Sheriff himself. I guess they want to savor their victory.

The case is announced and the Judge asks McKenney if he has any witnesses. McKenney says no, but he wants to introduce three letters to the court from the Bank of Lancaster employees and he asks the Judge to read them. I wonder to myself is this really the first time the Judge has seen the letters? We all sit while the Judge reviews the letters.

The Judge then asks Jim if he has any witnesses. Jim first calls Dr. Jarnecke. Dr. Jarnecke has been there all day, and Jim wants to be able to let him drive home to Fredericksburg as soon as his testimony is done. Jim focuses his questions on the doctor having agreed with the diagnosis of the other two experts. The doctor states that Chad has paranoid schizophrenia with somatic delusions and is in dire need of full psychiatric treatment, consisting of both medication and psychotherapy. Jim also establishes that the Northern Neck Regional Jail doesn't bother waking up inmates to take their medicine and that, at best, Chad had only one visit from a counselor for the entire year that he was incarcerated there. Jim then covers the arrangement that Dave Harmon has put together for Chad at the Saluda Jail and asks Dr. Jarnecke would that be the ideal arrangement. Dr. Jarnecke's answer will probably make the strongest point made in thirteen months on Chad's behalf.

The doctor emphatically states, "No, that is not the ideal arrangement for Chad. He should be in a mental health institution where he can get the help he needs." Keep in mind this is the psychologist that testified on behalf of the state. The doctor then goes on to say that given the fact that Chad is being incarcerated, the Saluda arrangement is a good one, and he would recommend this over any other of the few alternatives that are available.

Even though I feel that Dr. Jarnecke would probably agree that a majority of psychiatrists would have disagreed with his conclusion concerning Chad's accountability relative to the robbery, I take my hat off to him. What he did today took some courage and some character. *Thank you sir.*

When it becomes McKenney's turn to cross-examine the doctor, he focuses on what the doctor said about Chad's ability to tell the difference between right and wrong. Once again, it is brought out how Dr. Jarnecke thinks that Chad wearing a stocking mask and changing the license plates proved that he planned the whole thing and that he can tell the difference between right and wrong. I am hoping that Jim in his rebuttal will finally bring up in court why the other two experts, who spent much more time in analyzing Chad than Dr. Jarnecke, feel that Chad was incapable of controlling his actions that day. Not only was he incapable of controlling his actions, but also the schizophrenia had robbed Chad of his ability to understand the ramifications of his actions on himself or others. But I will be disappointed.

McKenney also goes over Dr. Jarnecke's point that the "vast majority of the sufferers of paranoid schizophrenia do not engage in illegal conduct." This same point was brought up at Chad's conviction. There is only one important fact that McKenney leaves out every time he states it in court and the *Northumberland Echo* runs it for him. The statement includes everyone who has this diagnosis. But if you remove those who are under effective treatment, the percentage of paranoid schizophrenics who do end up committing crimes goes up dramatically. But let's don't confuse the issue with the facts!

Jim calls up one of the witnesses from our church, and quite frankly, I am amazed at how well she does. She speaks with clarity and forcefulness as she describes what a good family we are, how long she has known us, and how she has interacted with Chad during our home-teaching visits. She describes the night that Chad comes over to help her set up her new computer and printer. She also explains how shocked she was when she heard the news about Chad. When Jim finishes, McKenney declines to cross-examine her. I don't blame him.

Jim then calls President Rasmussen to the stand. The purpose for calling the President of our branch to the stand is to testify to what programs we have available to help those in need and to indicate how the branch has been supporting us and Chad and will continue to so in the future.

To everyone's surprise, when it comes time for McKenney to cross examine, he starts baiting the President and setting him up with a lot of ridiculous questions such as; "Are you Christians? Do you believe in the Bible? Do you teach the Ten Commandments? Was Chad taught the difference between right and wrong?" He closes the questioning with some sort of question/comment like, "So even though he was taught Christian principles, he stilled robbed the bank?"

President Rasmussen leaves the stand looking a little perplexed. Would someone please tell the prosecuting attorney that Chad is severely mentally ill and what that usually means is that the person is having some major difficulties with their thought processes. I don't know if McKenney was trying to demonstrate his prosecuting prowess or if he had some point to make. I think all he accomplished was to lose the Mormon vote for next year's election.

Debra is next. I find that I get so emotionally involved at this point that I only remember a few of the questions that Jim asks her.

Jim, through a series of questions, leads Debra through a timeline of the events that lead up to the robbery. Debra is doing a good job of maintaining her composure and giving direct answers to the questions. She does break down when Jim inquires why Chad wanted Lidocaine and she explains that Chad tried to perform surgery on himself. I am fighting back the tears at this point also. This is all so beyond my comprehension! It almost feels like I'm having an "out-of-the-body" experience and I'm looking at this mother and father who are in a courtroom trying desperately to help their son! The feeling of despair is indescribable!

Jim also asks Debra a few questions concerning Chad's background, which brings out some of Chad's accomplishments before he is hit by the schizophrenia. Jim's final question is an open-ended question asking Debra to take a few minutes to explain how she feels about her son and what she would like to say on his behalf. At this point Debra is overcome with emotion and just starts to cry. She struggles to regain her composure and does try to explain through a trembling voice that Chad was a good kid, who always did what he was supposed to do and would do anything for you.

Debra has done a great job. *But Jim, I think you would have been surprised how well I would have done if given the chance to respond to the same open question you gave Debra.*

I am surprised that McKenney wants to ask Debra a few questions, especially given the fact that she is still struggling to regain her composure. I cannot understand what McKenney is up to. There are no visitors from the other side. Chad has already been convicted. The only people present, beside court personnel and counsel, are Chad's supporters, deputies, and newspaper reporters. Then it hits me! This guy is putting on a show for both the deputies and the reporters!

I can tell he is trying to set Debra up for his last question. He asks Debra whether Chad was taking his medicine before the robbery. I can tell immediately what he is up to and it burns me that he is going after Debra in this manner. He considers this question a win-win situation for himself. If Debra answers in the affirmative, McKenney will point out that even if Chad is on his medicine he is still capable of committing a crime and therefore should be incarcerated for as long as possible. If Debra answers in the negative, McKenney will point out that Chad is a danger to himself and society because he refuses to take his medicine and therefore should be incarcerated for as long as possible.

But Debra is confused by the question and for good reason. What McKenney failed to consider is that we really don't know the answer to it, though we are pretty sure that he was not taking his medicine as prescribed, but there is also the matter of dosage. Chad was on a much lighter dosage at the time, so who can say what the impact would have been if he had been properly medicated. It is most likely that the robbery wouldn't have occurred at all.

Debra shows her confusion as she is still trying to gain her composure and asks McKenney to repeat the question. Debra tells him she is not sure and shrugs her shoulders. Unwittingly, Debra has effectively blunted McKenney's question, and McKenney can tell he is not scoring any points. He quickly says he has no more questions. I thought all lawyers were taught in their first year of law school to never ask a witness a question they don't already know the answer to. Not that any of this matters. The Judge is only a few minutes away from confirming what Debra has been saying all along.

The Judge then asks McKenney if he has anything more to say. McKenney gets up, refers to the letters submitted by the Bank of Lancaster employees and says something to the effect that he believes, "that throughout this process, that all the attention has been focused on what was best for the defendant. Let us not forget about the nice ladies who had fear brought into their lives!" Oh really! I've been attending hearing after hearing for over a year now. Not once have I heard anyone raise their voice in defense of Chad - not even his own attorneys. All I've ever heard is Jim and the Judge agreeing to McKenney's most recent request for a postponement. And let's not forget that the only person who was really in any physical danger at the time of the robbery was Chad himself - Middleton and his merry men were only yards away. In addition, the *Northumberland Echo* has been running front page articles every month, which are full of self serving quotes from McKenney, degrading Chad and praising the bank employees (keep those advertising dollars coming!) But I'm sure the newspaper reporters who are present today are eating it up.

McKenney continues along this vein for a few minutes, and then recommends to the Judge that the defendant get the maximum time available under the guidelines. It was just a few nights before that Jim told us that McKenney wouldn't do this.

Jim is next and you can tell that he also desperately wants his remarks to make a difference. He his doing a great job, and I can tell that he really has been working hard on Chad's case lately. Jim is concentrating his remarks around the importance of Chad serving his time at Saluda. I would have preferred that he would have also focused his remarks on asking the Judge to choose a time less then the midpoint range. Saluda will probably do a good job of seeing that Chad takes his medicine, but Chad will still be without proper psychotherapy. What strikes me, as Jim is giving his remarks, is that Taliaferro doesn't even appear to be listening! He is certainly not looking at Jim. He seems to be looking at some papers and is writing some notes. I can't believe it! I continue to watch the Judge, and he continues to look through some papers and doesn't appear to be listening to Jim at all.

As Jim gives his closing remarks, the Judge looks up and says he has a few question for Jim. The questions center around the fact that Taliaferro doesn't think he has the authority to tell the Department of Corrections on where Chad should be incarcerated. It actually takes a few minutes to reassure the Judge that it is okay to make a recommendation. I can only shake my head. If this man is afraid to do this...! We then all sit and wait for the Judge to make his decision.

After about five to ten minutes, the Judge looks up and starts to tell us how serious a bank robbery is and in many cases it can lead anywhere from twenty-five years to life. It is almost as if the Judge feels the need to lecture Chad's supporters, though I also know he is laying the groundwork for his decision. Once again, the fact that Chad wore a stocking mask and changed license plates is cited by the Judge as demonstrating "the calculated nature of the robbery." *My god! You mean to tell me that even the Judge is ignoring the other two expert opinions! Have you forgotten the other facts sir, that Chad chose to rob the bank that is located across the street from the Sheriff's Department and he chose to do it without a weapon, while there were a dozen police cruisers all within a hundred yards.* Why is it these facts are never repeated over and over again! Or how about this one: the frontal lobe of his brain is no longer functioning as it should! Not only will the two other experts attest to this, but there is physical evidence as well!

The Judge then feels it is necessary to read out the names of the bank employees who have submitted the victim impact statements. I guess he also feels that Chad's supporters need to have his victims personalized. It has become pretty obvious that the Judge has no intention of coming in under the mid-point. Debra was right; nothing that anyone did or said today would have made any difference. The Judge seems to be an advocate for the prosecutor. The question now is will he actually pick a point above the mid-range. Another question, why did we have to wait two months for this?

The Judge then refers to the fact that several of the victims impact statements state that "things like that don't happen here on the Northern Neck." Actually, just in the last two years, five bank branches belonging to four different banks have been robbed on the Northern Neck. A bank officer was murdered by crooks waiting for him to come home from a bank. I guess the letter writers and the Judge must have overlooked this. But, once again, no sense confusing the issue with the facts.

He again starts telling us how serious a bank robbery is. Boy! We really must be dumb!

The Judge then starts discussing the importance of the sentencing guidelines and what a great resource it is for someone in his position. He actually rekindles a little ray of hope in me that, because there is no provision for the mentally ill in the guidelines, he will sentence below the suggested midpoint. In other words, the score that Chad has, 43 points out of a possible 174 points, has not been adjusted to allow for his mental illness. I assume that whoever is responsible for the rating leaves that up to the discernment of the Judge. The fact that the sentencing guidelines allows no provision for the mentally ill is archaic – all part of a disastrous and unfair system.

He takes a minute to look over his papers and then announces his verdict. "I sentence the defendant to twenty-five years for bank robbery," he lets that hang in the air for about three or four seconds and then says, "Suspended!" He then says, "I sentence the defendant to ten years for grand larceny!" He lets that hang in the air for a few seconds and then says, "...Suspended to three years and seven months." This is the exact mid point of the sentencing guideline. Not only did the Judge not rock the boat, he didn't even create a ripple. Chad does get credit for time already served, leaving him with two-and-half years.

I am disappointed but not surprised. It wasn't enough to just make him a felon for the rest of his life; they also took away any chance he had left of fully recovering. To be truthful, we are going to be lucky now if Chad will ever be able to function on his own in society. Another two-and-half years without proper treatment will leave him as a shell of his former self. The Saluda Jail alternative provides some hope, but Chad has had his fill of jails, he is convinced he will be much happier in a prison where the inmates have more freedoms. I felt I could convince Chad to stick it out in Saluda if his remaining term were close to one year. Now, I don't know.

It is hard to believe that the Judge could not even come down just a few months on his sentence. The sentencing guidelines and the psychiatric reports gave him the ammunition he needed. I think the combination of his inexperience, his desire to be known as a tough Judge, and public opinion played a big role.

What Chad needed today was an extraordinary man. What he got was an ordinary one.

EPILOGUE

What have I learned? Enough to make me want to keep a detailed journal and share my experience with others. I am hoping that this journal gives people a point of reference and helps prepare other parents whose children have been stricken with a mental disease, particularly schizophrenia, for the rough ride ahead. I also hope it will increase people's sensitivity to the suffering that this horrible disease can cause its victims. Maybe people will be a little more forgiving if someone who is possessed by its demons ever wrongs them. I also have a silly dream that somehow this journal will be widely read by members of our society and work as an impetus for social change, or at least provide a different viewpoint for those who are far to the right in their political thinking. When times are hard, it is always the programs that are meant to help the mentally ill and those who have been incarcerated that are cut. Would it be too much to hope that, one day, society will be willing to help its mentally ill citizens as much it does those who are stricken by physical illnesses?

Having had these experiences, I am now aware of our judicial system's fallacies and weaknesses. Our judicial system is only as strong, honorable, and merciful as those who have been selected for its administrative positions. The selection process is far too politically biased against the principles that mainstream America espouses. Just look at what we had to endure while our son was being held for trial. At a time when it was imperative for him to receive medical attention, he was effectively denied bail, his parents were not allowed visitation rights, and he was paraded around and photographed while in shackles and chains by those eager to promote their stories and professional careers.

Any accused person who is brought to trial in Northumberland County has two strikes against him before he even gets to bat. There is a young, ambitious prosecuting attorney who wants to further his political career, as well as a new Judge who wants to develop a reputation for being tough on crime. Often the witnesses brought against the accused are the Sheriff's deputies, upon whom the prosecutor and the judge depend for their own personal safety in the courtroom. The defense attorneys are afraid to aggressively pursue the defense because they know they are at the judge's mercy every time they represent a client in his courtroom, and it's the only courtroom in the county. Add to this equation a large cadre of older, retired persons who want to make sure their politicians are tough on crime. Mercy takes a back seat in this county. It makes one wonder how many counties in this country are similar.

What ever happened to that concept of both sides working together to establish the facts and to come up with a fair verdict?

We need to start attracting a higher level of talent to our police departments. I think the only way this will happen is by increasing salaries to the level that is needed. The police hold a crucial position in the smooth functioning of our democratic society. I know that rural budgets are tight and the funds are just not available. Solution: Hire fewer policemen at higher pay. Require college degrees and give an edge not only to those who have criminal justice degrees, but also to those who have degrees in the humanities and the social sciences. Improve the training for recruits and create a career path that is going to attract the best and the brightest. People who are dedicated to a social cause don't mind putting in long hours because they are doing something worthwhile for which they are being adequately compensated. I would much rather have a well trained, competent, off-duty police officer being paged to respond to a call, than an on-duty police officer who is incompetent or prejudiced.

It also should be easier for citizens to hold police officers accountable for their actions. Their current sovereign immunity must end if the quality of their work is to be improved. The statute of limitations to file a complaint against an officer needs to be extended to however long it takes for the bureaucratic court system to finish processing a loved one. It also should be against the law for any prosecutor or sheriff to threaten that things are going to go worse for your loved one if you do file a complaint, and if they make good on their threats, they should go to jail. They should be held to a higher standard.

I have no tolerance for individuals who seek to further their political and professional careers at a mentally ill teenager's expense.

It is absolutely archaic how the mentally ill are treated in most of our jails. They receive exactly the same treatment as the other prisoners. They are left to their demons, with those in charge making very little effort to see that they receive the proper medication and therapy. It costs more for a jail to treat an inmate as mentally ill, so they take the attitude that the mentally ill person is no sicker than any of the other inmates. Resources are so scarce that it takes an act of God before the State will classify someone as mentally ill. We have been told that unless a state psychiatrist finds the inmate standing on a chair with a rope tied around his neck, he will give the okay to "warehouse" the inmate with all the others.

If your loved one is incarcerated, he or she is at the mercy of those in charge. Subsequent to Chad's sentencing, I found out that the Northern Neck Regional Jail Superintendent takes great pride in the fact that he can warehouse an inmate at less cost than other jails. It is this type of administration that leads to the discouragement of visitors, less visiting time, and the filthy conditions that the inmates must endure. This also explains why there are no programs for the inmates and why they lack proper medical treatment. The Northern Neck Regional Jail superintendent refers to the inmates as furniture that need to be processed further along the assembly line. What's more, the politicians love him for this attitude, because he keeps costs low! I don't think that even the most conservative of Americans would agree with this type of treatment; but once again, I don't think most members of our society are even aware that this is happening. At least I hope not. It is a sad commentary if they do know and they don't do anything about it.

As a defendant, my son was supposed to have had some fundamental rights. The Bill of Rights is supposed to guarantee that everyone has a right to reasonable bail, a right to due process of the law, and a right to be free from cruel and unusual treatment. The collective actions of the Northumberland County criminal justice system, the *Northumberland Echo*, and the Northern Neck Regional Jail effectively denied my son these rights.

I also learned a lot about the accuracy, honesty, and fairness of the press. These are three traits that some don't worry about. The *Northumberland Echo* is a cross between a tabloid and a public relations arm for both the Sheriff and the prosecuting attorney. I had no idea how vicious they could be and get away with it. These guys are experts of walking that fine line between fiction and defamation. Privacy laws need to be strengthened to stop this abuse of free speech and to make it easier for someone who has been abused or harassed to have some means of recourse.

As my wife and I have been going through this ordeal, I have become more aware of how little attention is given to the mentally ill. Championing their cause is not sexy! How many politicians and celebrities have you seen on national TV asking for donations to programs for the mentally ill? Have you ever seen a telethon or a walk-a-thon conducted on the behalf of the mentally ill? While it is very easy to observe and identify with the pain and suffering of someone who suffers from a physical disease or ailment the inner disease of the mentally ill is impossible to see, making it much more difficult, if not impossible for people to empathize.

* * * * *

I love my son. I admire his courage and willingness to resist the demons that plague him. He is doing the best he can to fight a good fight. As he has done his whole life, he is trying to do this on his own, trying to muster everything he has to return to normal. Even now, he will try to be optimistic when we see him and tells us not to worry. Everything is going to be okay once he gets out, he says. I know now it's a fight he can't win. The schizophrenia has robbed him of his greatest asset, his mind. Once he gets out, every time he fails to take his medicine, the schizophrenia will bring him down another notch, and the voices will return. The year we lost in the Northumberland County Court System was critical to his success. The three-and-a-half years that he will spend in jail without proper psychotherapy and a constant monitoring of his medication have sealed his fate. Early intervention was key to helping Chad. The experts tell us that the best thing we can hope for now is that Chad might be able to live away from home and exist on disability payments. He will never be able to hold a job and will never be able to interact in a normal way with others.

Some of the facts that the experts didn't tell us, but that I was able to research on my own, are even more sobering. The average, expected life span of a paranoid schizophrenic is about half that of a normal citizen. One out of ten will commit suicide.

Many will resort to alcohol and drugs as a means to escaping the demons, and they will neglect their physical well-being. Drug overdoses, alcohol poisoning, and heart failure are common killers of schizophrenics. Many will end up in jail and others will turn to the streets before they die.

The experts tell us that it is impossible for a normal citizen to appreciate the horror and confusion that a schizophrenic experiences every day. The voices that torment a schizophrenic are usually destructive, telling their victims that they are worthless and a burden to all those around them. For those with somatic delusions, the effects are overwhelming. It is no wonder that so many schizophrenics end up committing suicide.

What happened to Chad was not fair! I am referring to both the schizophrenia and receiving the verdict that was handed down by society in our little neck of the woods. Once the facts were known, Chad should have been sent to a mental institution immediately and kept as long as it took to get him healthy, whether it was six months or six years. At least he would have had a shot at a normal life and some happiness. At that early stage, Chad still had a chance to make a positive contribution to society. What is ironic is that it would have been mostly Debra and I that would have ended up paying for Chad's treatment, yet society insisted on extracting more than its fair share of Chad's flesh before it was satisfied that justice had been done. Now society will be paying for Chad's upkeep for the rest of his life. That, perhaps, is the only fair part of the outcome.

Debra and I are trying to come to grips with the reality of the situation. We are trying to let go of the dreams and aspirations that we had for our son, of whom we are so proud. We are preparing for the worst and hoping for the best.

Chad Wegkamp, Senior High School photo.

Ali Wegkamp, as a junior, decked out in her
Northumberland High School basketball uniform.

Not only were Chad and Ali brother and sister, they were also the best of friends. This photo was taken at our home in Northern Virginia, when Ali was two years old and Chad was four.

Deana Wegkamp and beau's wedding invitation, March, 2001.

Paul and Debra Wegkamp, outside of their home in January of
2003. They have just learned that U.S. Attorney John Davis has
indicted Chad in the U.S. District Court on six counts of
counterfeiting charges. Each count carries a $250,000 fine and a
maximum sentence of twenty years.

Larry and Linda Wegkamp on their wedding day. Larry is my Dad
and Linda is my step-mom.
Their support never wavered during the ordeal.

"Northumberland Commonwealth's Attorney R. Michael
McKenney recommended that Wegkamp receive the most severe
sentence under the guidelines in part because of the impact the
robbery had upon bank employees."

Rappahannock Record – September 26, 2002.

APPENDIX

Where families can go for help

In the aftermath of the bank robbery, we were entirely bewildered and second-guessing ourselves regarding what we should have done differently. Hindsight is a wonderful thing – too bad it is useless. I would like to make the reader aware of the best practical resources that we found in the aftermath, ones that we wish we had known about when Chad first began exhibiting signs of schizophrenia.

Believe it or not, there are only a few organizations that offered any real, immediate help. The best one is the National Alliance for the Mentally Ill, more commonly referred to as NAMI (www.nami.org), a nonprofit organization with headquarters in Arlington, Virginia. NAMI maintains a toll–free help line (800-950-6264), and it has state and local affiliates all over the country. Its expressed purpose is to be an advocate for the mentally ill and their families. Its local offices have family support groups and provide educational programs.

Each state and U.S. territory has a Protection and Advocacy agency that provides services for its citizens with disabilities, including all types of mental illness. These agencies are congressionally mandated by the federal government and supported by federal appropriations. These agencies can assist with litigation and case law advice, and they also offer experts in all areas of social services, such as housing, Medicaid, and special education. You can reach your state agency by contacting the National Association of Protection and Advocacy Systems located in Washington, DC (202-408-9514/www.napas.org).

The best resource we found is the book, *Surviving Schizophrenia*, by Dr. E. Fuller Torrey, which, in my opinion, is the Bible for families who are dealing with schizophrenia. Dr. Torrey, one of the best-known psychiatrists in the country, has been on a crusade most of his life to find a cure for schizophrenia. During this crusade, he has been a tremendous advocate for the mentally ill and their families. He is the president of the Treatment Advocacy Center and has authored sixteen books. As a result of all of his efforts, he has received numerous awards for his work in psychiatry and has appeared on such programs as *60 Minutes* and *Oprah*.

The book covers just about everything you could possibly want to know about schizophrenia, in lay terms, with chapters covering the causes, treatment, and impact of schizophrenia. My favorite chapters are the ones that deal with the rehabilitation, problems, and care of someone who is schizophrenic. There is also an excellent chapter on how family members can cope with the reality of living with a schizophrenic loved one on a daily basis. Perhaps the most valuable part of the book is the appendixes, which list an array of available resources, such as recommended books and videos that both instruct and share the experiences of others dealing with schizophrenia.

Another good book is *I Am Not Sick I Don't Need Help* by Xavier Amador with Anna-Lisa Johanson. Dr. Amador is an Associate Professor at Columbia University College of Physicians and Surgeons in New York City and a world-renowned expert on the problems associated with schizophrenia and bipolar disorder. Ms. Johanson, a Georgetown University Law School graduate, is a leading mental health advocate who is actively involved in developing legal resources for families of the seriously mentally ill. She is the daughter of Margaret Mary Ray, the woman most people know as "David Letterman's stalker." This book is a practical resource on how to deal with a mentally ill family member who refuses to take their medicine or seek help because they don't think they need it.

The best website we found was www.schizophrenia.com. This comprehensive website contains many valuable links. The feature we like the best are the chat rooms; there are different chat rooms for schizophrenics, siblings, and parents. These chat rooms are well monitored and are a great source for someone who just needs to talk with someone who has had similar experiences.

A word of caution when you search for a competent psychiatrist, most of the psychiatric community in private practice avoid dealing with those who have been stricken with the severest brain diseases. The money to be made is in assisting the wealthy "worried well" (a phrase coined by Dr. Torrey) with their everyday problems of living. Unfortunately, for this reason, the best and brightest of this profession have very little experience with handling patients that have a severe mental disease. Often the most competent psychiatrist can be found at your local Department of Social Services. This is where you will find psychiatrists and social service workers who have had extensive experience in dealing with schizophrenia and bipolar disease.

I would also encourage families to be proactive in determining what medications have been selected for a family member. Doctors like to play it safe. Zyprexa (Eli Lilly & Co./www.zyprexa.com), part of the second generation of drugs for treating psychosis, has been on the market the longest and has proven to be usually very effective with treating the positive symptoms (delusions and hallucinations). Because this drug has a track record of success, it is the one most often prescribed by doctors. However, every patient is different and there is no way to tell how each patient will respond to his or her medication. For this reason, your doctor should be experimenting as to which combination of drugs is best. Our son gained ten pounds a month while on Zyprexa, and it did very little for his negative symptoms (apathy, no emotion). We have found that in our son's situation that a combination of Geodon (Pfizer Inc./www.pfizer.com) and Abilify (Bristol-Myers Squibb Co./www.abilify.com) has proven to be the most effective in controlling both the positive and negative symptoms of schizophrenia, without any serious side effects.

Resources and Alternatives for Judges and Lawyers

The criminal courts punished our son with the harshest sanction available: incarceration with no allowances made for proper medical treatment. The other alternatives that are available run all the way from declining to prosecute to seeking a civil commitment to a mental hospital or other type of diversion program. Here are some examples:

1. Decline or delay prosecution, pending the defendant submitting to and receiving the mental health treatment he needs;

2. Allow the defendant to plead guilty, but defer a finding of guilt and sentencing contingent upon the defendant

entering into treatment and not being re-arrested within a specified time period;

3. As part of a guilty plea, recommend that the defendant's entire sentence be suspended contingent upon the defendant engaging in treatment and not re-offending; and

4. Send the defendant to a diversion program that insures that proper medical attention is received under the supervision of special community/probation programs.

All of these alternatives provide a pathway for defendants to get the help they need, allowing them to retain the potential to become a contributing member of society. These alternatives also enable prosecutors to fulfill their duty to protect the public safety.

Most of the state agencies for Protection and Advocacy are actively involved in providing advice and recommendations to public defenders and other court officers on matters related to alternative sentencing options for the mentally ill. Some of these agencies have taken the next step and have helped form community diversion programs. Some of these diversion programs involve mental health courts and crisis intervention teams. More information can be obtained by contacting the Protection and Advocacy offices of Florida, New Jersey, Pennsylvania, and South Carolina.

Also, a number of counties and local communities have formed their own diversion programs. For example, Jefferson County, Kentucky has formed a diversion program for nonviolent mentally ill defendants. If these defendants successfully complete a six-month intensive treatment program, their charges are dismissed. In New York City, the Center for Alternative Sentencing and Employment Services (CASES) targets seriously mentally ill defendants that have been charged with both violent and nonviolent felonies. Instead of incarceration, these defendants are placed in a two-year intensive case management program that involves mental health professionals and periodic monitoring by the courts. If the defendant successfully completes the program, the charges are dismissed.

There are a number of nonprofit organizations that are great resources for those in the legal profession. The Bazelon Center for Mental Health Laws (www.bazelon.org/202-467-5730), based in

Washington, DC, provides technical support on mental health law issues, as well as co-council on selected lawsuits with private lawyers, legal services programs, ACLU chapters, and state protection and advocacy agencies. This organization has staff attorneys that can provide advice, research, and litigation support for any cases that involve the criminal prosecution of the mentally ill and/or their rights under the American with Disabilities Act.

The Treatment Advocacy Center (TAC) (www.psychlaws.org/703-294-6001), based in Arlington, Virginia, works on changing and improving state-assisted treatment laws for the mentally ill. The TAC has provided a model law for assisted treatment that has been used by many governmental units in forming their own assisted treatment programs. It can provide legal articles and case digests covering key issues impacting the rights of the mentally ill, as well as a summary of the assisted treatment standards for every state.

*   *   *   *   *

For families, citizens, and those within the criminal justice system who want to become advocates for the mentally ill, any of the above mentioned organizations would be a good place to start looking for more information.

The Psychotic Bank Robber

A Schizophrenic Teen Takes Desperate Measures. His Parents Want Help. The Law Wants Prison.

By Peter Carlson
Washington Post Staff Writer
Sunday, January 26, 2003; Page F01

HEATHSVILLE, Va.

Chad Wegkamp woke up and decided to rob a bank.

He figured he had no choice. He'd already tried to solve his problem by operating on himself with a pair of scissors, but that proved so painful and bloody he had to stop. After that, he tried to make the $4,000 he needed to pay for the operation by printing it on his computer. But his homemade money looked fake so he stuffed most of it into a paper bag and threw it down the hill outside his parents' house in Mila, a little town on Virginia's Northern Neck.

Now, on the morning of Aug. 13, 2001, Wegkamp decided to hit a bank. He'd been thinking about it for a week, ever since he read about a bank robber who stole $10,000 in the next county.

Wegkamp, then 18, got up early, not long after his father left for his job as an accountant. His sister was already at basketball practice. His mother, a nurse who'd worked a 12-hour shift, was still sleeping. He took a black knit cap and cut eye holes in it. He replaced the license plates on his mother's silver Honda CRV with plates from the Toyota he'd totaled a month earlier. Then he took off.

He drove to Heathsville, about 20 miles away, and pulled into the parking lot of the Bank of Lancaster, which happens to sit across the street from the Northumberland County sheriff's office.

He put on black gloves and the cap, picked up a backpack and hustled into the bank. He had no gun, no knife, no weapon of any kind.

"Put your hands up," he yelled. "This is a holdup."

For a moment, the tellers thought Wegkamp was joking. But he seemed so agitated -- pacing, cursing, demanding money -- that they quickly realized he was serious.

He tossed his backpack to teller Donna Jewell.

"Put the money in there!" he ordered. "Put it *all* in there and don't hit any alarms."

Frightened, Jewell and another teller stuffed about $6,000 into the backpack and handed it back. Wegkamp walked over to Nancy Hamilton, who was sitting at a desk near the vault.

"Give me the keys to the vault," he demanded.

She told him she didn't have the keys.

"Get up against the wall, face first, or I'll kill you!" he yelled. Then he ran out and drove away.

He went home and put his mother's license plates back on her Honda. He stashed the knapsack of money in the laundry room, behind the dryer.

When his mother woke up, shortly after 10, he was sitting in the living room, watching TV. She was thrilled to see him there. It was the first time in weeks he'd left his bedroom before she demanded that he get up.

"Maybe his medication is working," she thought. "Maybe he's getting better."

Parents' Worries

Debra Wegkamp worried about her son. She had been the first person to suggest that he was schizophrenic -- even before psychiatrists made the diagnosis -- and she was terrified that he'd kill himself.

She had looked back over his life, searching for clues to his illness. His birth had been complicated and he hadn't breathed for his first few minutes outside the womb. Could that have something to do with it?

Chad was always a bit odd. As a baby, he used to bang his head against the side of the crib. When he got older, he'd rub his head on the grass until it bled. Then there were his little rituals -- he always knocked on a chair before he sat down in it. Before he could go to sleep, he'd repeat to himself, "I'm not going to die, I'm not going to die."

But Debra and Paul Wegkamp had dismissed those eccentricities because Chad was a smart kid who did well academically. In elementary school in Fairfax County, he was recommended for a program for gifted students. And after the family moved to the Northern Neck in 1995, he excelled at Northumberland High, earning a 3.55 GPA and graduating ninth among the 97 members of the Class of 2000.

He was a classic high school nerd. He didn't date. He didn't play sports like his sister, Ali, who is three years younger. But he was a computer prodigy. At 12, he was selling computers he built from parts he'd bought online, earning enough by his senior year to buy a used red Audi.

So when Chad went off to James Madison University in the fall of 2000 to study business and computer science, his parents were confident he'd succeed.

The first indication that something was wrong came in April 2001 when Chad called home to say he and some friends had been arrested for drunk and disorderly conduct. A few days later, he confessed in an e-mail that he'd also been charged with possession of marijuana.

"It was a shock to us," Paul Wegkamp recalls. "We're Mormons. We don't drink. We don't smoke. And drugs are out of the question."

Paul and Debra feared that Chad had fallen in with the proverbial bad crowd. But the truth was far worse. He was, it later became apparent, psychotic.

It began when he was working out. Riding an exercise bike at the school gym, he felt something unusual in his crotch. Back in his dorm room, he examined himself and concluded that his scrotum was abnormally large. He went to a doctor, who told him there was nothing physically wrong. But Chad was convinced that his scrotum was too big and that it made his pelvis tip forward, which caused his back to become rigid, which caused his head to tip back.

273

And people could tell. He heard them talking about him, calling him "nerd" or "faggot" behind his back. Sometimes he'd confront them and they'd say, "I don't know what you're talking about." He asked his friends if people were talking about him. They told him he was crazy.

"I'm getting paranoid," he wrote in an e-mail to his father on April 19. "I always think everybody's talking about me and my eyes are always glassy white and I can see all sorts of blood vessels in my eyes."

He didn't mention his scrotum but he complained about his rigid back, the trouble he had keeping his head still.

"Maybe I have some whack condition or something," he wrote. "I'm sure it will pass but maybe mom can tell me exactly what is going on."

Paul showed the e-mail to Debra. She figured Chad was having some kind of anxiety attack. She called him and suggested he see the school nurse. She called again the next day, and Chad told her the nurse said there was nothing wrong.

By then, he'd stopped attending classes. He holed up in his dorm room, fiddling on the computer. His grades plummeted. He ended up with an F, three D's and a C.

On May 4, when the school year ended, his parents came to pick him up. Chad had a baseball cap pulled low over his eyes. He barely looked at them and answered all questions with a vague mumble.

Back home, he rarely left his room and seldom bathed. He spent all day sleeping and all night on the computer. He'd be alone in his room and Debra would hear him saying, "Shut up!" When she asked whom he was talking to, he'd say, "I'm only messing with you, Mom."

After 10 days, he told his mother about his scrotum, how it was affecting his whole body, how people were talking about it. He began cutting holes in his underwear so he could tape his scrotum up, then pulling on the tightest jockstrap he could find.

Debra took him to the family doctor, who said there was nothing wrong with Chad's scrotum. Chad didn't believe it so she took him to a urologist, who said the same thing. Chad still didn't believe it.

Debra suspected that Chad was schizophrenic. Working as a nurse in a nearby jail, she'd seen many schizophrenics and she knew that the symptoms included hearing voices, paranoia and delusions.

She made an appointment with Mario Gomez, a Richmond psychiatrist. On June 8, Paul drove Chad to see Gomez, who made a preliminary diagnosis: "symptoms of a delusional nature and depressive obsessions." He prescribed Prozac and a schizophrenia drug called Zyprexa. But Chad didn't always take his medication, and on June 29 Gomez noted that Chad showed "minimal improvement."

His parents agreed: Chad wasn't getting any better. He complained to Ali that wherever he went, he heard people mocking him. He took a job cleaning carpets but he complained that his co-workers were talking about him. After a couple of weeks he quit.

One day Debra heard him outside screaming toward a dock on the Great Wicomico River, a couple hundred yards away: "Shut up!" Horrified, she ran out and asked Chad what was going on. Trembling with anger, he told her the oystermen were yelling at him. But there were no oystermen there.

Still obsessed with his groin, he'd walk around constantly pulling up on his pants to keep his scrotum tightly bound. He told his mother he'd gone online and found a plastic surgeon who would operate on him for $4,000. After that, he kept asking for $4,000. He asked every day, sometimes six or seven times a day.

The scariest moment came in late July. Debra found surgical tape in Chad's room. He told her that he'd numbed his scrotum with ice and tried to operate on himself, stopping only because it hurt so much.

She was stunned. Immediately she worried about suicide, which she knew was common among schizophrenics, but she couldn't bring herself to utter the word.

"Chad," she said, "you're not going to hurt yourself, are you?"

He didn't answer.

"Please," she said. "I couldn't stand it. I really couldn't stand it."

That day, she started looking for a new psychiatrist. Somebody recommended one in Richmond and she called to beg for the earliest possible appointment. She got one for Aug. 14.

As it turned out, that was the day after Chad robbed the Bank of Lancaster.

License Tagged

Debra parked the Honda in front of her house and saw two policemen waiting there.

"I'm not the bank robber," she told them, smiling.

She'd been pulled over by cops twice the previous day -- the day of the bank robbery -- because her car matched the description of the getaway vehicle. Now she'd just returned from taking Chad to his new psychiatrist.

While Debra was telling the police that they could search the vehicle, Chad got out and walked toward the house. The cops stopped him. He had his baseball cap pulled low and he seemed nervous.

At that point, Paul came home from work. The police wanted to know about the license plates from their Toyota. Paul explained that the car had been totaled but he had the plates in the house. He retrieved them, and the cops' eyes lit up. They told him the plates matched those seen on the getaway car. They also said Chad matched the description of the bank robber.

Paul told Chad to get in the house. Inside, he asked his son, "What the hell have you done?"

Chad started crying. "Dad," he said, "I needed the money for my scrotum."

Caught in the Headlights

When the police asked if they could search the house, Paul said he wanted to call a lawyer first. When the lawyer advised him not to let the cops in without a search warrant, Paul handed the phone to a policeman so the lawyer could relay that message directly.

At that point, the Wegkamps say, the police warned that if they heard a toilet flushing or saw any signs of destruction of evidence, they'd storm the house.

Paul opened the living room curtains, and the whole family -- Paul, Debra, Chad and Ali -- sat in front of the window, so the cops could see that nobody was destroying evidence. Outside, the police pulled their cars up on the lawn and trained their high beams into the living room.

For nearly three hours, the Wegkamps sat, waiting. Finally, the sheriff arrived with a search warrant. A dozen cops swarmed in. They strip-searched the entire family, the Wegkamps say, then started searching the house.

For three more hours, the Wegkamps watched as the police foraged for clues. Chad, who had taken his antipsychotic medicine, fell asleep. The rest of the family sat rigid and nervous. The dog paced.

A loud yell came from the laundry room: The police had found the knapsack full of loot. At that point, the Wegkamps says, the cops celebrated with high-fives.

Soon the police announced that they'd found fake money Chad had made using his computer, as well as the green food coloring he'd used to dye it. Hearing that, Debra remembered the day Chad used his computer and scanner to copy some photos of flowers for her. She'd seen the "money" he'd created, but it didn't look real and she thought nothing of it. Now it was evidence of counterfeiting.

Sometime after midnight, a half-dozen police gathered around Chad, who was slumped on the couch. "Chad," one announced, "you are under arrest for -- "

He stopped. Chad was fast asleep.

His parents woke him up. The cops handcuffed him and led him off to jail.

The Letter of the Law

That was the start of what Paul Wegkamp calls a "nightmare that has no end."

First came the newspapers. The Northern Neck News and the Northumberland Echo both printed front-page photos of Chad wearing prison stripes, handcuffs and shackles. In big red type, the Echo said: "Wegkamp could face life in prison if convicted."

That was true. Under Virginia law, robbing a bank -- even without a weapon -- carried a penalty of five years to life. Under federal law, counterfeiting could mean another 20 years.

Paul hired James Breeden, a prominent local attorney, and took a second mortgage on his house to make a $10,000 down payment for his services. A judge set Chad's bail at $100,000, but the Wegkamps no longer had enough equity in their house to use it as collateral. So Chad would have to remain in jail until his trial, scheduled for Dec. 18, 2001.

Breeden asked Northumberland County prosecutor R. Michael McKenney to consider the possibility that Wegkamp was not guilty by reason of insanity. McKenney said he'd study the psychiatric evaluations to see if Chad's mental illness prevented him from telling right from wrong, which is Virginia's legal standard for judging insanity in criminal cases.

On Sept. 10, Chad was taken to Richmond's Chippenham Medical Center for evaluation by Gomez, the psychiatrist. A CAT scan of Chad's brain revealed an enlarged ventricle, a condition frequently associated with schizophrenia.

"Mr. Wegkamp has schizophrenia, paranoid type," Gomez concluded in his official report. The illness caused such powerful delusions that "Chad could not distinguish between right and wrong with respect to his act."

Breeden hoped that Gomez's report would convince McKenney that Chad should be hospitalized, not imprisoned. But McKenney was unswayed. "Gomez's evaluation was poor," McKenney explained in a recent interview. "It rushed to a conclusion without any facts to support it."

Breeden offered to have another expert evaluate Chad, and McKenney agreed. Chad's trial was postponed until Feb. 26, 2002.

At Breeden's suggestion, Paul Wegkamp hired Richmond psychologist Edward A. Peck III to evaluate Chad. Peck studied

Gomez's report, interviewed Chad twice and administered various psychological tests. He concluded that Chad suffered from a "Paranoid Schizophrenic Disorder" coupled with "overwhelming" delusions that rendered him "unable to distinguish between right and wrong." He recommended that Chad be sent to a mental hospital.

McKenney wasn't convinced. "I was suspicious that Dr. Peck was giving the results he was paid to give," McKenney says. "There was a hired-gun look to his report."

McKenney hired Roy W. Jarnecke, a Fredericksburg psychologist, to evaluate Chad. Jarnecke studied the earlier reports and interviewed Chad. He agreed that Chad was a paranoid schizophrenic. But he concluded that Chad "was aware of the wrongfulness of his actions" and "was able to control and direct his actions."

After that, McKenney told Breeden that he would proceed with the case and demand a jury trial.

That decision put Chad in a dilemma. If a jury found him not guilty by reason of insanity, he would be sent to a mental hospital. But if the jurors voted to convict, they would then sentence him to a punishment somewhere between five years and life. On the other hand, if Chad pleaded guilty, a judge would sentence him under state guidelines that recommended a sentence between two and 4 1/2 years.

Breeden advised Chad to plead guilty. Chad took the advice. On Sept. 24, 2002, Judge Harry T. Taliaferro sentenced him to 35 years in prison, with all but three years and seven months suspended.

"I am disappointed but not surprised," Paul Wegkamp wrote in the diary he'd been keeping since his son's arrest.

Paul and Debra believed that Chad's psychosis had been worsened by his incarceration without psychiatric treatment. "We are going to be lucky now if Chad is ever able to function on his own in society," Paul wrote. "Another two years without treatment will leave him as a shell of his former self."

But the worst was still to come. In December 2002, a federal grand jury indicted Chad Wegkamp on three counts of manufacturing counterfeit money and three counts of possessing counterfeit money. At issue are 10 $10 bills and 36 $20 bills he printed on his home computer -- $820 in bills that McKenney says were too crude to fool him.

Chad faces a possible 40 years in prison and fines totaling $500,000. His trial is scheduled for March 19.

Why is the federal government prosecuting an already-imprisoned psychotic for making pathetically crude counterfeit money that he never tried to spend?

Paul J. McNulty, U.S attorney for the Eastern District of Virginia, declines to discuss the matter. "It would be inappropriate to comment," a spokesman says, "because it's an ongoing case."

The Letter of the Law

"This is Virginia," says Mike McKenney. "We still take crime seriously."

McKenney, 44, is wearing a gray suit with an American flag lapel pin. The prosecutor is sitting behind his desk, flanked by an American flag, a Virginia flag and busts of George Washington, Thomas Jefferson and Theodore Roosevelt.

"This is a bank robbery in a rural area," McKenney says. "It's a crime that concerned people. Chad is mentally ill but he knows right from wrong. Even though he has mental problems, he has to be punished. I'm sorry his parents didn't identify his problem before that and take steps to address it. But I can't be held responsible for that."

McKenney figures Chad got off easy: The last bank robber prosecuted in Northumberland County got 27 years.

"I actually think that Chad should have gotten more time because he clearly knows right from wrong," McKenney says. "He did everything to conceal himself. He wore a mask. He wore gloves. He changed his license plate. He secreted the money."

He also sliced into his scrotum because he thought he heard people talking about it.

"That only proves he's mentally ill," McKenney says. "It doesn't prove that he doesn't know right from wrong." He shrugs. "I don't make the rules. I just follow them."

Isn't there some better way to handle cases like this?

"I'll bet there is," he says. "But I'm not sure what that is."

In Chad's Words

As Chad Wegkamp shuffles into the visiting room at the Northern Neck Regional Jail, his right hand is yanking the top of his prison pants to pull his scrotum up.

He's wearing a faded black-and-white striped prison uniform. His hair is a crude crew cut styled by inmate barbers. His sparse goatee fails to make him look mature, perhaps because he still suffers from adolescent acne. He's 20.

He sits in a chair and picks up a telephone so he can talk to the reporter on the other side of the glass divider. His voice is soft. His answers are terse.

How are they treating you here?

"It's all right," he says. "Not too bad."

He reads, plays cards, keeps mostly to himself, he says. He takes his medicine most of the time -- at least when he remembers to wake up early enough to get it.

Asked why he robbed the bank, he looks down, rubs his left hand over his eyes.

"It seemed like my world was falling apart," he says softly. "I thought if I got the money to do what I needed to do, I could go back to college and live a normal life."

What did you need to do?

"I don't want to say it out loud here," he whispers. "I basically had enough of feeling people were talking about me all the time and I decided to rob that bank."

Why did you try to operate on yourself?

"I just felt that because of the problem, I needed to fix it. I know it sounds crazy."

Are you mentally ill?

"I got to the point where I was so obsessed with my problem that I let it eat at me," he says. "I was mentally ill." He pauses. "I think I'm fine now."

Was his sentence just?

He shakes his head no. "I think I should have got some time because I did something wrong," he says, "but I think I got too much time. Two years was the minimum. I think I should get that. But I definitely should get *some* time."

Are you worried about the time you're facing for counterfeiting?

"Yes," he says. "Because with me having paranoid schizophrenia, every day is like 20 days, you know?"

Why is every day like 20 days?

"Because you think people are talking about you," he says.